FOR ALL THOSE WHO FREED THEMSELVES
BY CUTTING THE ROPE.

STRANGE FRUIT

VOLUME II

More Uncelebrated Narratives from BLACK HISTORY

words and pictures by
Joel Christian Gill

FULCRUM

Library of Congress Cataloging-in-Publication Data

Gill, Joel Christian.
Uncelebrated narratives from Black history / words and pictures by Joel Christian Gill;
foreword by Henry Louis Gates, Jr.

pages cm -- (Strange fruit ; volume 1)
Summary: "Strange Fruit, Volume I, Uncelebrated narratives from Black history is a collection of stories from African American history that exemplifies success in the face of great adversity. This unique graphic anthology offers historical and cultural commentary on nine uncelebrated heroes whose stories are not often found in history books. Among the stories included are: Henry 'Box' Brown, who escaped from slavery by mailing himself to Philadelphia; Alexander Crummel and the Noyes Academy, the first integrated school in America, established in the 1830s; Marshall 'Major' Taylor, a.k.a. the Black Cyclone, the first Black champion in any sport; and Bass Reeves, the most successful lawman in the Old West. Written and illustrated by Joel Christian Gill, the diverse art beautifully captures the spirit of each remarkable individual and opens a window into an important part of American history"-- Provided by publisher.

Audience: Age 12 to 18.
       ISBN 978-1938486579 (paperback)
1. African Americans--Biography--Juvenile literature. 2. African Americans--Biography--Comic books, strips, etc. 3. Heroes--United States--Biography--Juvenile literature. 4. Heroes--United States--Biography--Comic books, strips, etc. 5. African Americans--History--Anecdotes--Juvenile literature. 6. African Americans--History--Anecdotes--Comic books, strips, etc. 7. Graphic novels. I. Title.
  E185.96.G54 2014
  973.04960730092'2--dc23
  [B]
                              2014010803

Production Assistant: Shannon Scott
Editor: Larisa Hohenboken

Printed in the United States
0 9 8 7 6 5 4 3 2 1

Fulcrum Publishing
4690 Table Mountain Dr., Ste. 100
Golden, CO 80403
800-992-2908 • 303-277-1623
www.fulcrum.bookstore.ipgbooks.com

Contents

Foreword

One of my favorite things as a little girl was to hear my family and elders telling stories about how they grew up. I was especially spellbound by the stories of my grandparents, Sara and Eugene Barnett, who dropped little memories, pearls of their youth, into my eager ears. My grandparents, who grew up in Leary, Georgia, and Athens, Georgia, kept their history alive by passing memories down from mouth to ear like their elders before them. As a little girl, I learned quickly the power of oral storytelling in African American communities, especially in the Deep South.

With Joel Christian Gill's second volume of *Strange Fruit*, he visualizes those oral traditions in vibrant, accessible, and striking ways. This volume takes up the important work of reclamation, presenting the stories of little-known Black folks who get skipped in the history books, Black History Month skits and speeches, and everyday conversations about "the struggle." Like speaking truth to power, Gill draws these heroes to life, helping us recognize that their efforts to help themselves and others were the norm rather than exceptions. That is what makes this volume stand out the most: Gill's understanding that Black excellence is not a reaction to the racial biases imposed by white American history and culture, but is in fact quite commonplace.

The people the reader will meet in this book faced extraordinary circumstances. We are introduced to selfless and courageous Black women like Millie and Christine McCoy, Cathay Williams, and Mary Fields. We learn about the valiant Eugene Bullard. We catch a glimpse of one of the most gracious clapbacks in history, a letter by ex-slave Jourdon Anderson to his former master that debunks the notion of Black inferiority. We get to hear the beauty of the world through the ears of Blind Tom Wiggins. We also recognize the challenge of Black people traveling in Jim Crow America via Victor Green's *Green Book for the Negro Motorist*, which marked safe spaces for Black folks on the road.

Together, these stories offer multiple views of Black people seeking and achieving freedom in the most dire circumstances. Gill illustrates these acts of self-liberation for both young and old, an offering that crosses generations to offer hope for the future and honor our ancestors. Ase.

Regina Bradley

Assistant Professor of English and African Diaspora Studies Kennesaw State University November 2017

Introduction: E Pluribus Unum

E pluribus unum: out of many, one. That is the story of Black people in America. People from different tribes, languages, and cultures; people who were stolen from different societies, brought to this country and forced to build a new nation. Over time, these disparate peoples exerted a strong cultural influence in their new land. Their traditions are now woven into the fabric of America; their food preferences, their music, and their customs are ubiquitous in American society.

By now, the descendants of those many forced migrants, now free, have become one. Some would say they came together out of a sense of community; others would say due to shared struggle. The truth is that it was because of force. These many people were forced into a group based on something as trivial as the amount of melanin in their skin. However, the thing that most profoundly connects these people is their stories. Their stories of struggle and success, heartbreak and triumph; their stories that so often mirror the beloved American rags-to-riches tale.

It is these stories that tell the larger story of America and what it means to be an American. So often, however, these people and their stories have been ignored and forgotten. Every American has heard of Elvis, but how many have heard of Willie "Big Mama" Thornton, who wrote and performed the original "Hound Dog"? Or Sister Rosetta Tharpe, the "godmother of rock and roll"?

This whole undertaking began as a way to say that Black History is more than 28 days in February, as my hashtag #28daysarenotenough indicates. Now it is about how our stories, the stories of all Americans, are connected in ways we often forget due to our obsession with skin tone.

Our humanity is shared through our stories, but the humanity of Black people is placed in a box labeled "Other" that we only open and admire in February. We need these stories to be a larger part of the American story so that people, all people, will realize that there isn't just "Black History" and "White History," but one American history, shaped by all of us.

If we cherish and share these stories, we will increase our connection to each other. When we build strong connections, we will build a better society. A society where the credo *E Pluribus Unum* is a truth we feel in our relationships with each other, not just a slogan on our currency.

Joel Christian Gill
Author, Historian,
Cartoonist, Story Sharer
#28daysarenotenough

JOURDON ANDERSON

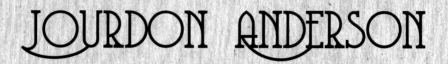

$11,680

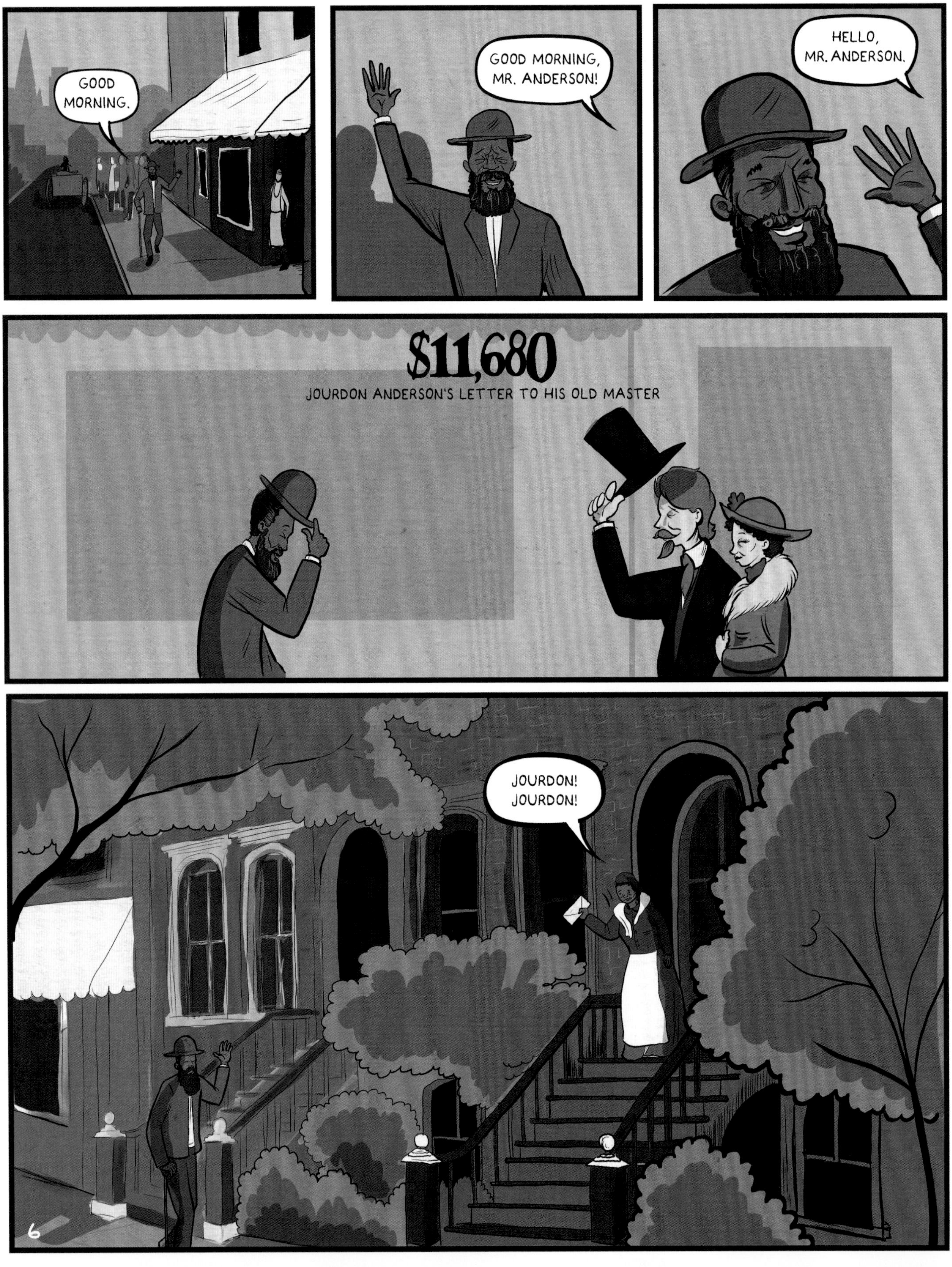
GOOD MORNING.
GOOD MORNING, MR. ANDERSON!
HELLO, MR. ANDERSON.
$11,680
JOURDON ANDERSON'S LETTER TO HIS OLD MASTER
JOURDON! JOURDON!

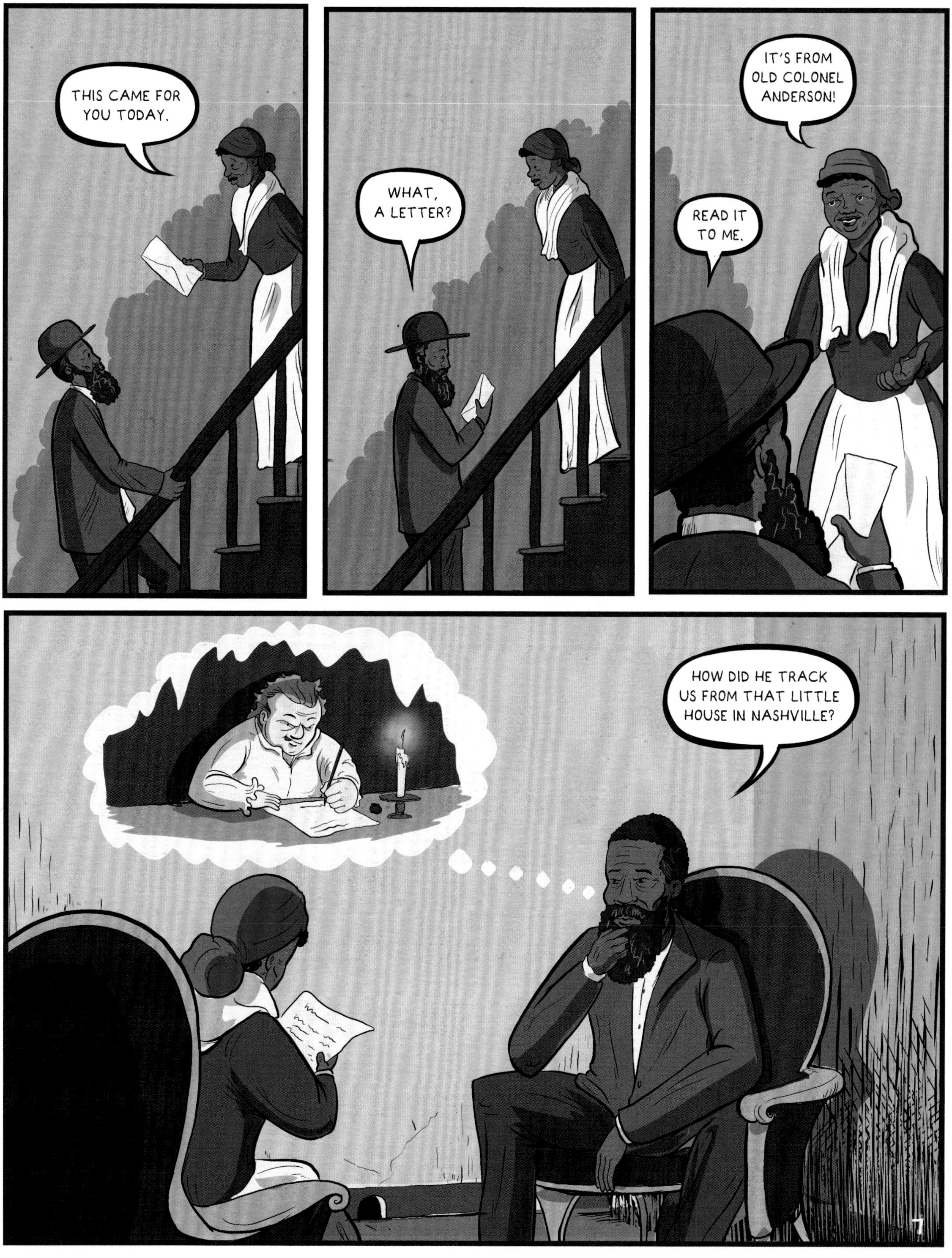
THIS CAME FOR YOU TODAY.
WHAT, A LETTER?
IT'S FROM OLD COLONEL ANDERSON!
READ IT TO ME.
HOW DID HE TRACK US FROM THAT LITTLE HOUSE IN NASHVILLE?

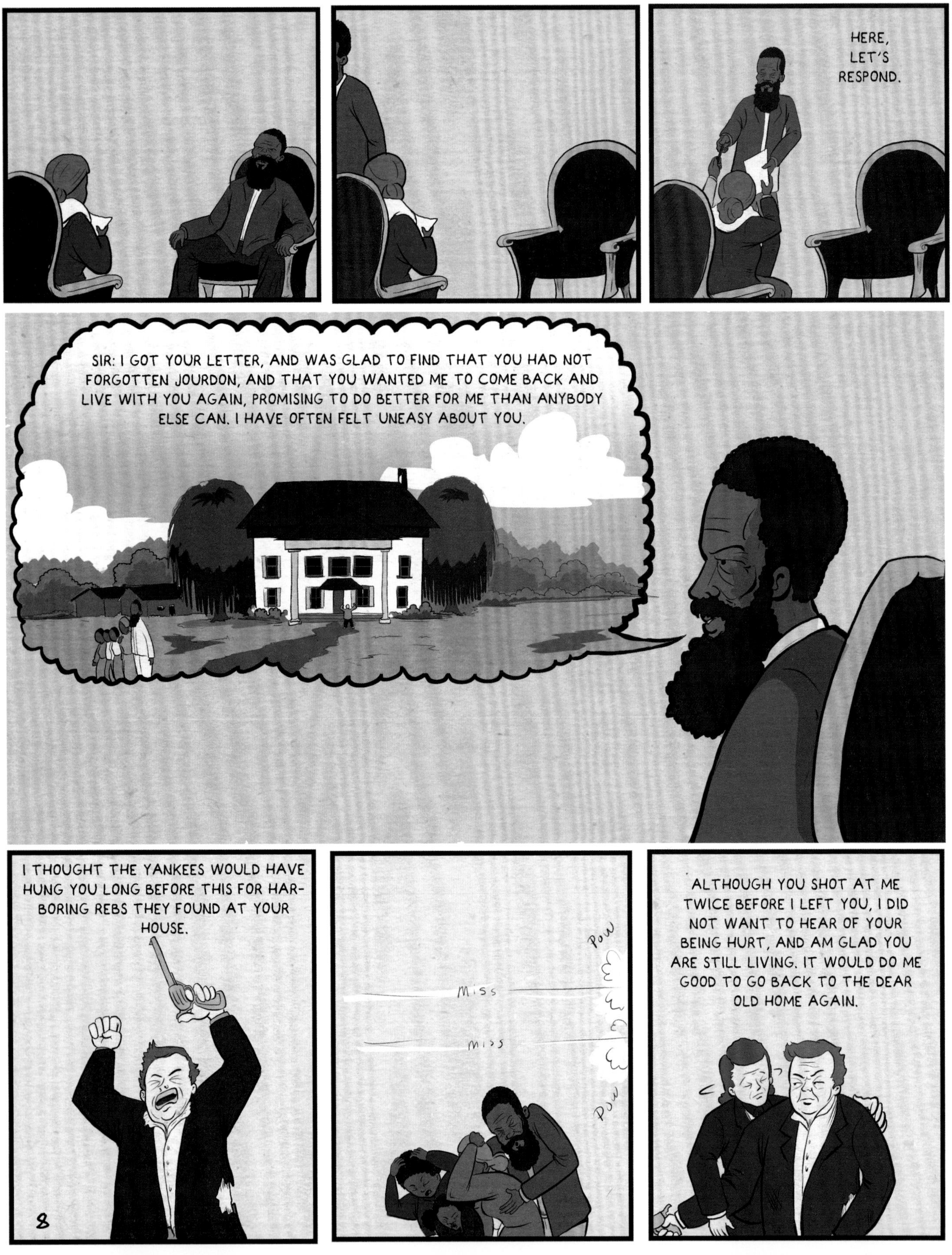
HERE, LET'S RESPOND.
SIR: I GOT YOUR LETTER, AND WAS GLAD TO FIND THAT YOU HAD NOT FORGOTTEN JOURDON, AND THAT YOU WANTED ME TO COME BACK AND LIVE WITH YOU AGAIN, PROMISING TO DO BETTER FOR ME THAN ANYBODY ELSE CAN. I HAVE OFTEN FELT UNEASY ABOUT YOU.
I THOUGHT THE YANKEES WOULD HAVE HUNG YOU LONG BEFORE THIS FOR HAR-BORING REBS THEY FOUND AT YOUR HOUSE.
POW
MISS
MISS
POW
ALTHOUGH YOU SHOT AT ME TWICE BEFORE I LEFT YOU, I DID NOT WANT TO HEAR OF YOUR BEING HURT, AND AM GLAD YOU ARE STILL LIVING. IT WOULD DO ME GOOD TO GO BACK TO THE DEAR OLD HOME AGAIN.

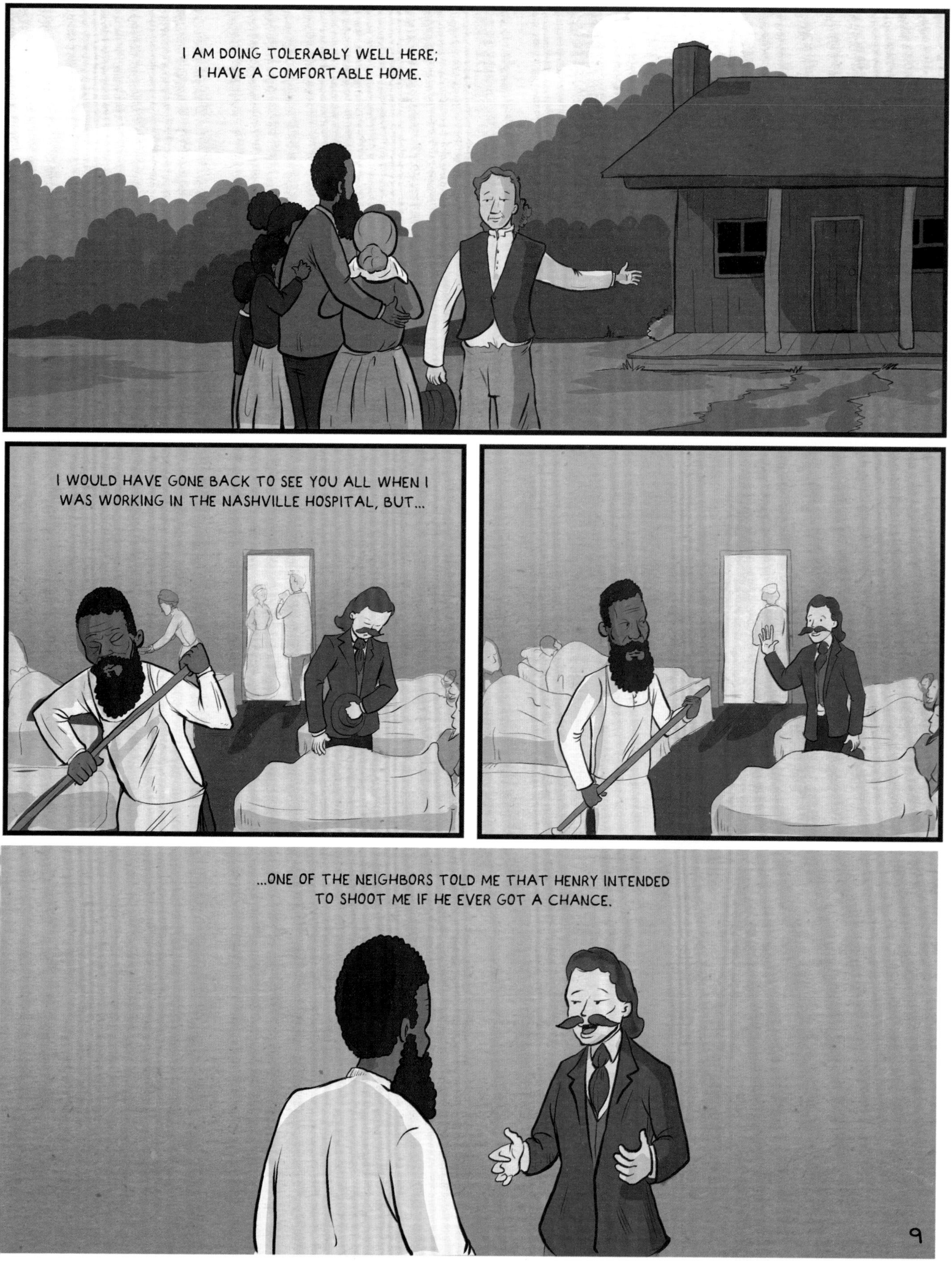
I AM DOING TOLERABLY WELL HERE; I HAVE A COMFORTABLE HOME.
I WOULD HAVE GONE BACK TO SEE YOU ALL WHEN I WAS WORKING IN THE NASHVILLE HOSPITAL, BUT...
...ONE OF THE NEIGHBORS TOLD ME THAT HENRY INTENDED TO SHOOT ME IF HE EVER GOT A CHANCE.

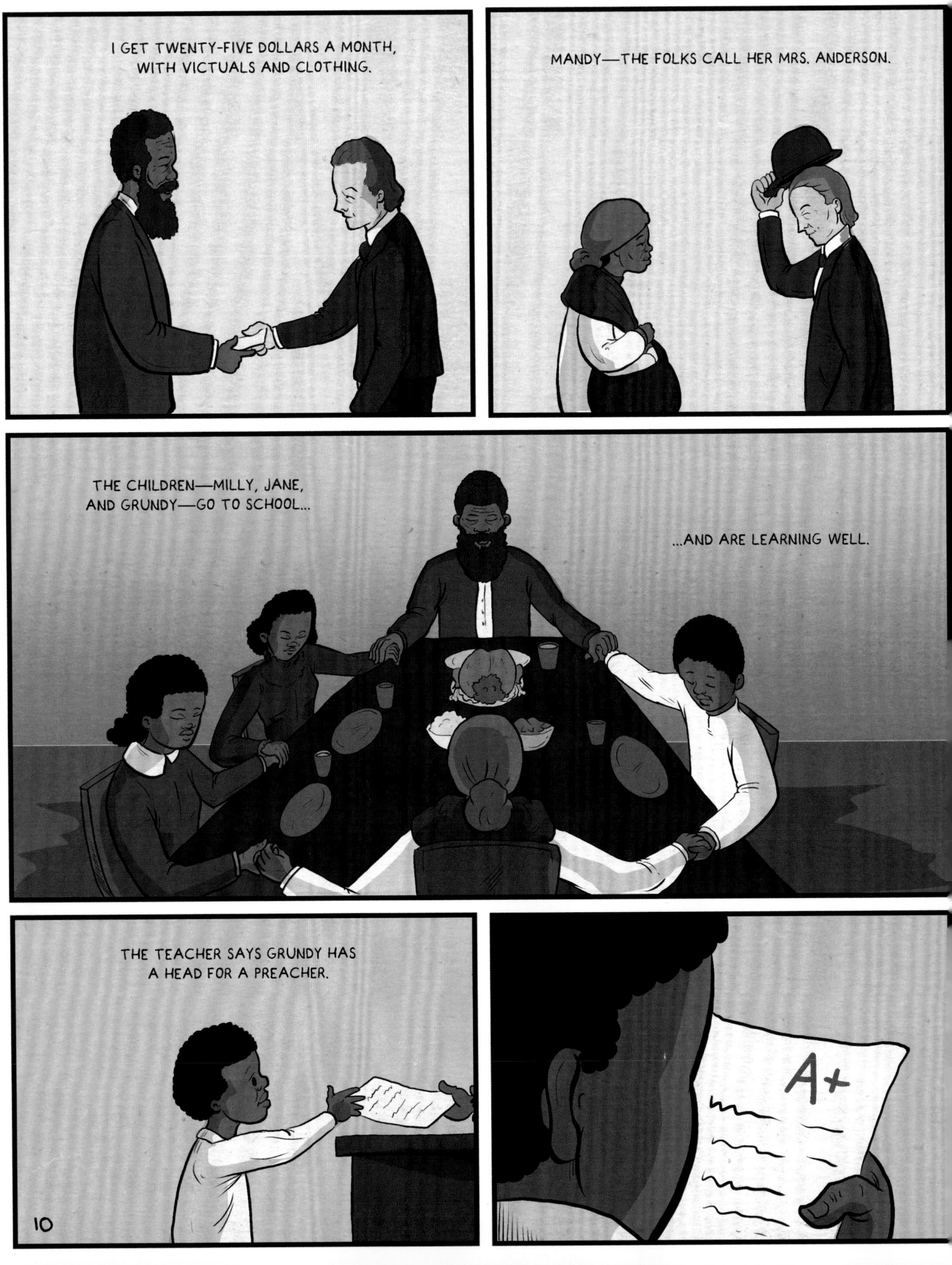
I GET TWENTY-FIVE DOLLARS A MONTH, WITH VICTUALS AND CLOTHING.
MANDY—THE FOLKS CALL HER MRS. ANDERSON.
THE CHILDREN—MILLY, JANE, AND GRUNDY—GO TO SCHOOL...
...AND ARE LEARNING WELL.
THE TEACHER SAYS GRUNDY HAS A HEAD FOR A PREACHER.
A+

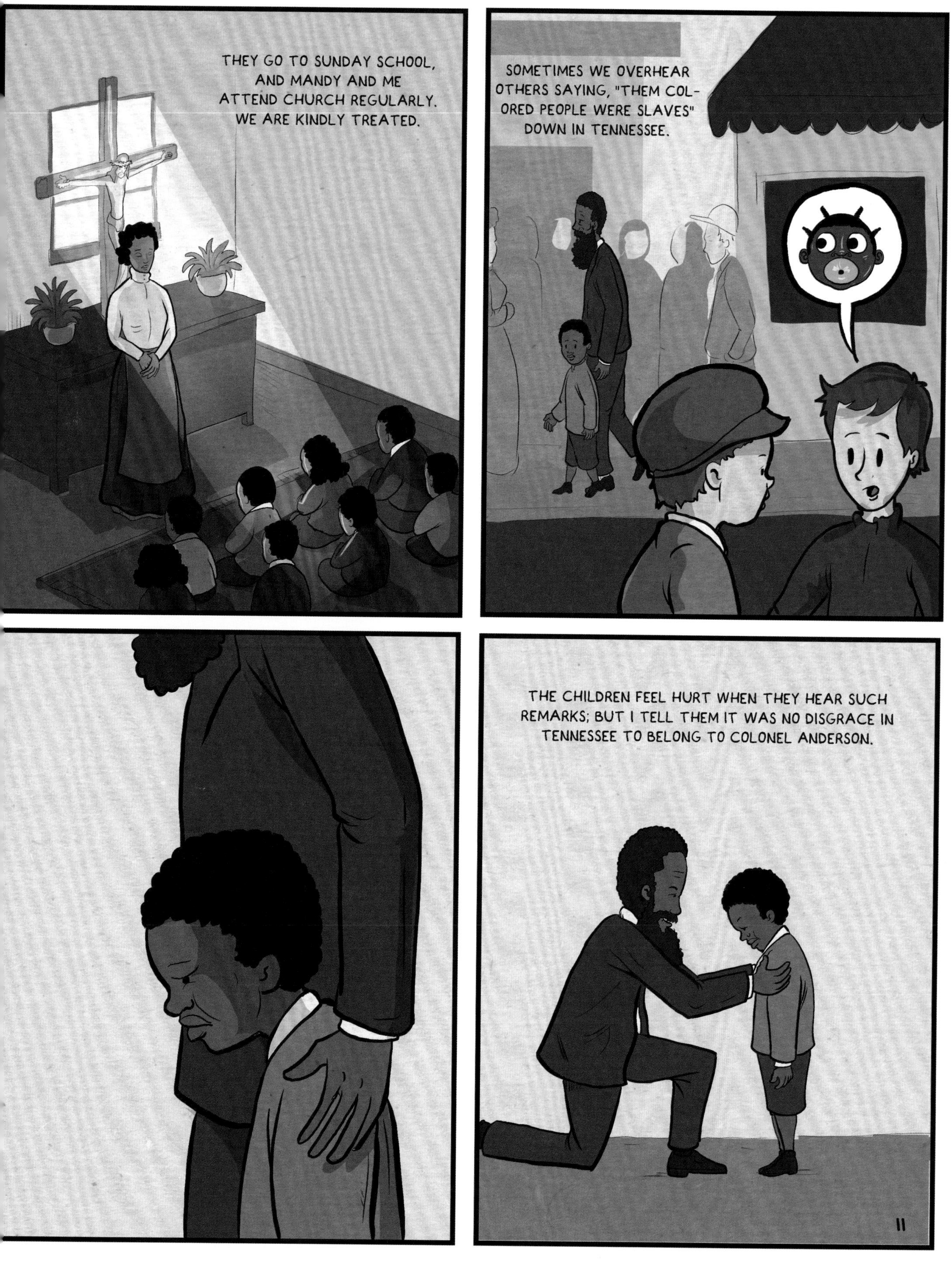
THEY GO TO SUNDAY SCHOOL, AND MANDY AND ME ATTEND CHURCH REGULARLY. WE ARE KINDLY TREATED.
SOMETIMES WE OVERHEAR OTHERS SAYING, "THEM COL-ORED PEOPLE WERE SLAVES" DOWN IN TENNESSEE.
THE CHILDREN FEEL HURT WHEN THEY HEAR SUCH REMARKS; BUT I TELL THEM IT WAS NO DISGRACE IN TENNESSEE TO BELONG TO COLONEL ANDERSON.

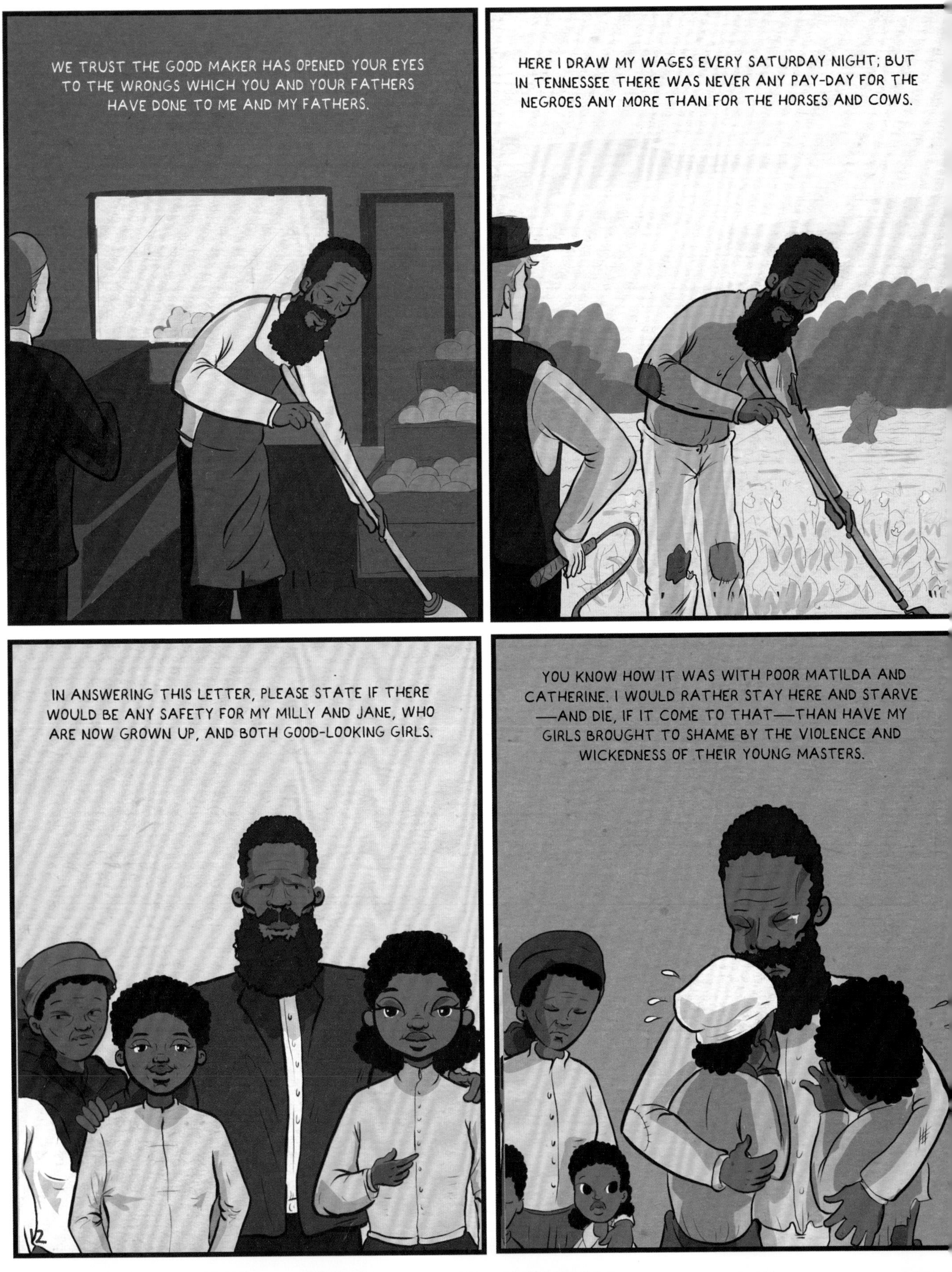
WE TRUST THE GOOD MAKER HAS OPENED YOUR EYES TO THE WRONGS WHICH YOU AND YOUR FATHERS HAVE DONE TO ME AND MY FATHERS.
HERE I DRAW MY WAGES EVERY SATURDAY NIGHT; BUT IN TENNESSEE THERE WAS NEVER ANY PAY-DAY FOR THE NEGROES ANY MORE THAN FOR THE HORSES AND COWS.
IN ANSWERING THIS LETTER, PLEASE STATE IF THERE WOULD BE ANY SAFETY FOR MY MILLY AND JANE, WHO ARE NOW GROWN UP, AND BOTH GOOD-LOOKING GIRLS.
YOU KNOW HOW IT WAS WITH POOR MATILDA AND CATHERINE. I WOULD RATHER STAY HERE AND STARVE—AND DIE, IF IT COME TO THAT—THAN HAVE MY GIRLS BROUGHT TO SHAME BY THE VIOLENCE AND WICKEDNESS OF THEIR YOUNG MASTERS.

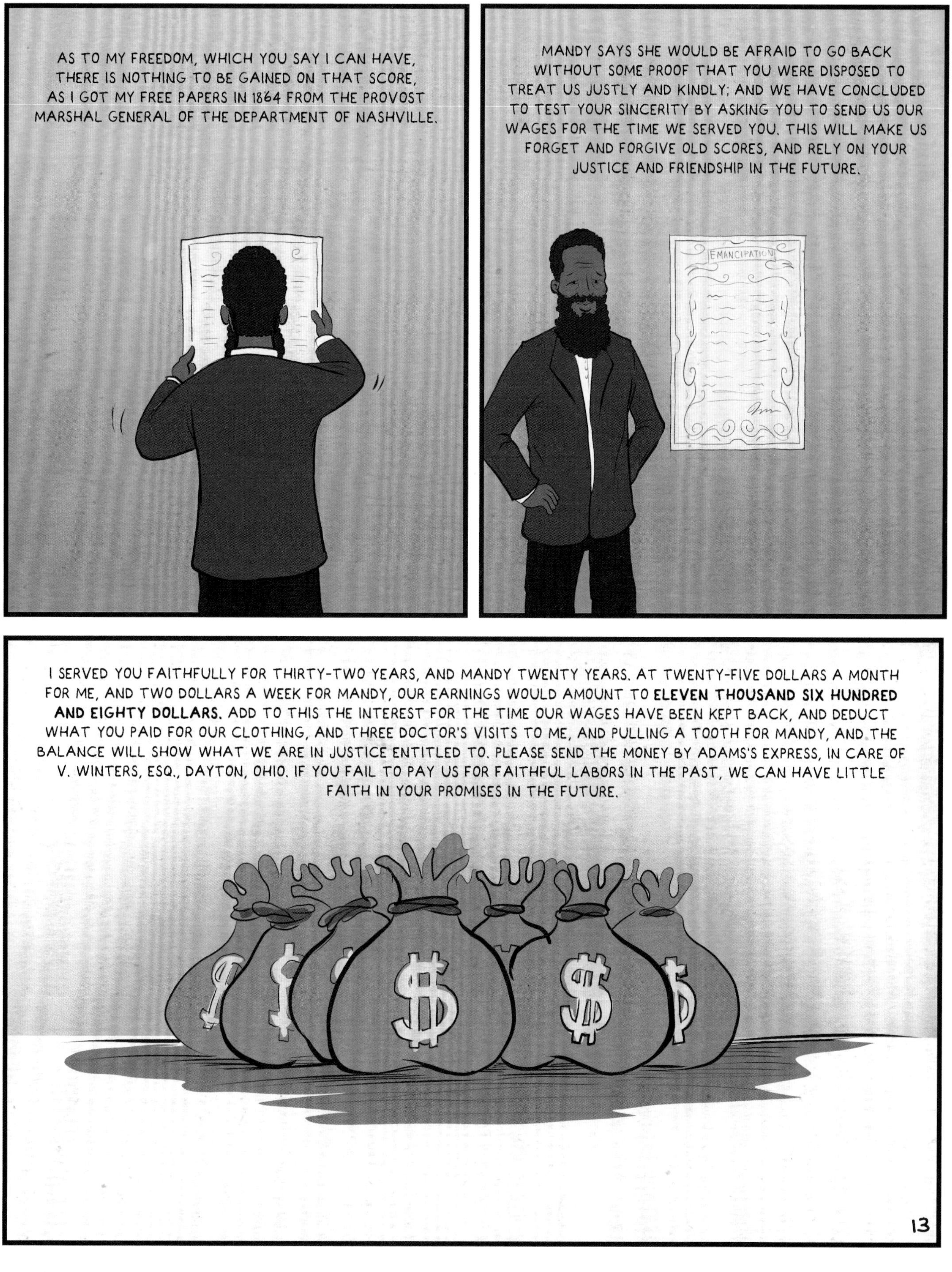
AS TO MY FREEDOM, WHICH YOU SAY I CAN HAVE, THERE IS NOTHING TO BE GAINED ON THAT SCORE, AS I GOT MY FREE PAPERS IN 1864 FROM THE PROVOST MARSHAL GENERAL OF THE DEPARTMENT OF NASHVILLE.
MANDY SAYS SHE WOULD BE AFRAID TO GO BACK WITHOUT SOME PROOF THAT YOU WERE DISPOSED TO TREAT US JUSTLY AND KINDLY; AND WE HAVE CONCLUDED TO TEST YOUR SINCERITY BY ASKING YOU TO SEND US OUR WAGES FOR THE TIME WE SERVED YOU. THIS WILL MAKE US FORGET AND FORGIVE OLD SCORES, AND RELY ON YOUR JUSTICE AND FRIENDSHIP IN THE FUTURE.
EMANCIPATION
I SERVED YOU FAITHFULLY FOR THIRTY-TWO YEARS, AND MANDY TWENTY YEARS. AT TWENTY-FIVE DOLLARS A MONTH FOR ME, AND TWO DOLLARS A WEEK FOR MANDY, OUR EARNINGS WOULD AMOUNT TO **ELEVEN THOUSAND SIX HUNDRED AND EIGHTY DOLLARS.** ADD TO THIS THE INTEREST FOR THE TIME OUR WAGES HAVE BEEN KEPT BACK, AND DEDUCT WHAT YOU PAID FOR OUR CLOTHING, AND THREE DOCTOR'S VISITS TO ME, AND PULLING A TOOTH FOR MANDY, AND THE BALANCE WILL SHOW WHAT WE ARE IN JUSTICE ENTITLED TO. PLEASE SEND THE MONEY BY ADAMS'S EXPRESS, IN CARE OF V. WINTERS, ESQ., DAYTON, OHIO. IF YOU FAIL TO PAY US FOR FAITHFUL LABORS IN THE PAST, WE CAN HAVE LITTLE FAITH IN YOUR PROMISES IN THE FUTURE.

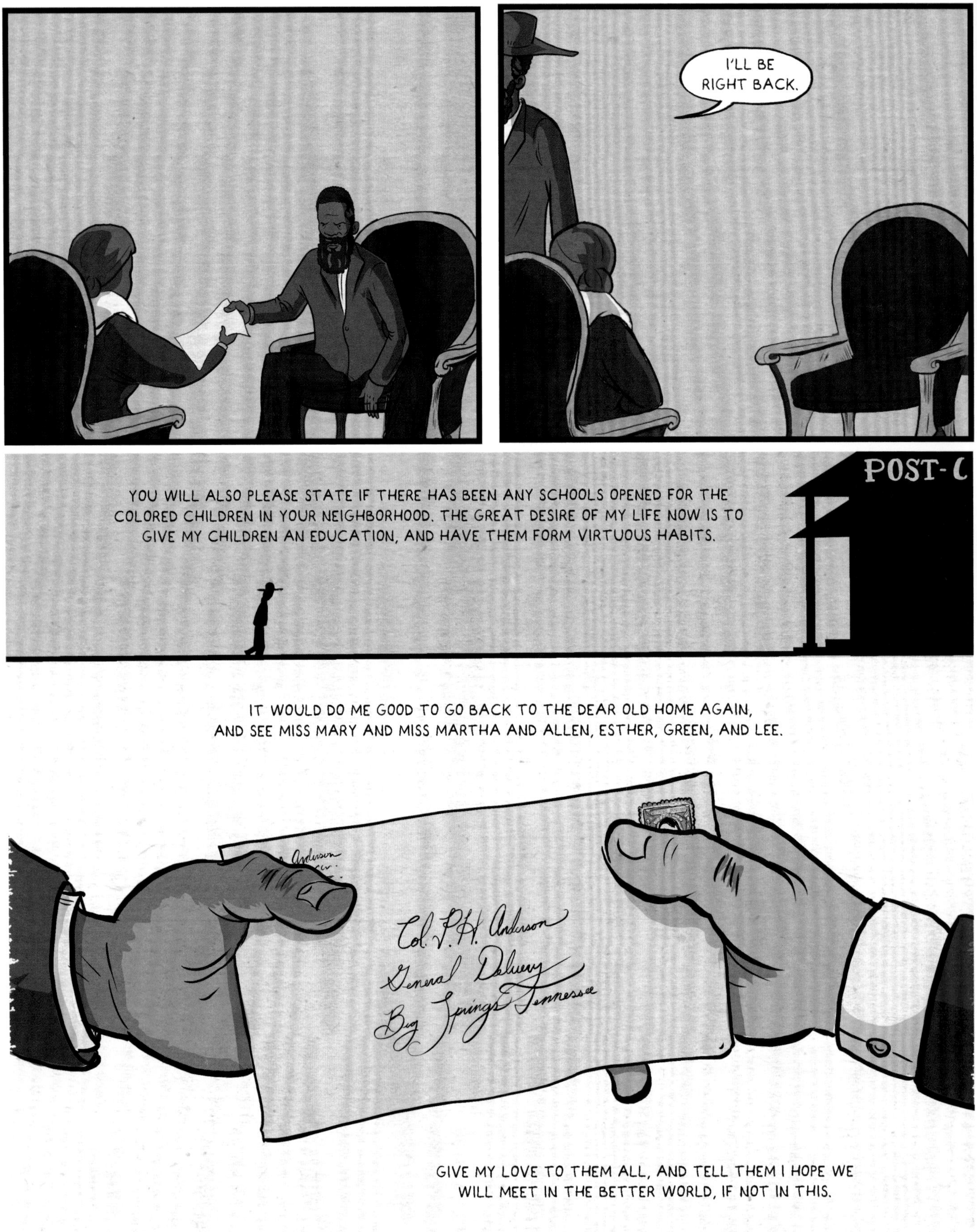
I'LL BE RIGHT BACK.
POST-
YOU WILL ALSO PLEASE STATE IF THERE HAS BEEN ANY SCHOOLS OPENED FOR THE COLORED CHILDREN IN YOUR NEIGHBORHOOD. THE GREAT DESIRE OF MY LIFE NOW IS TO GIVE MY CHILDREN AN EDUCATION, AND HAVE THEM FORM VIRTUOUS HABITS.
IT WOULD DO ME GOOD TO GO BACK TO THE DEAR OLD HOME AGAIN, AND SEE MISS MARY AND MISS MARTHA AND ALLEN, ESTHER, GREEN, AND LEE.
Col. P.H. Anderson
General Delivery
Big Springs Tennessee
GIVE MY LOVE TO THEM ALL, AND TELL THEM I HOPE WE WILL MEET IN THE BETTER WORLD, IF NOT IN THIS.

SAY HOWDY TO GEORGE CARTER FOR ME, AND THANK HIM FOR TAKING THE PISTOL FROM YOU WHEN YOU WERE SHOOTING AT ME.

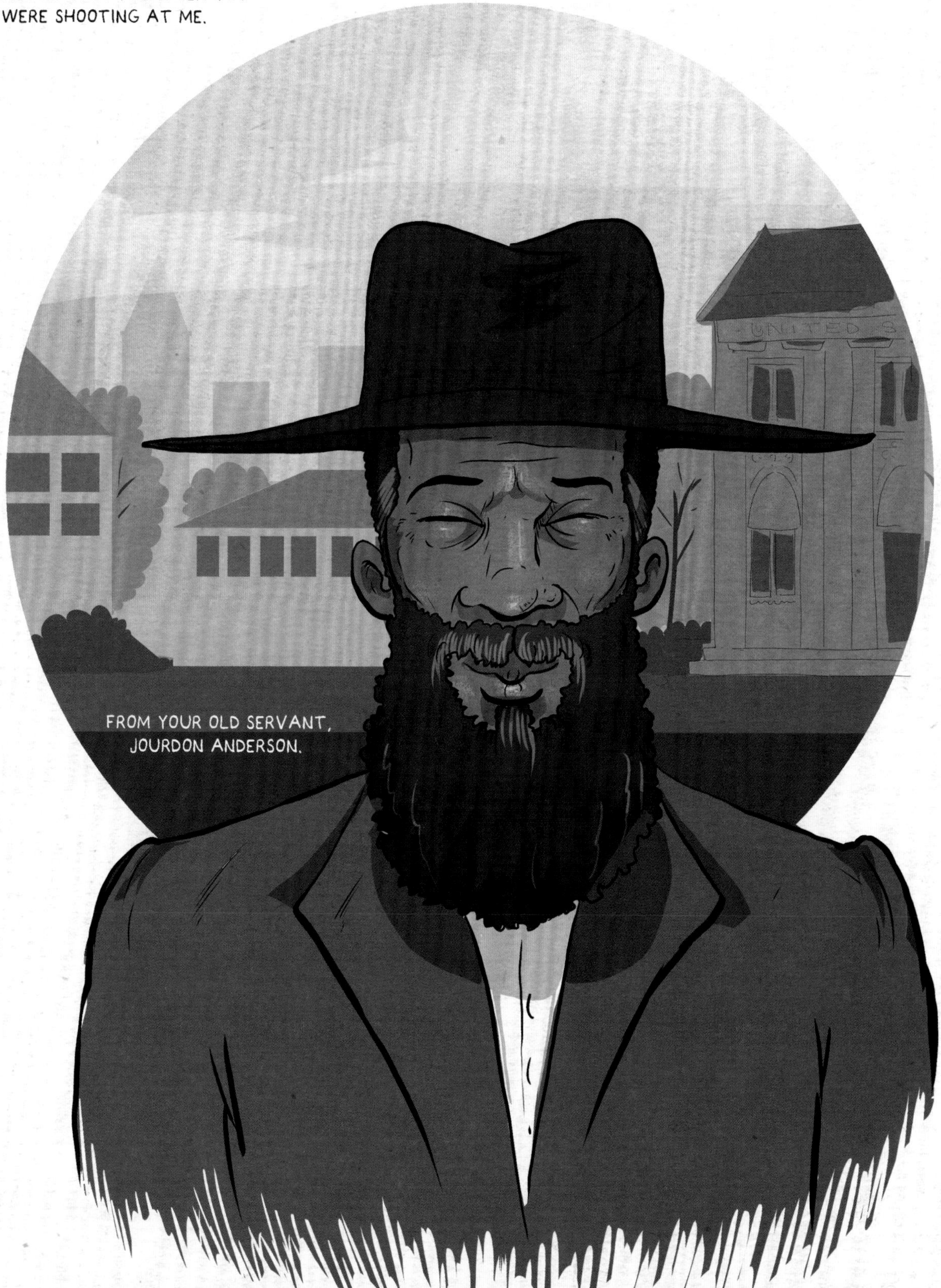
FROM YOUR OLD SERVANT,
JOURDON ANDERSON.

STAGECOACH MARY FIELDS

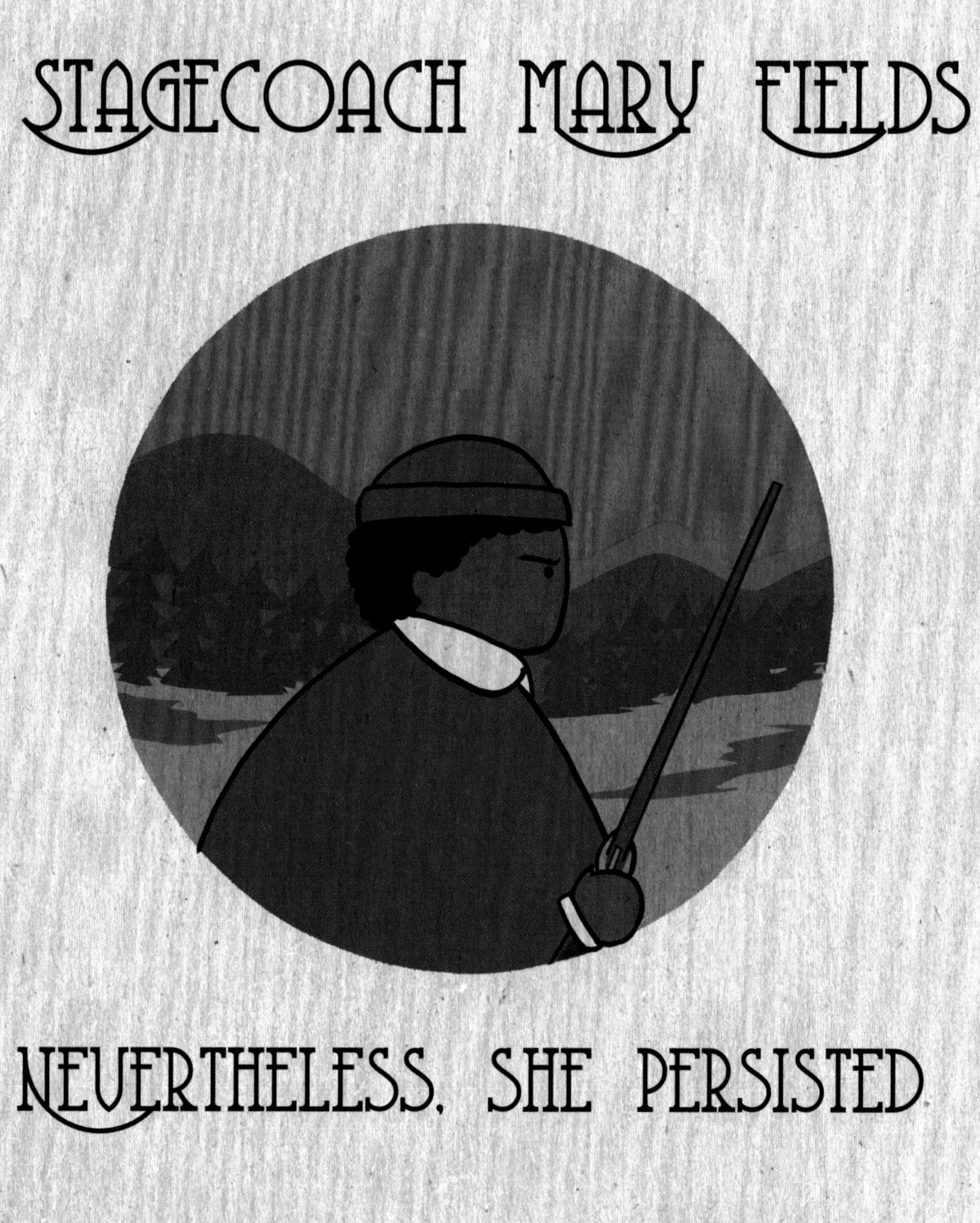

NEVERTHELESS, SHE PERSISTED

NEVERTHELESS, SHE PERSISTED

THE STORY OF STAGECOACH MARY FIELDS

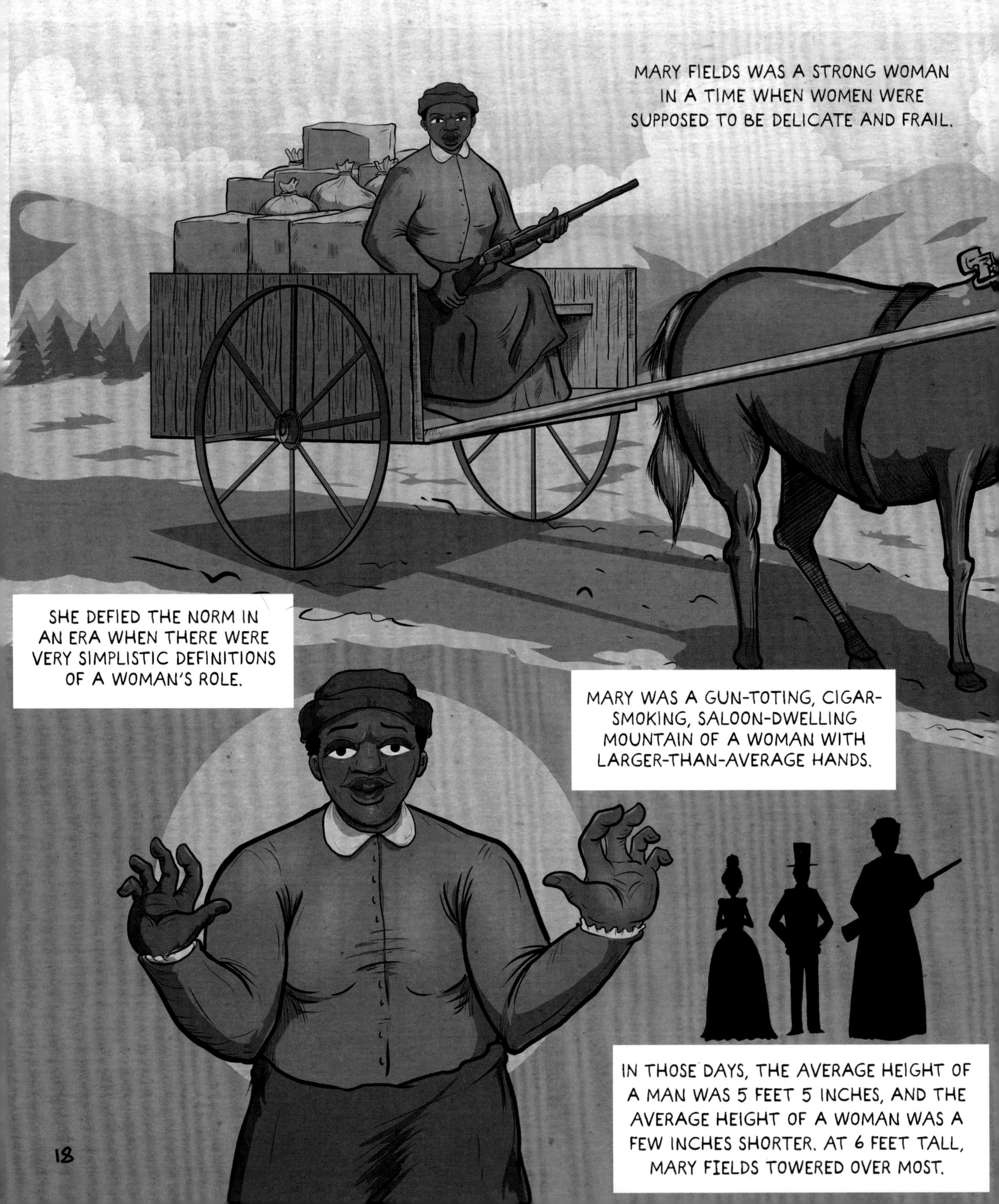
MARY FIELDS WAS A STRONG WOMAN IN A TIME WHEN WOMEN WERE SUPPOSED TO BE DELICATE AND FRAIL.
SHE DEFIED THE NORM IN AN ERA WHEN THERE WERE VERY SIMPLISTIC DEFINITIONS OF A WOMAN'S ROLE.
MARY WAS A GUN-TOTING, CIGAR-SMOKING, SALOON-DWELLING MOUNTAIN OF A WOMAN WITH LARGER-THAN-AVERAGE HANDS.
IN THOSE DAYS, THE AVERAGE HEIGHT OF A MAN WAS 5 FEET 5 INCHES, AND THE AVERAGE HEIGHT OF A WOMAN WAS A FEW INCHES SHORTER. AT 6 FEET TALL, MARY FIELDS TOWERED OVER MOST.

MARY WAS NOT BOUND BY CONVENTION. SHE WORE A DRESS LIKE THE "PROPER" LADIES...

...BUT THERE WAS ALWAYS A PAIR OF TROUSERS ON UNDERNEATH.

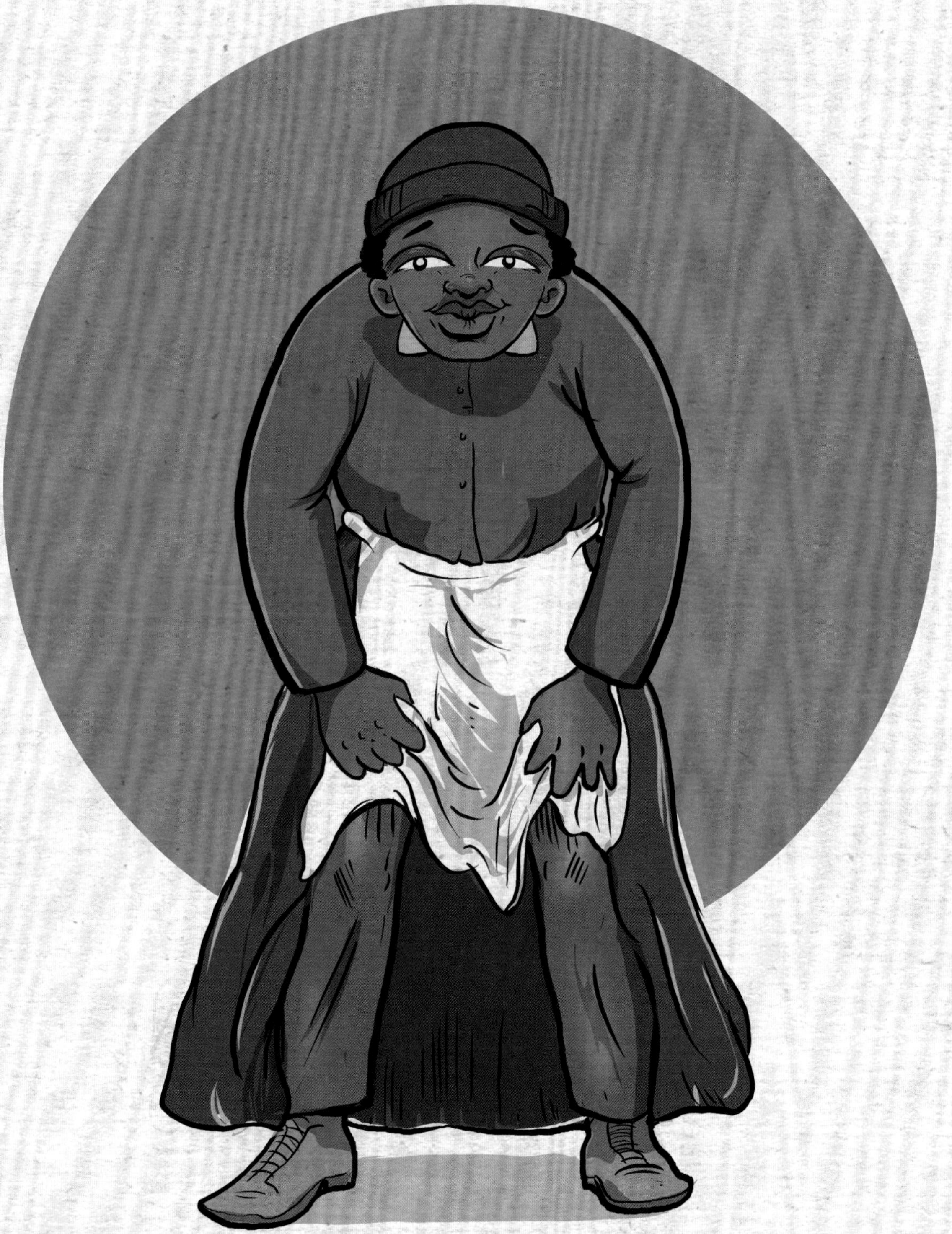

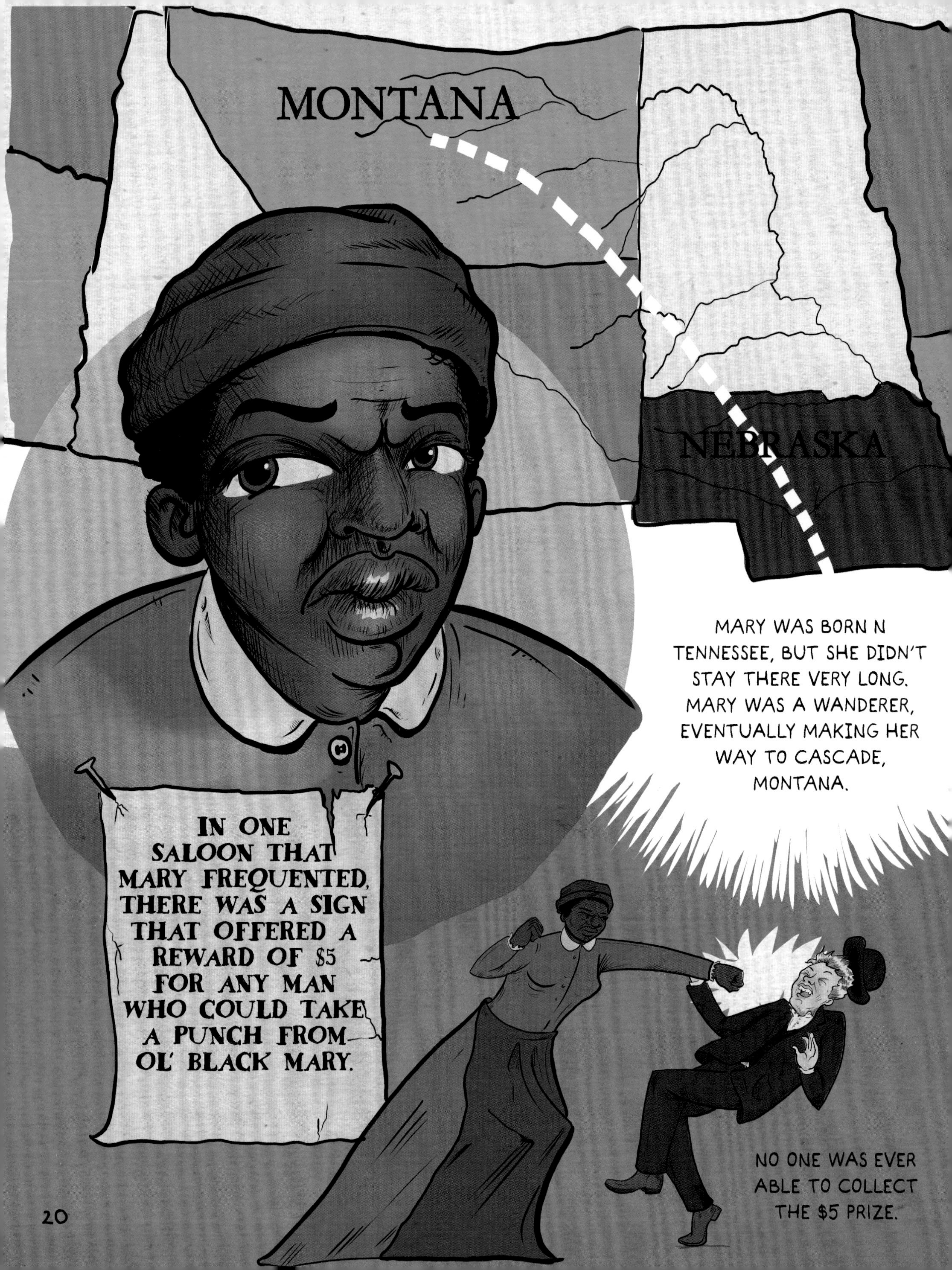

MONTANA
NEBRASKA
MARY WAS BORN N TENNESSEE, BUT SHE DIDN'T STAY THERE VERY LONG. MARY WAS A WANDERER, EVENTUALLY MAKING HER WAY TO CASCADE, MONTANA.
IN ONE SALOON THAT MARY FREQUENTED, THERE WAS A SIGN THAT OFFERED A REWARD OF $5 FOR ANY MAN WHO COULD TAKE A PUNCH FROM OL' BLACK MARY.
NO ONE WAS EVER ABLE TO COLLECT THE $5 PRIZE.

MARY'S FIRST JOB IN MONTANA WAS AT A SCHOOL RUN BY NUNS. ONE OF THE NUNS, MOTHER AMADEUS, WAS MARY'S CHILDHOOD FRIEND, AND HAD ASKED HER TO COME HELP OUT.

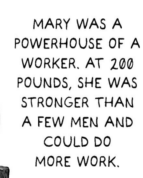

MARY WAS A POWERHOUSE OF A WORKER. AT 200 POUNDS, SHE WAS STRONGER THAN A FEW MEN AND COULD DO MORE WORK.

SOME OF THE MEN BRISTLED AT THE THOUGHT OF A WOMAN, AND A BLACK WOMAN AT THAT, WORKING HARDER THAN THEY COULD.

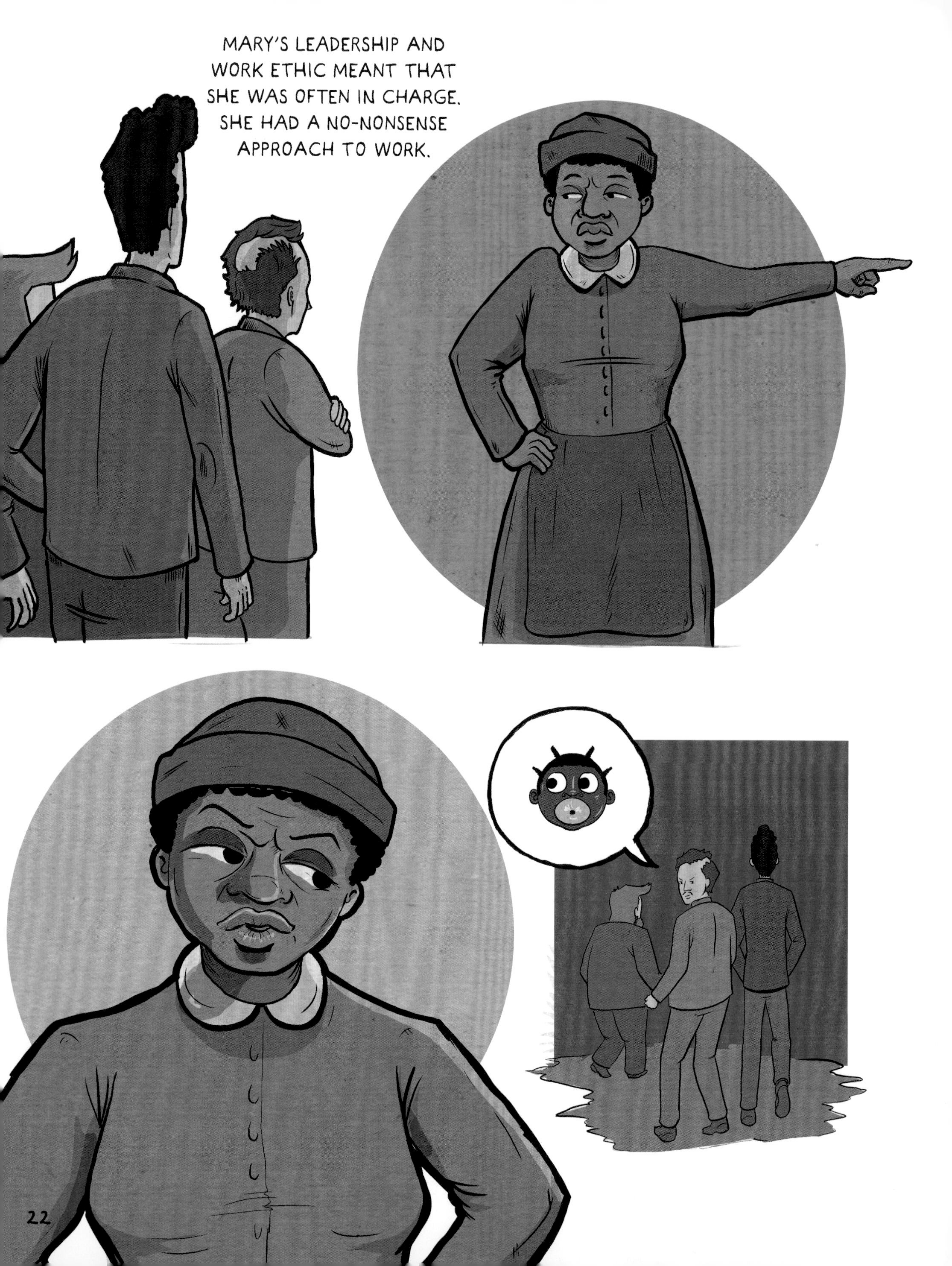
MARY'S LEADERSHIP AND WORK ETHIC MEANT THAT SHE WAS OFTEN IN CHARGE. SHE HAD A NO-NONSENSE APPROACH TO WORK.

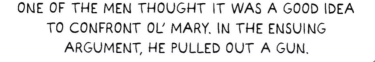

ONE OF THE MEN THOUGHT IT WAS A GOOD IDEA TO CONFRONT OL' MARY. IN THE ENSUING ARGUMENT, HE PULLED OUT A GUN.

LITTLE DID HE KNOW, MARY WAS ALWAYS PREPARED.

MARY ALWAYS KEPT A PISTOL HOLSTERED JUST UNDER HER APRON. THE GUNFIGHT WAS INTENSE, BUT IN THE END, MARY FIELDS CAME OUT VICTORIOUS, WITH HER ATTACKER SHOT IN HIS... WELL, LET'S JUST SAY HE WOULDN'T BE SITTING FOR A FEW WEEKS. BUT HER VICTORY CAME AT A COST.

ONE OF THE PRIEST'S SHIRTS, LEFT OUT TO DRY, WAS DAMAGED IN THE SHOOT-OUT. HE THOUGHT MARY UNRULY AND DEMANDED THAT SHE BE SENT AWAY.

23

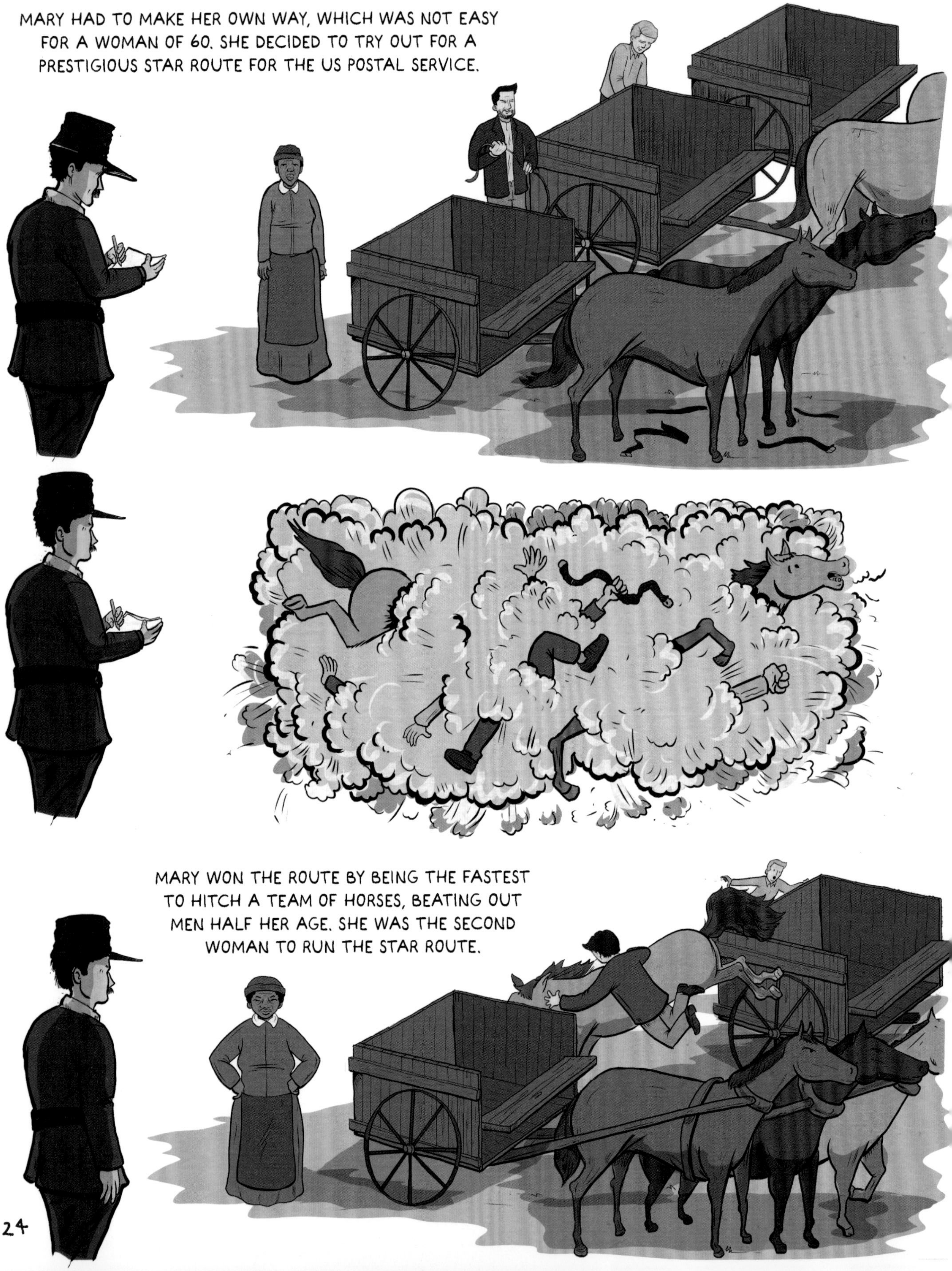
MARY HAD TO MAKE HER OWN WAY, WHICH WAS NOT EASY FOR A WOMAN OF 60. SHE DECIDED TO TRY OUT FOR A PRESTIGIOUS STAR ROUTE FOR THE US POSTAL SERVICE.
MARY WON THE ROUTE BY BEING THE FASTEST TO HITCH A TEAM OF HORSES, BEATING OUT MEN HALF HER AGE. SHE WAS THE SECOND WOMAN TO RUN THE STAR ROUTE.

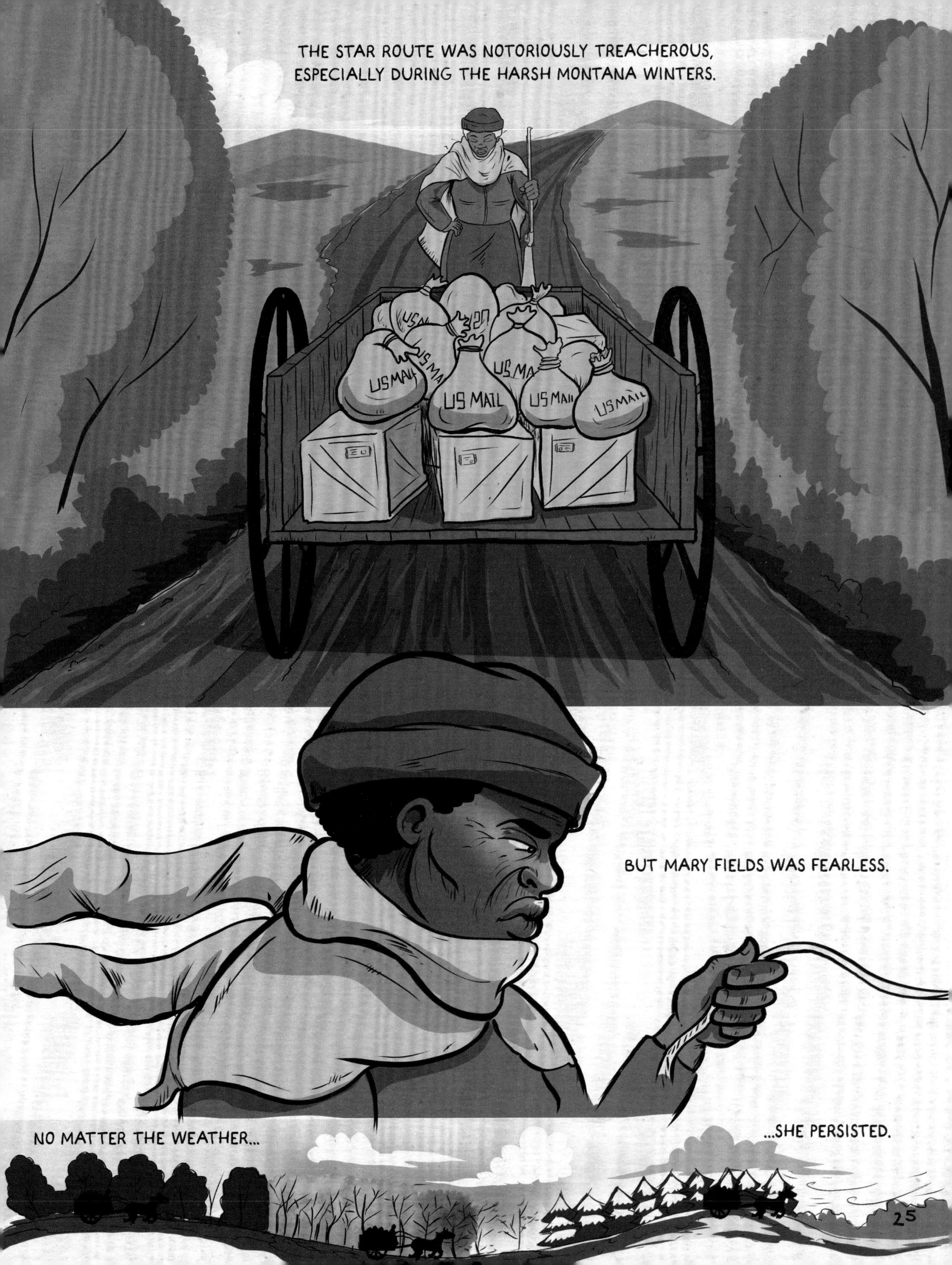

THE STAR ROUTE WAS NOTORIOUSLY TREACHEROUS, ESPECIALLY DURING THE HARSH MONTANA WINTERS.
US MAIL
BUT MARY FIELDS WAS FEARLESS.
NO MATTER THE WEATHER...
...SHE PERSISTED.

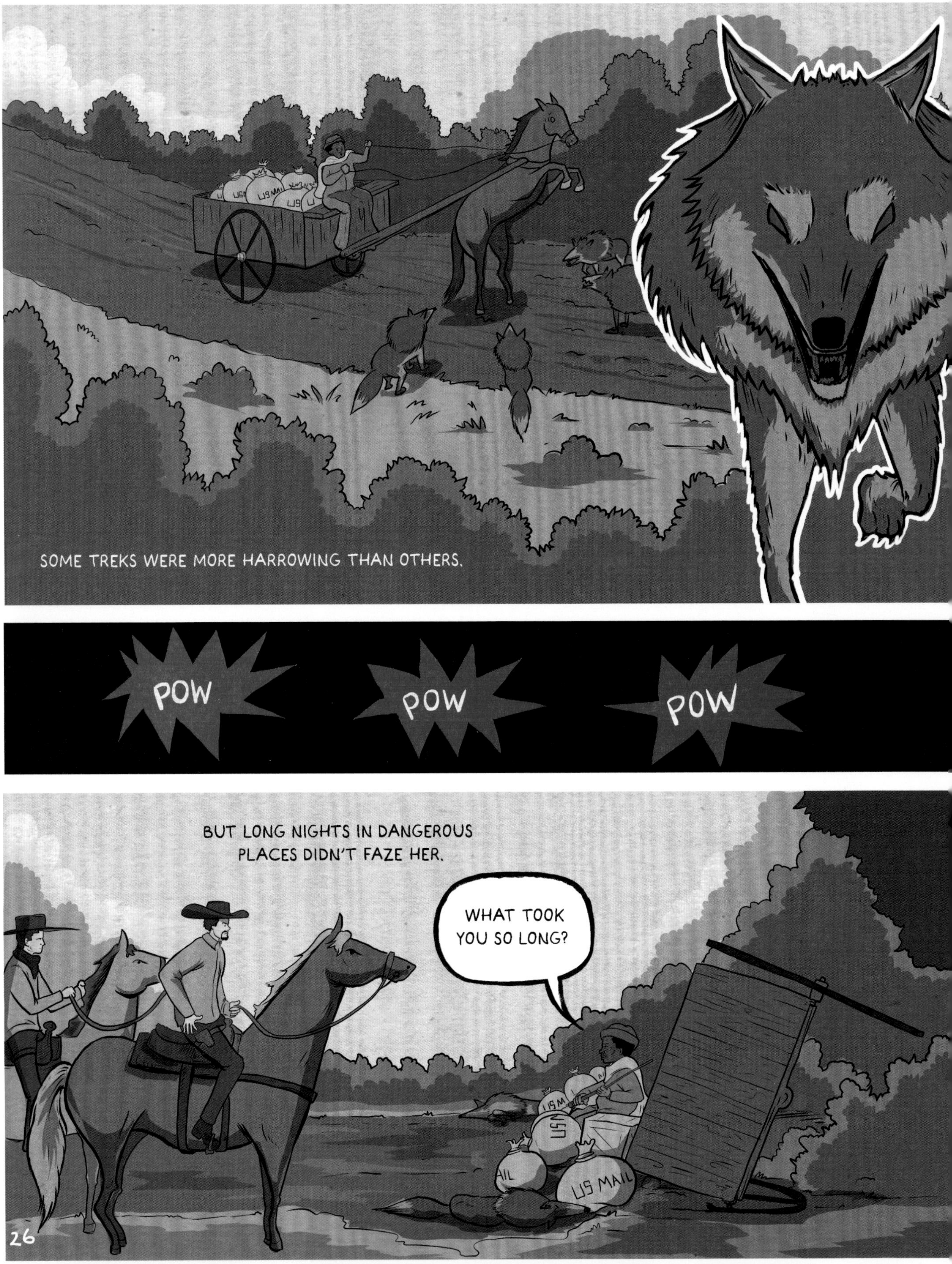
SOME TREKS WERE MORE HARROWING THAN OTHERS.
POW
POW
POW
BUT LONG NIGHTS IN DANGEROUS PLACES DIDN'T FAZE HER.
WHAT TOOK YOU SO LONG?
US MAIL

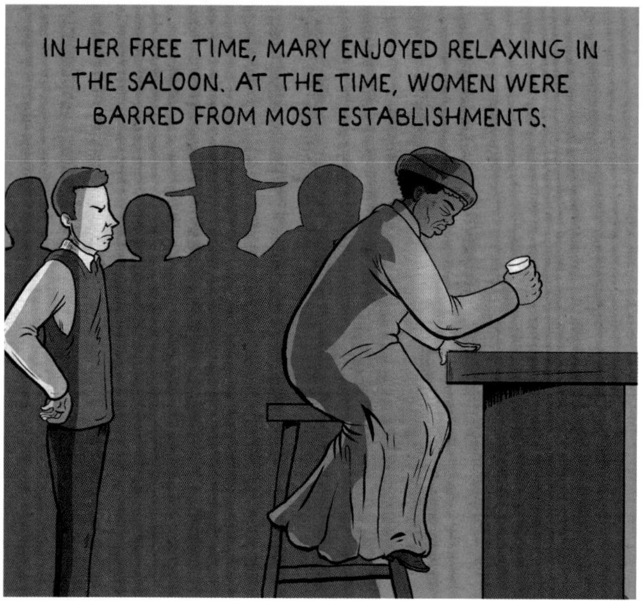
IN HER FREE TIME, MARY ENJOYED RELAXING IN THE SALOON. AT THE TIME, WOMEN WERE BARRED FROM MOST ESTABLISHMENTS.

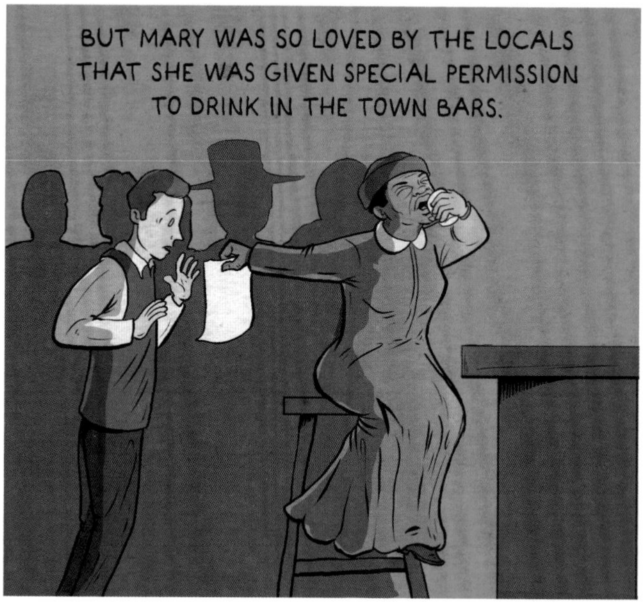
BUT MARY WAS SO LOVED BY THE LOCALS THAT SHE WAS GIVEN SPECIAL PERMISSION TO DRINK IN THE TOWN BARS.

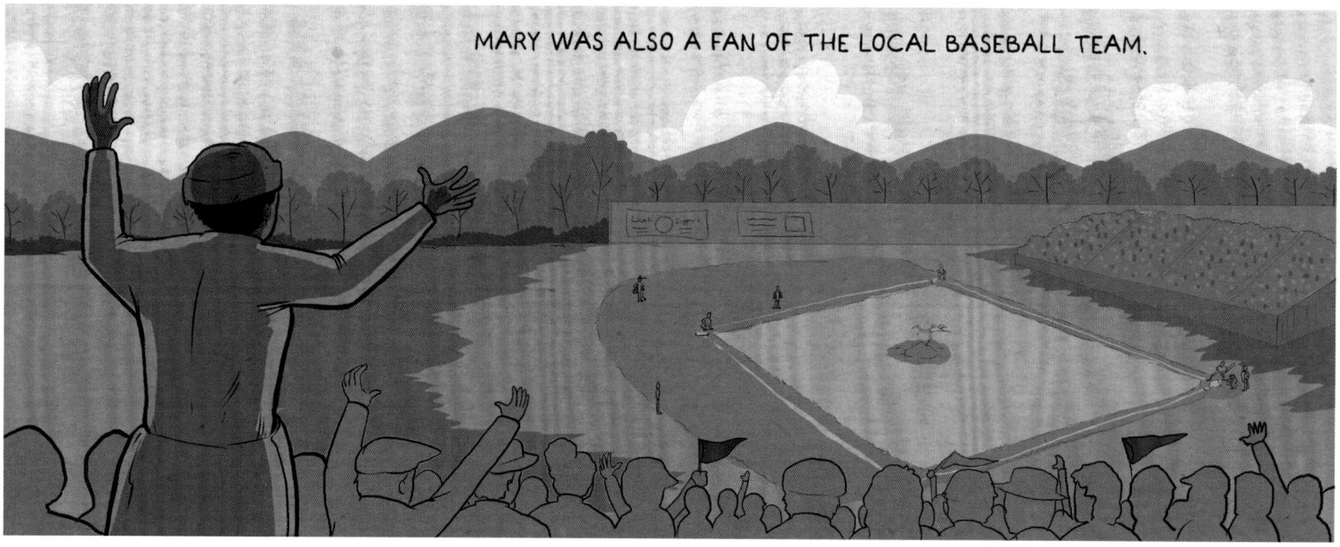
MARY WAS ALSO A FAN OF THE LOCAL BASEBALL TEAM.

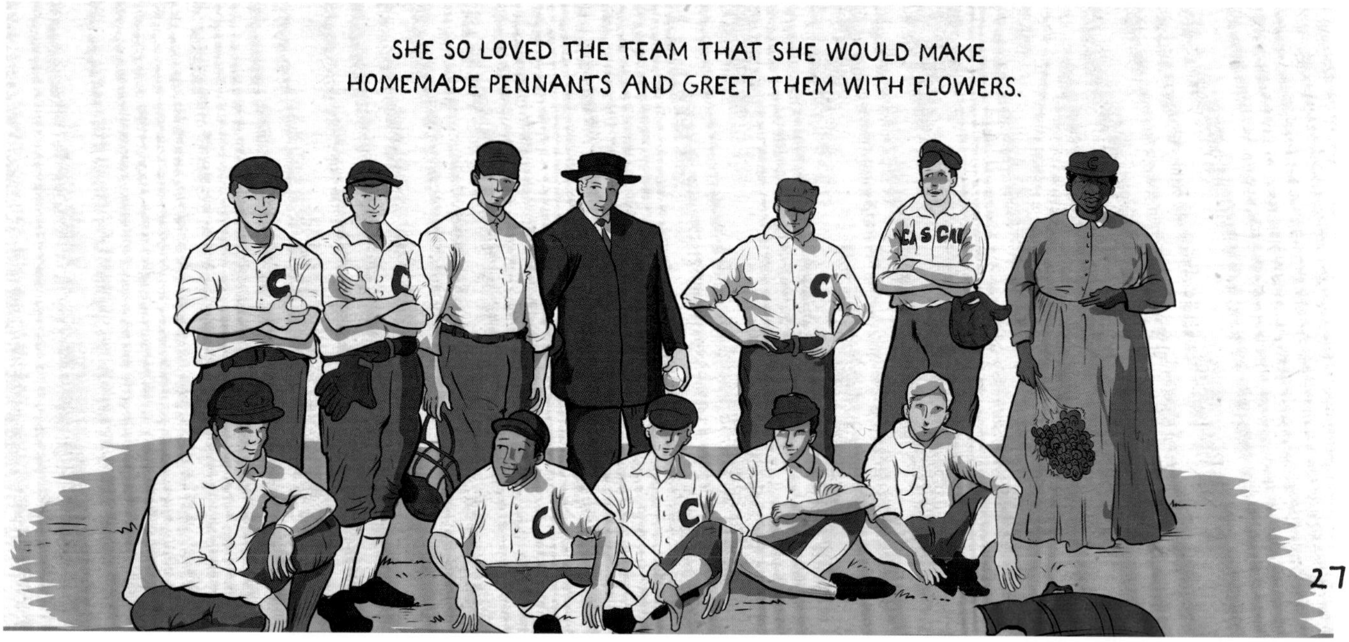
SHE SO LOVED THE TEAM THAT SHE WOULD MAKE HOMEMADE PENNANTS AND GREET THEM WITH FLOWERS.

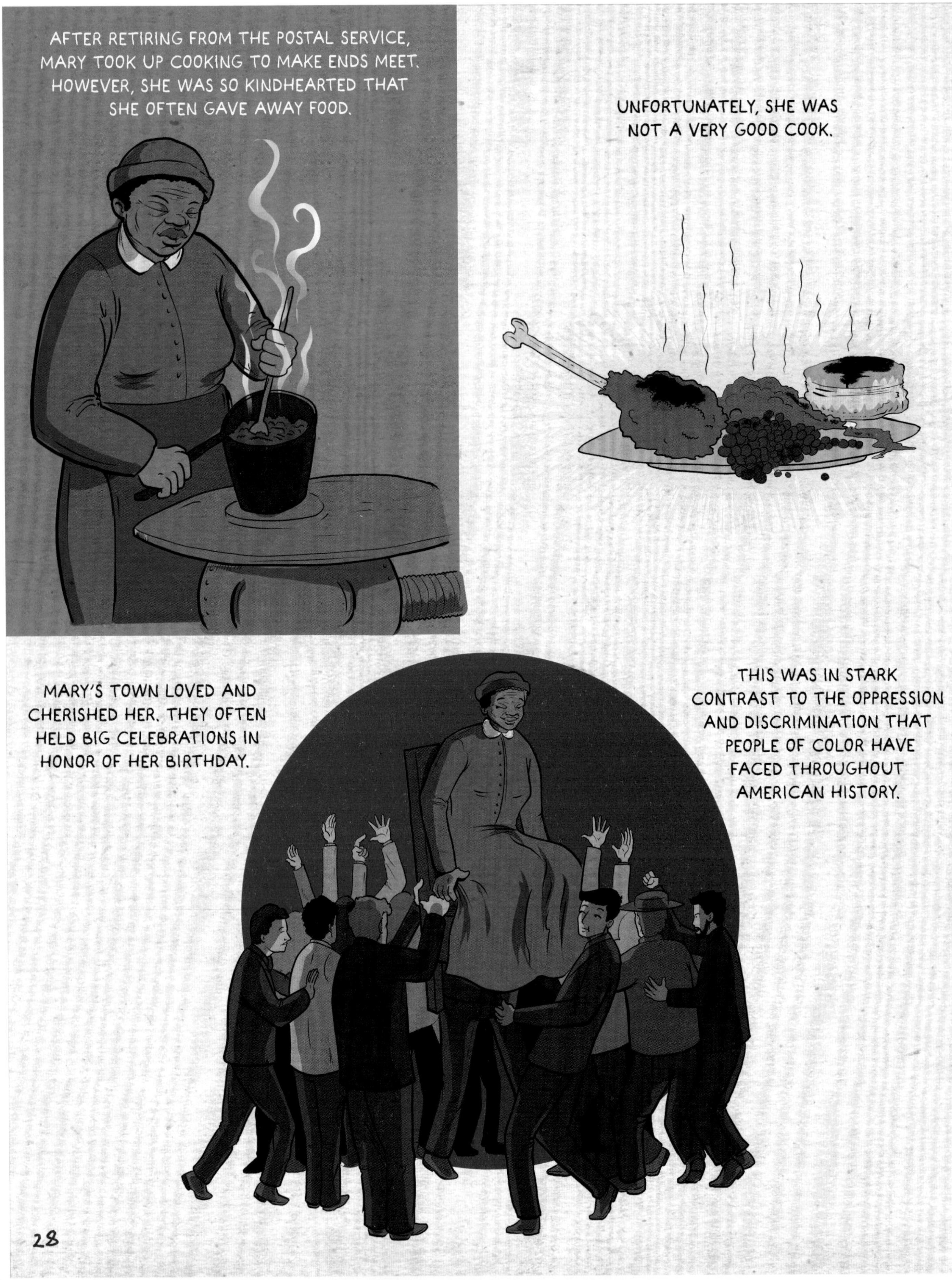
AFTER RETIRING FROM THE POSTAL SERVICE, MARY TOOK UP COOKING TO MAKE ENDS MEET. HOWEVER, SHE WAS SO KINDHEARTED THAT SHE OFTEN GAVE AWAY FOOD.
UNFORTUNATELY, SHE WAS NOT A VERY GOOD COOK.
MARY'S TOWN LOVED AND CHERISHED HER. THEY OFTEN HELD BIG CELEBRATIONS IN HONOR OF HER BIRTHDAY.
THIS WAS IN STARK CONTRAST TO THE OPPRESSION AND DISCRIMINATION THAT PEOPLE OF COLOR HAVE FACED THROUGHOUT AMERICAN HISTORY.

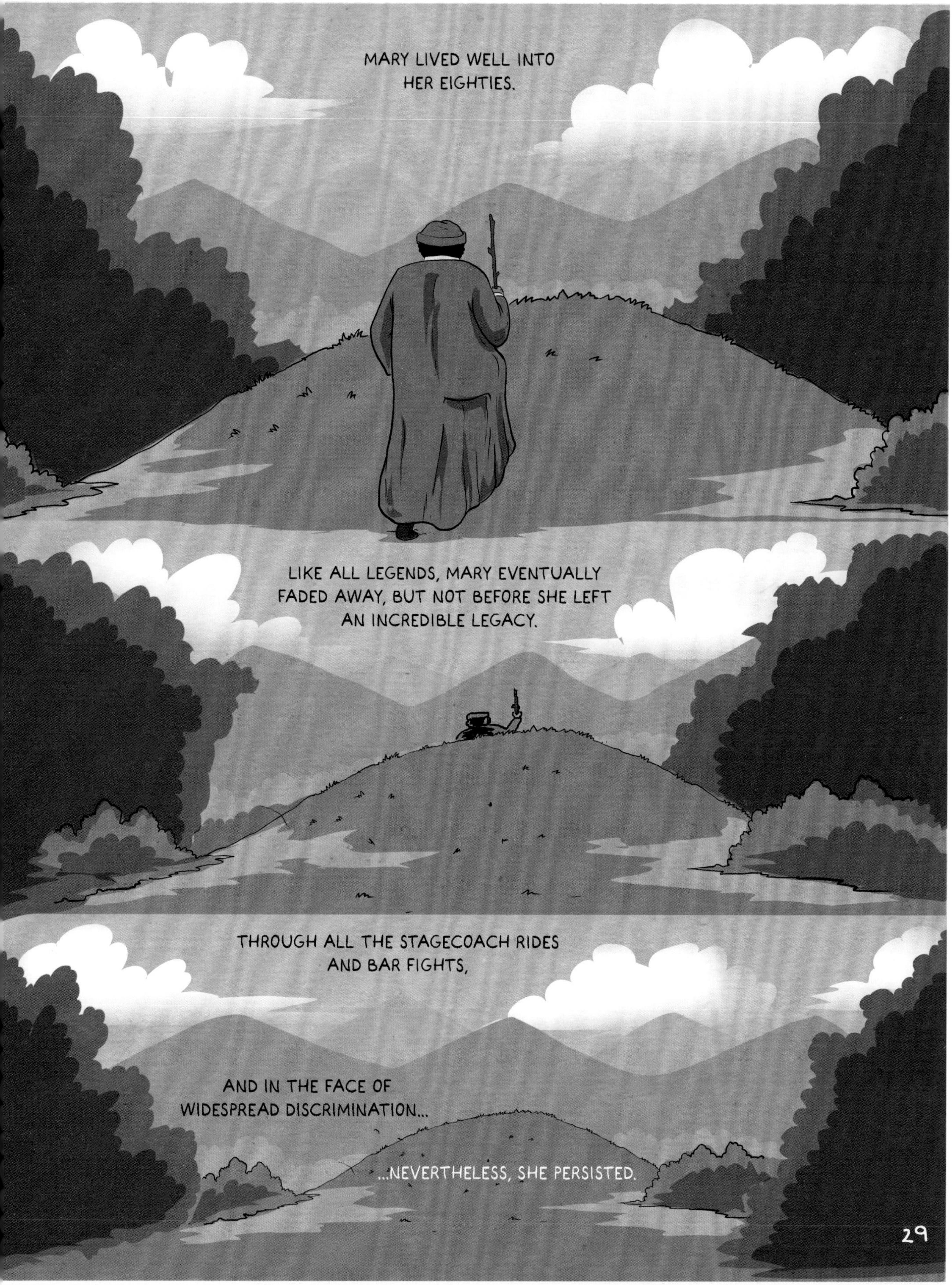
MARY LIVED WELL INTO HER EIGHTIES.
LIKE ALL LEGENDS, MARY EVENTUALLY FADED AWAY, BUT NOT BEFORE SHE LEFT AN INCREDIBLE LEGACY.
THROUGH ALL THE STAGECOACH RIDES AND BAR FIGHTS,
AND IN THE FACE OF WIDESPREAD DISCRIMINATION...
...NEVERTHELESS, SHE PERSISTED.

WILLIE KENNARD

THE SHERIFF OF YANKEE HILL

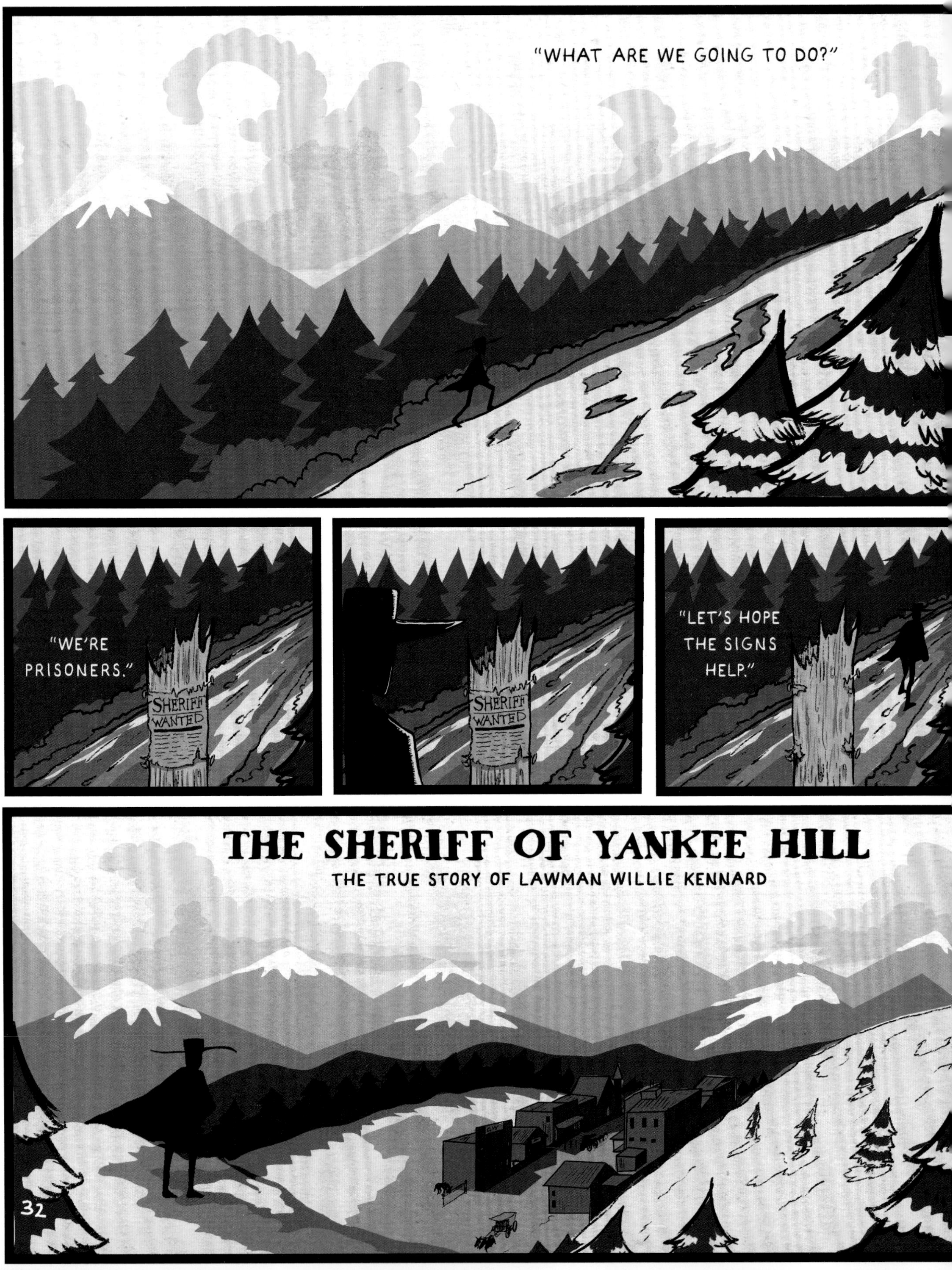
"WHAT ARE WE GOING TO DO?"
"WE'RE PRISONERS."
SHERIFF WANTED
SHERIFF WANTED
"LET'S HOPE THE SIGNS HELP."
THE SHERIFF OF YANKEE HILL
THE TRUE STORY OF LAWMAN WILLIE KENNARD

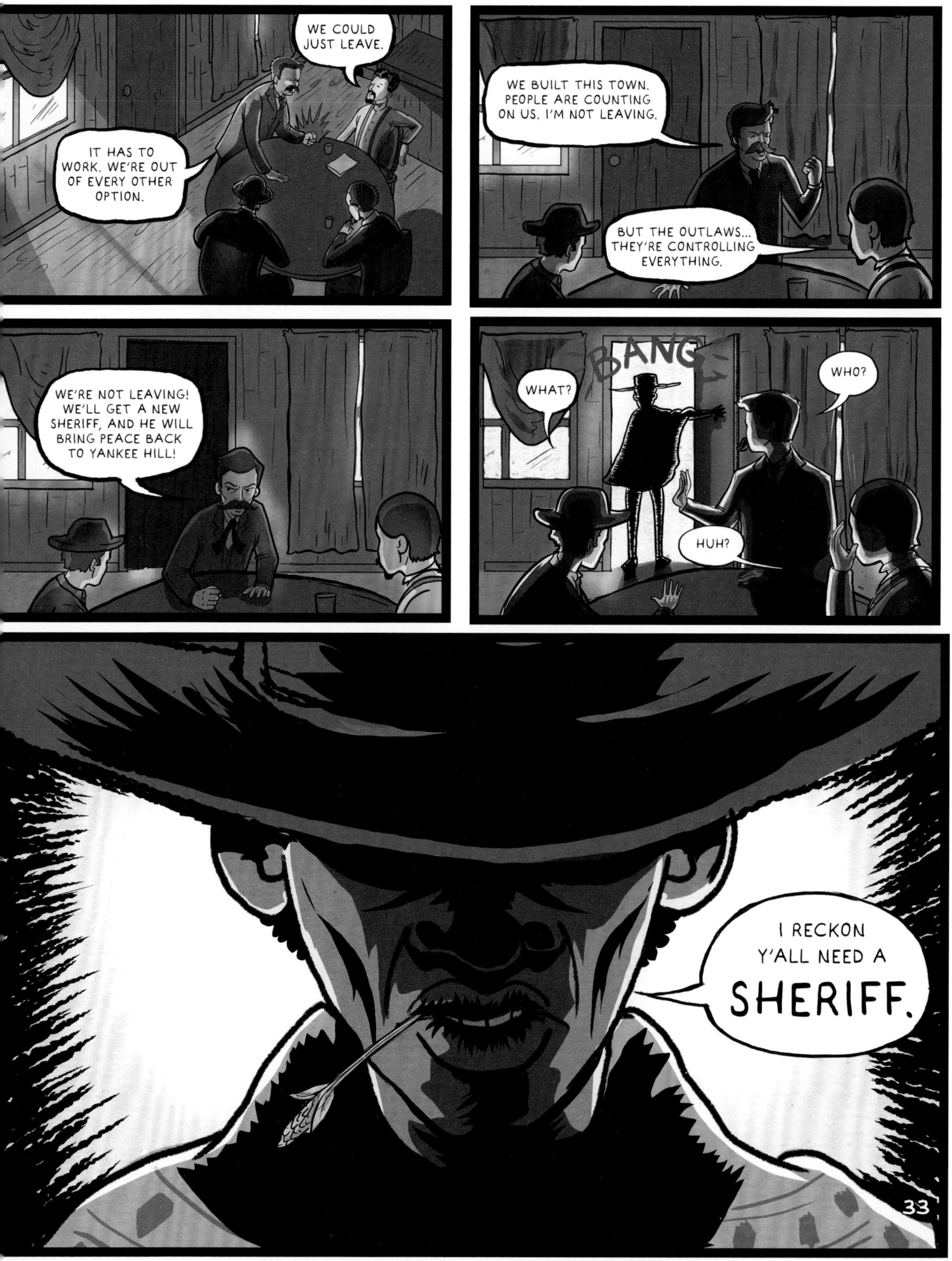
WE COULD JUST LEAVE.
IT HAS TO WORK. WE'RE OUT OF EVERY OTHER OPTION.
WE BUILT THIS TOWN. PEOPLE ARE COUNTING ON US. I'M NOT LEAVING.
BUT THE OUTLAWS... THEY'RE CONTROLLING EVERYTHING.
WE'RE NOT LEAVING! WE'LL GET A NEW SHERIFF, AND HE WILL BRING PEACE BACK TO YANKEE HILL!
BANG
WHAT?
WHO?
HUH?
I RECKON Y'ALL NEED A SHERIFF.

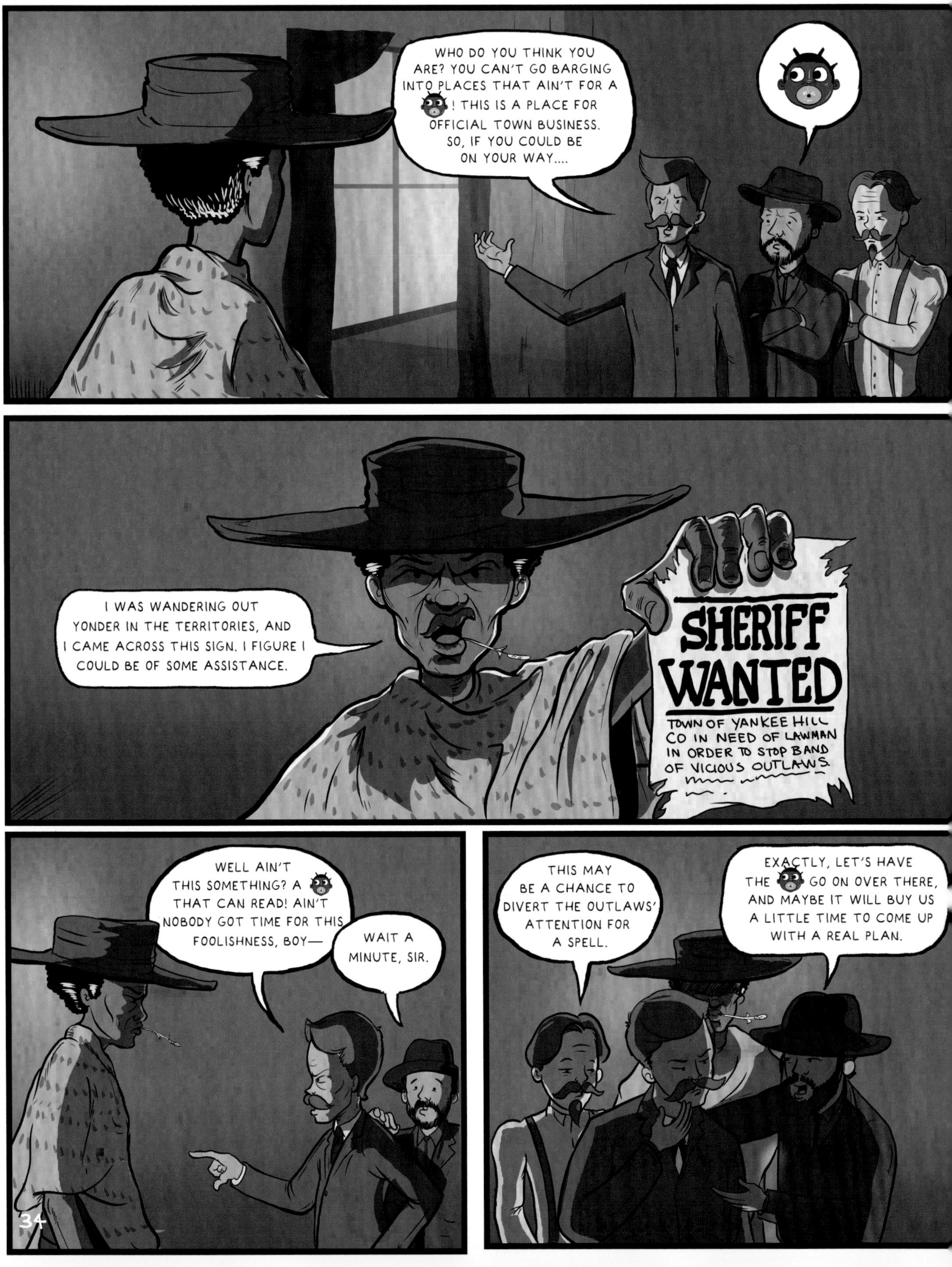
WHO DO YOU THINK YOU ARE? YOU CAN'T GO BARGING INTO PLACES THAT AIN'T FOR A ! THIS IS A PLACE FOR OFFICIAL TOWN BUSINESS. SO, IF YOU COULD BE ON YOUR WAY....
I WAS WANDERING OUT YONDER IN THE TERRITORIES, AND I CAME ACROSS THIS SIGN. I FIGURE I COULD BE OF SOME ASSISTANCE.
SHERIFF WANTED
TOWN OF YANKEE HILL CO IN NEED OF LAWMAN IN ORDER TO STOP BAND OF VICIOUS OUTLAWS.
WELL AIN'T THIS SOMETHING? A THAT CAN READ! AIN'T NOBODY GOT TIME FOR THIS FOOLISHNESS, BOY—
WAIT A MINUTE, SIR.
THIS MAY BE A CHANCE TO DIVERT THE OUTLAWS' ATTENTION FOR A SPELL.
EXACTLY, LET'S HAVE THE GO ON OVER THERE, AND MAYBE IT WILL BUY US A LITTLE TIME TO COME UP WITH A REAL PLAN.

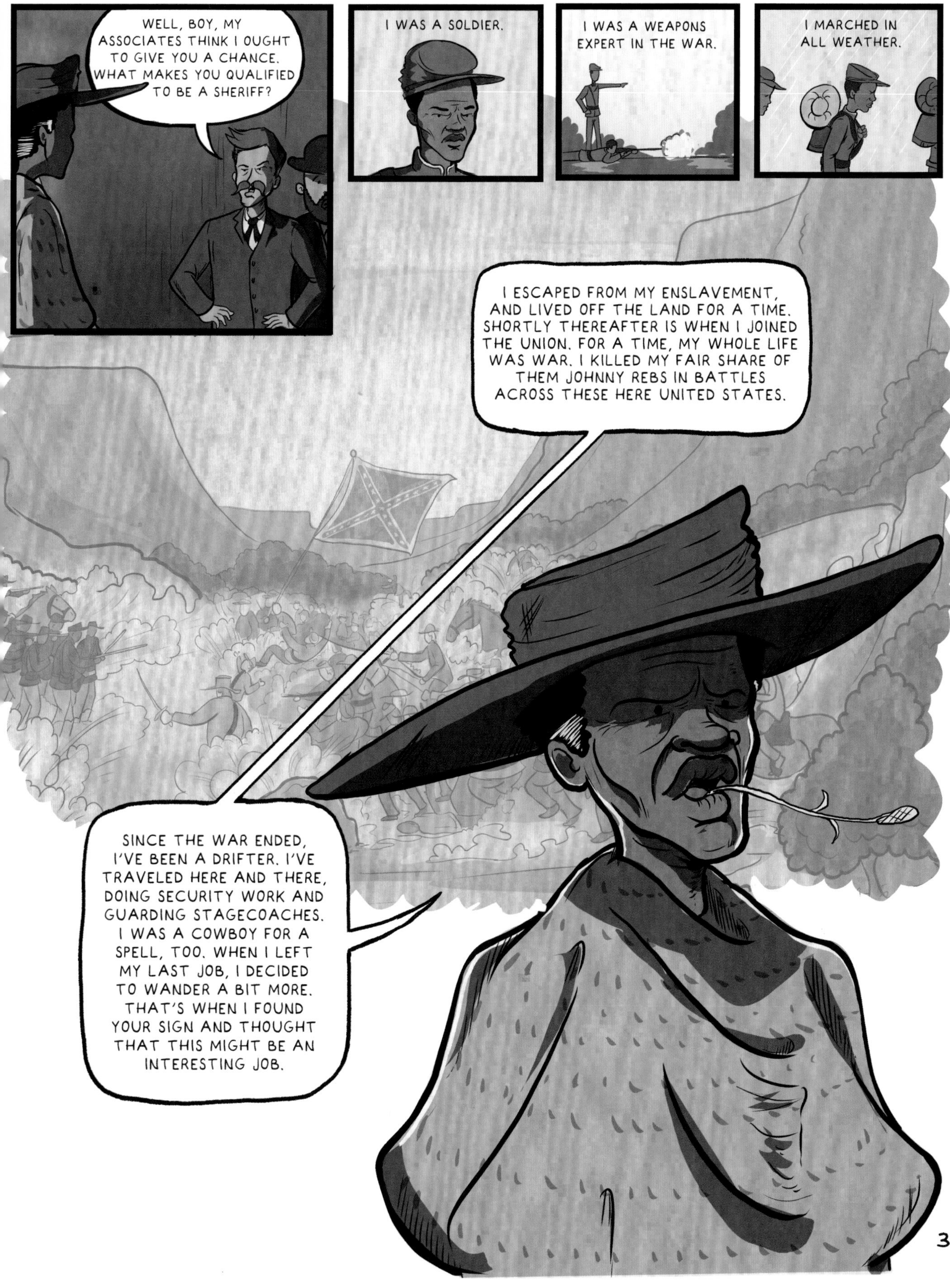
WELL, BOY, MY ASSOCIATES THINK I OUGHT TO GIVE YOU A CHANCE. WHAT MAKES YOU QUALIFIED TO BE A SHERIFF?
I WAS A SOLDIER.
I WAS A WEAPONS EXPERT IN THE WAR.
I MARCHED IN ALL WEATHER.
I ESCAPED FROM MY ENSLAVEMENT, AND LIVED OFF THE LAND FOR A TIME. SHORTLY THEREAFTER IS WHEN I JOINED THE UNION. FOR A TIME, MY WHOLE LIFE WAS WAR. I KILLED MY FAIR SHARE OF THEM JOHNNY REBS IN BATTLES ACROSS THESE HERE UNITED STATES.
SINCE THE WAR ENDED, I'VE BEEN A DRIFTER. I'VE TRAVELED HERE AND THERE, DOING SECURITY WORK AND GUARDING STAGECOACHES. I WAS A COWBOY FOR A SPELL, TOO. WHEN I LEFT MY LAST JOB, I DECIDED TO WANDER A BIT MORE. THAT'S WHEN I FOUND YOUR SIGN AND THOUGHT THAT THIS MIGHT BE AN INTERESTING JOB.

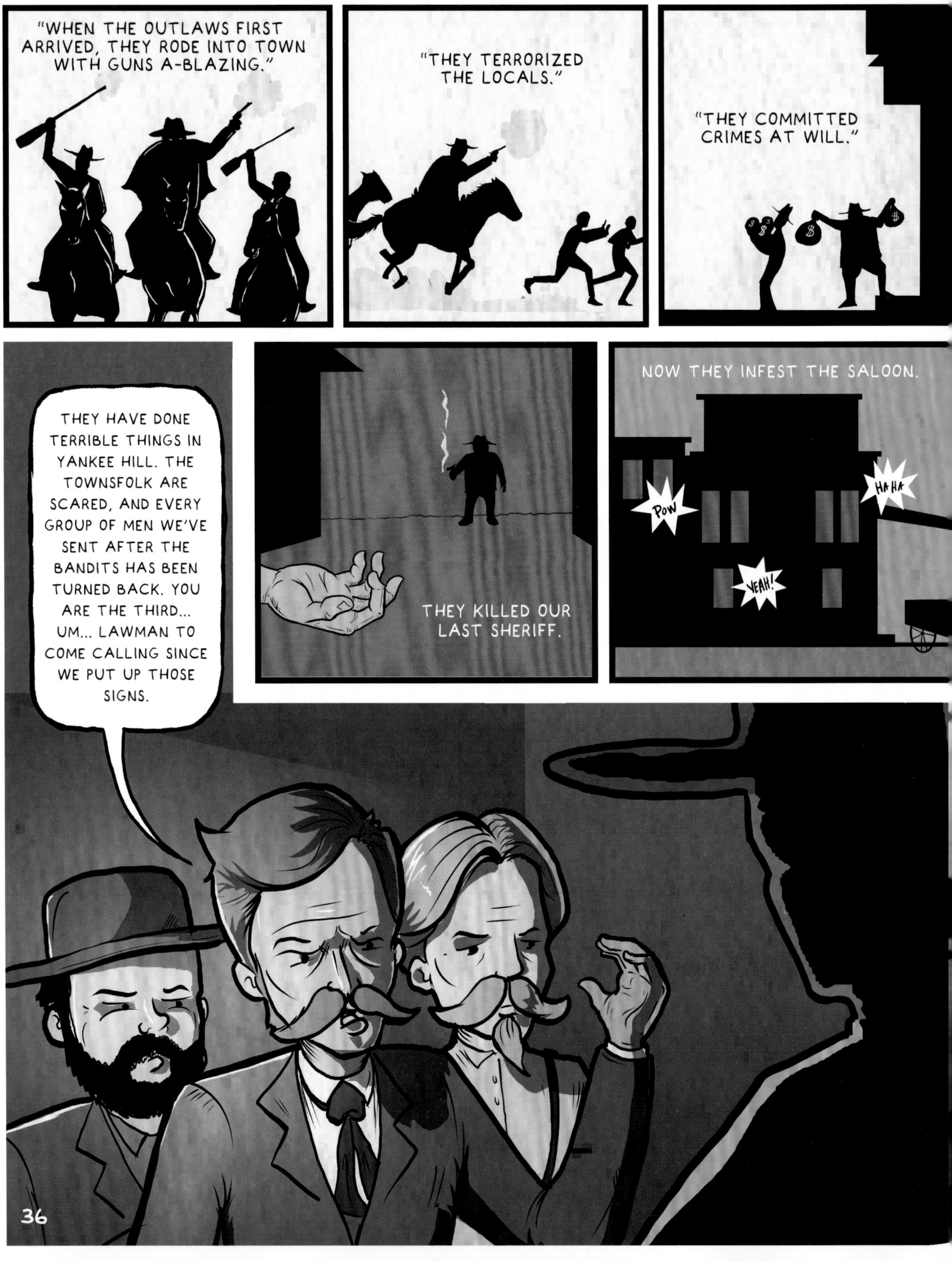
"WHEN THE OUTLAWS FIRST ARRIVED, THEY RODE INTO TOWN WITH GUNS A-BLAZING."
"THEY TERRORIZED THE LOCALS."
"THEY COMMITTED CRIMES AT WILL."
THEY HAVE DONE TERRIBLE THINGS IN YANKEE HILL. THE TOWNSFOLK ARE SCARED, AND EVERY GROUP OF MEN WE'VE SENT AFTER THE BANDITS HAS BEEN TURNED BACK. YOU ARE THE THIRD... UM... LAWMAN TO COME CALLING SINCE WE PUT UP THOSE SIGNS.
THEY KILLED OUR LAST SHERIFF.
NOW THEY INFEST THE SALOON.
POW
HAHA
YEAH!

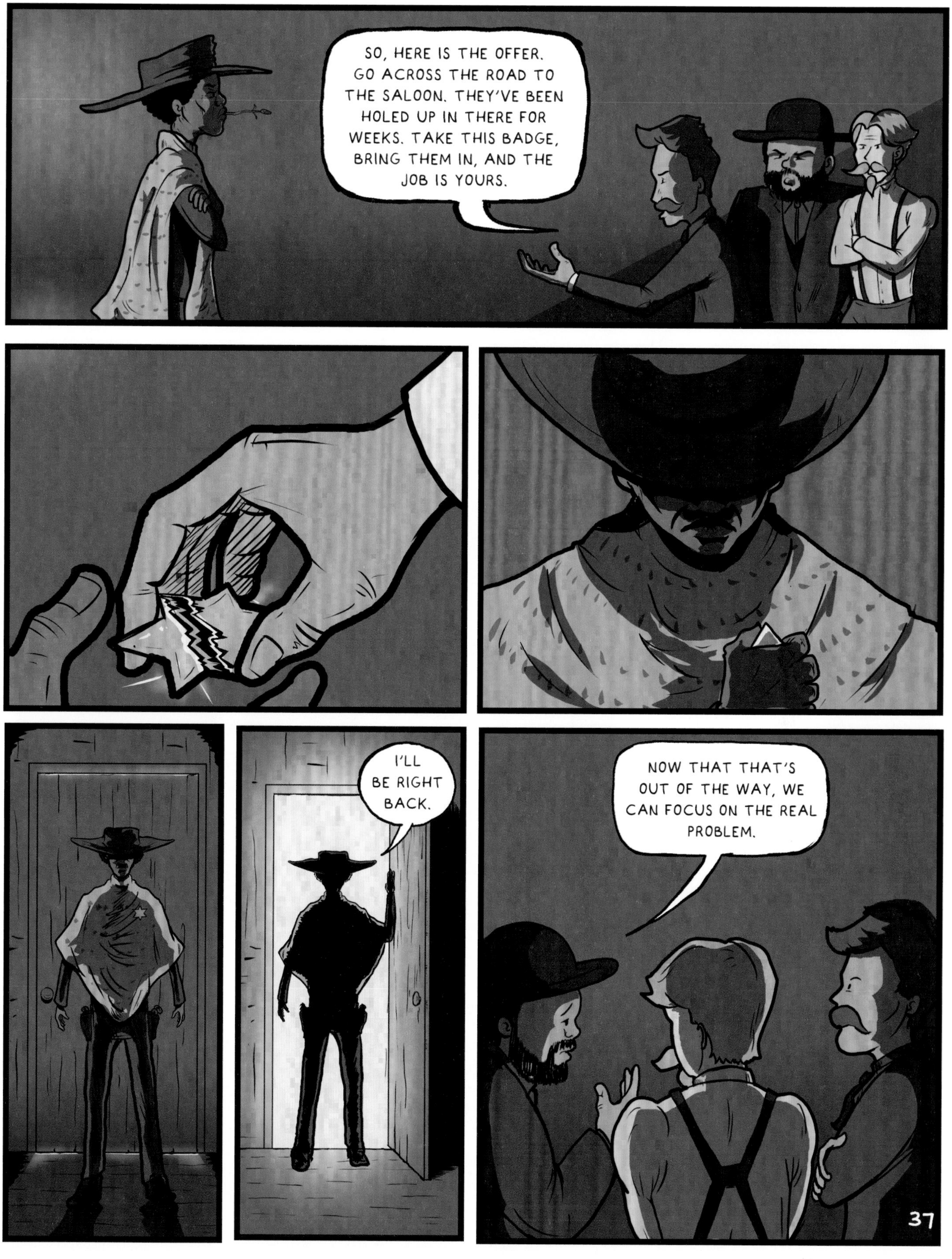
SO, HERE IS THE OFFER. GO ACROSS THE ROAD TO THE SALOON. THEY'VE BEEN HOLED UP IN THERE FOR WEEKS. TAKE THIS BADGE, BRING THEM IN, AND THE JOB IS YOURS.
I'LL BE RIGHT BACK.
NOW THAT THAT'S OUT OF THE WAY, WE CAN FOCUS ON THE REAL PROBLEM.

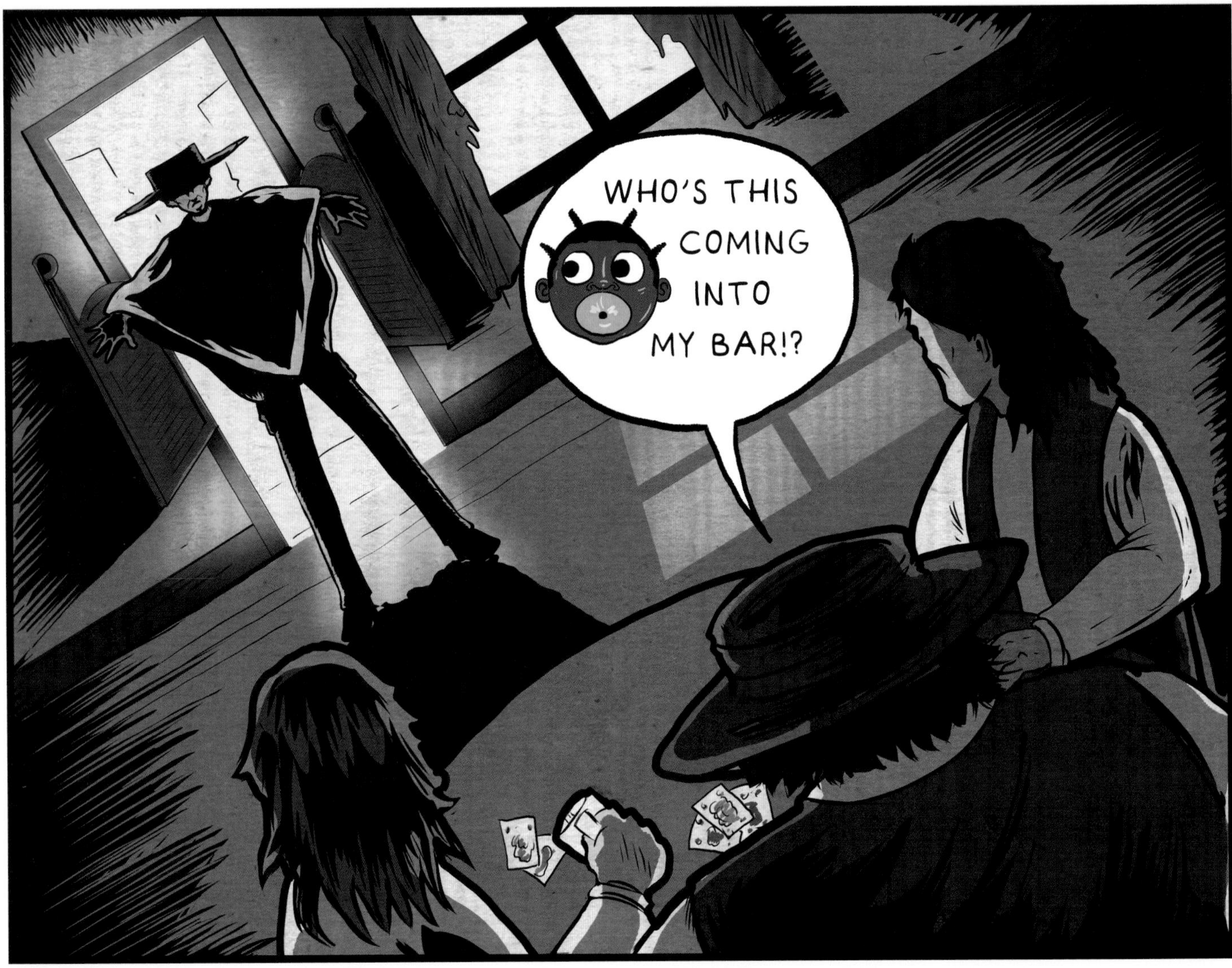
WHO'S THIS COMING INTO MY BAR!?

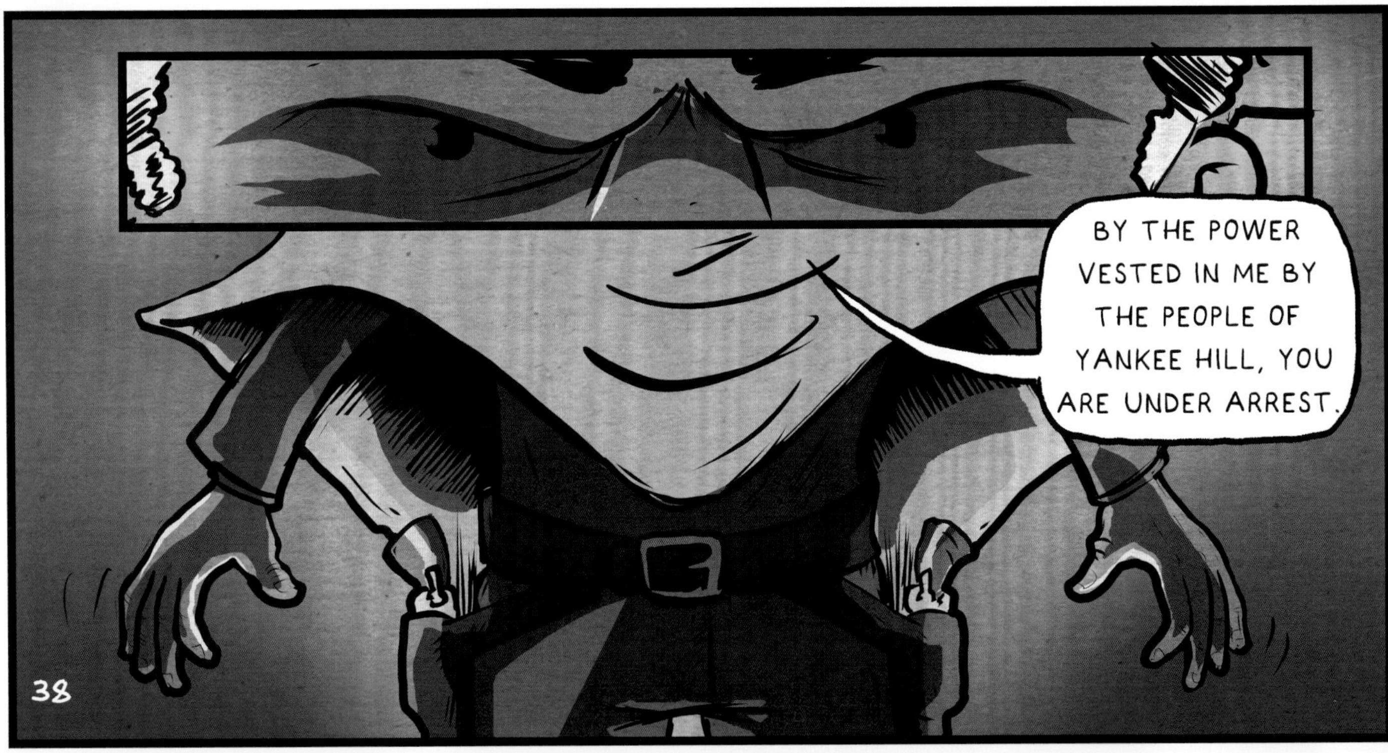
BY THE POWER VESTED IN ME BY THE PEOPLE OF YANKEE HILL, YOU ARE UNDER ARREST.

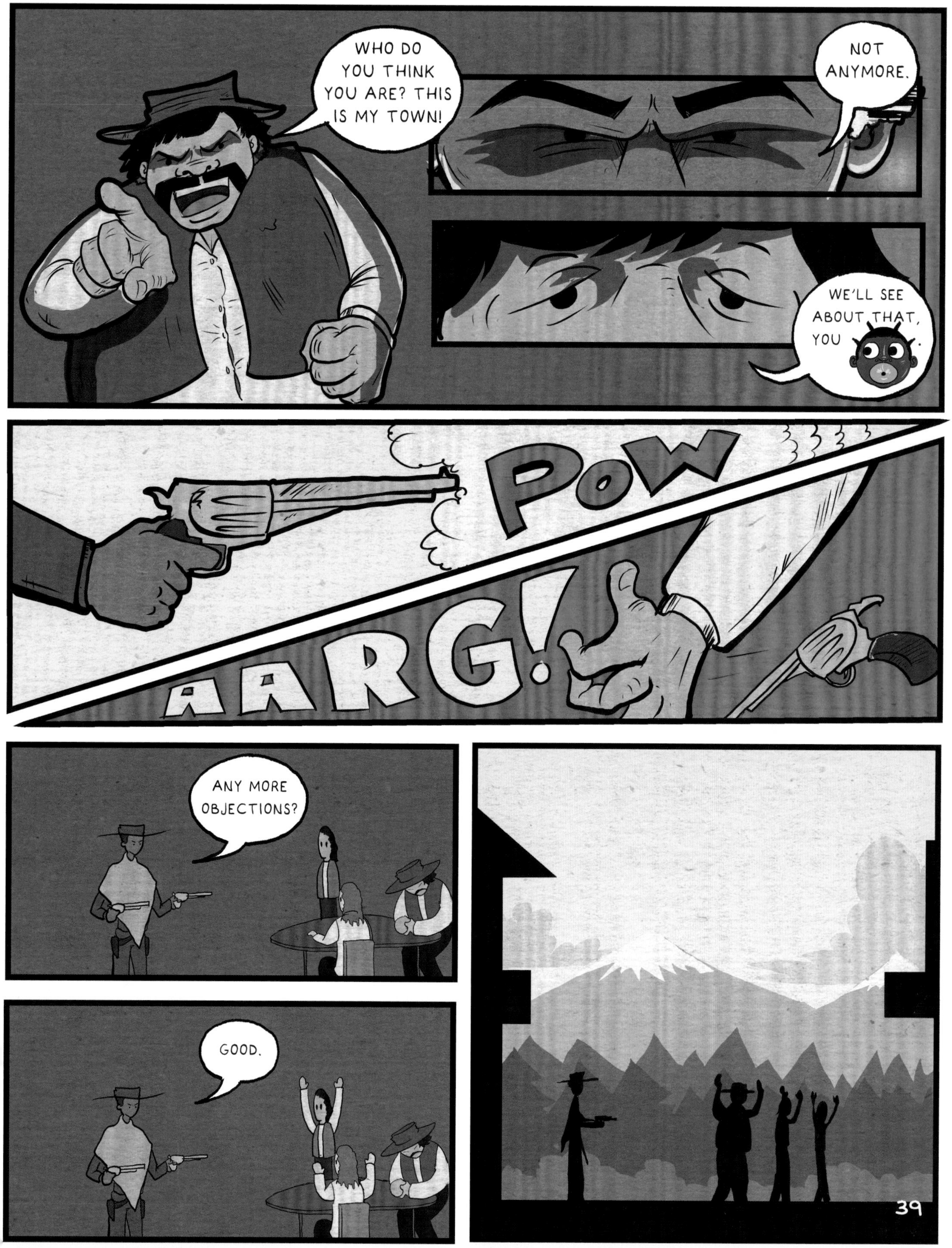
WHO DO YOU THINK YOU ARE? THIS IS MY TOWN!
NOT ANYMORE.
WE'LL SEE ABOUT THAT, YOU
POW
AARG!
ANY MORE OBJECTIONS?
GOOD.

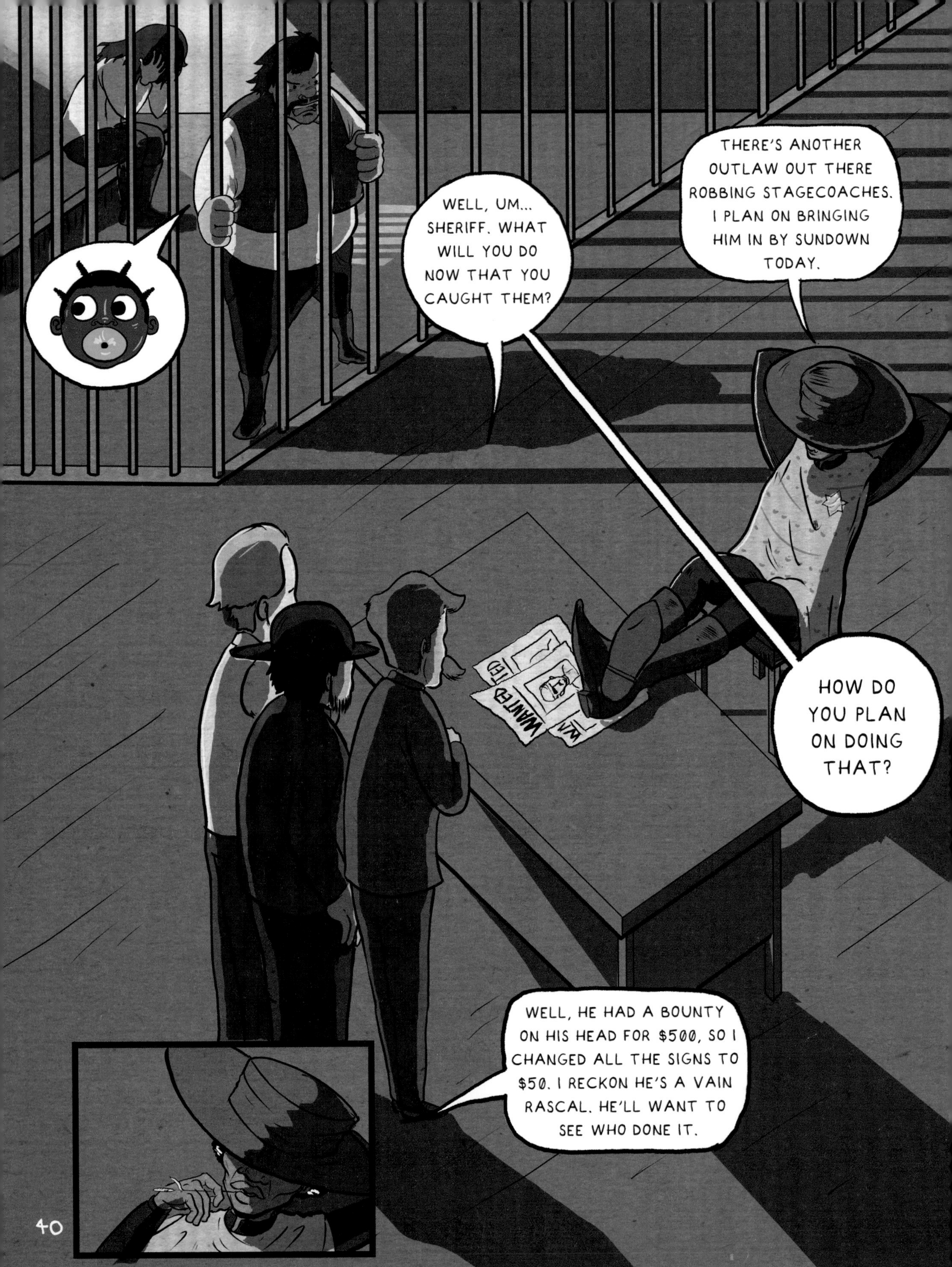
WELL, UM... SHERIFF. WHAT WILL YOU DO NOW THAT YOU CAUGHT THEM?
THERE'S ANOTHER OUTLAW OUT THERE ROBBING STAGECOACHES. I PLAN ON BRINGING HIM IN BY SUNDOWN TODAY.
WANTED
HOW DO YOU PLAN ON DOING THAT?
WELL, HE HAD A BOUNTY ON HIS HEAD FOR $500, SO I CHANGED ALL THE SIGNS TO $50. I RECKON HE'S A VAIN RASCAL. HE'LL WANT TO SEE WHO DONE IT.

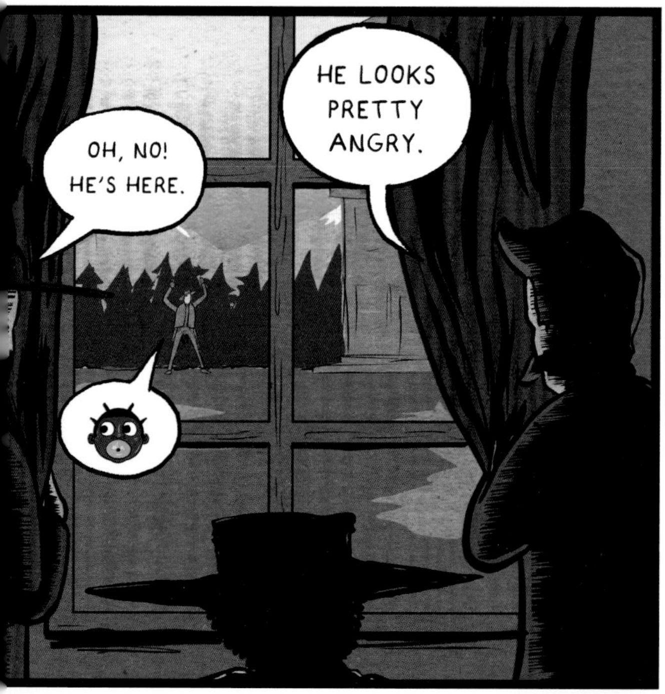
OH, NO! HE'S HERE.
HE LOOKS PRETTY ANGRY.

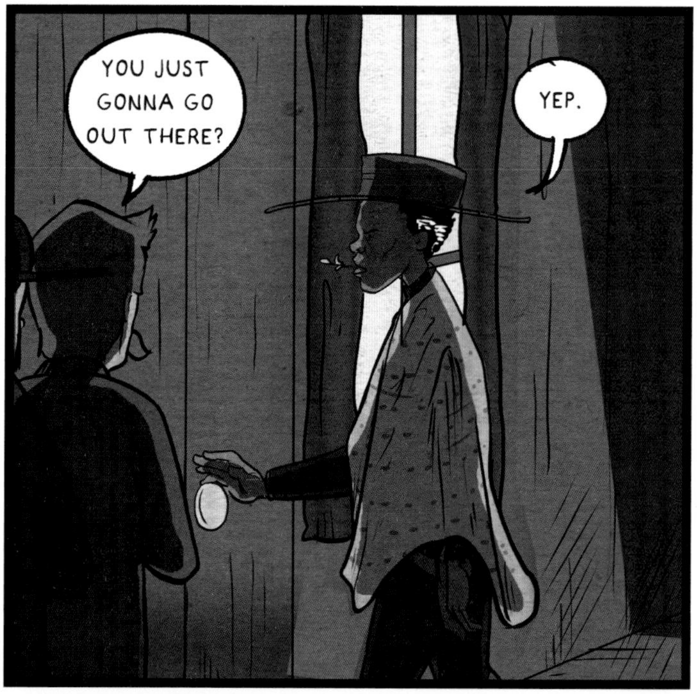
YOU JUST GONNA GO OUT THERE?
YEP.

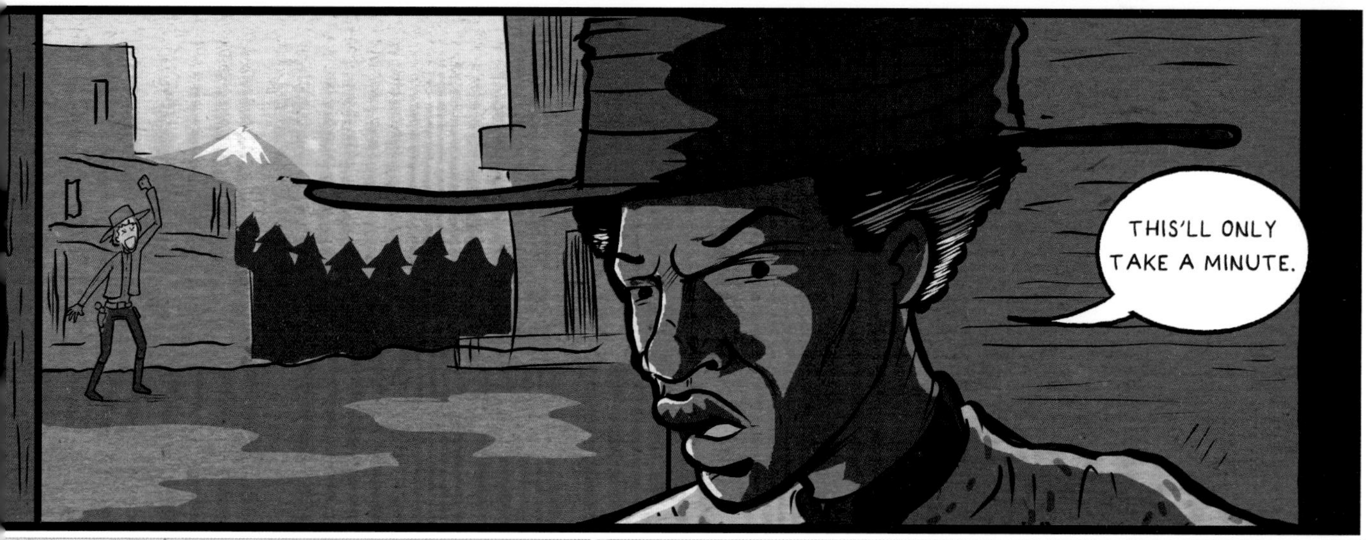
THIS'LL ONLY TAKE A MINUTE.

WILLIE KENNARD KEPT YANKEE HILL SAFE. AFTER HIS WORK WAS DONE, HE DRIFTED ON TO THE NEXT ADVENTURE.

NO ONE KNOWS HOW HIS STORY ENDED, BUT FOLKS NEVER FORGOT **THE SHERIFF OF YANKEE HILL.**

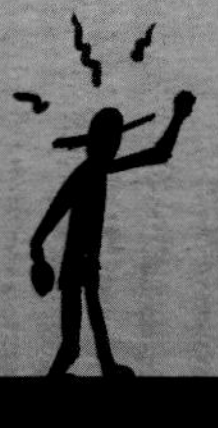

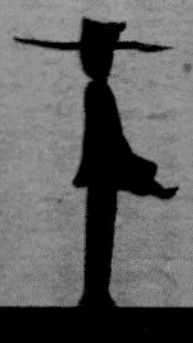

CATHAY WILLIAMS

CONTRABAND

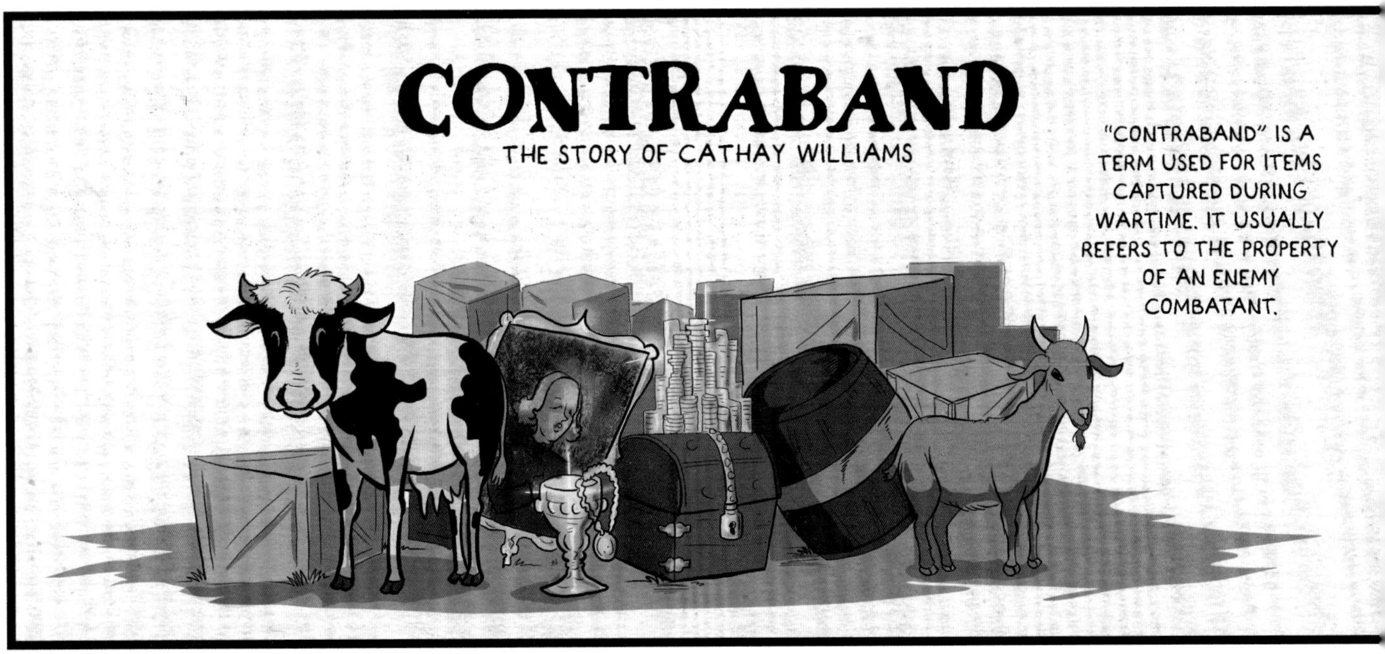
CONTRABAND
THE STORY OF CATHAY WILLIAMS
"CONTRABAND" IS A TERM USED FOR ITEMS CAPTURED DURING WARTIME. IT USUALLY REFERS TO THE PROPERTY OF AN ENEMY COMBATANT.

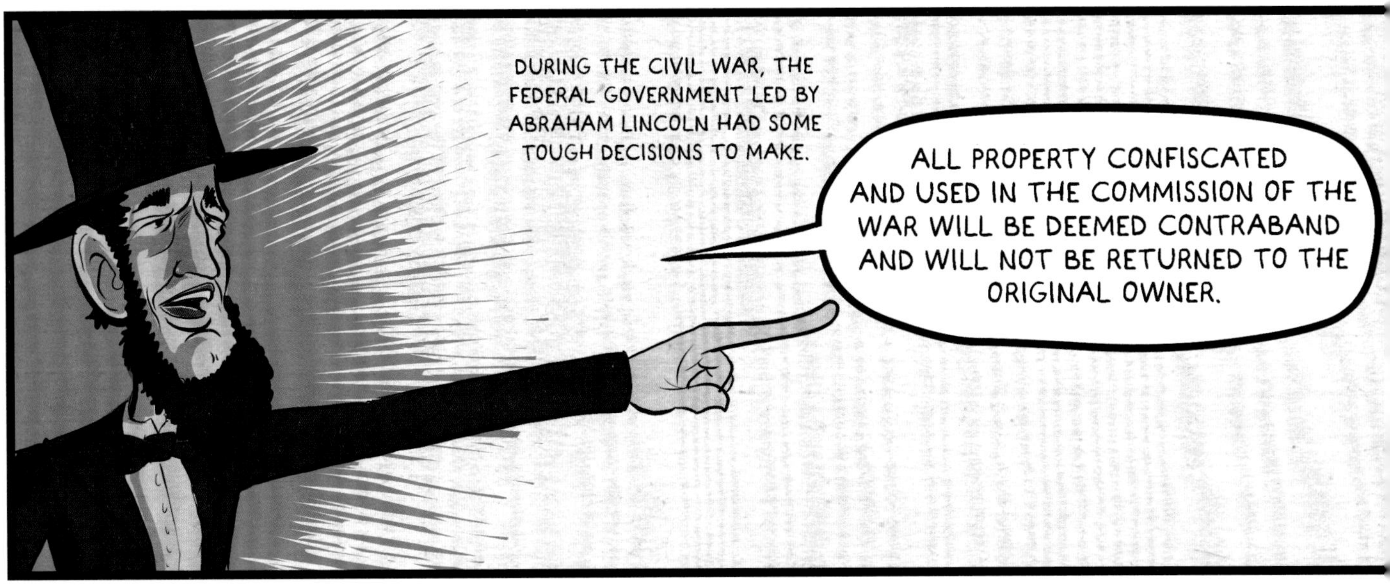
DURING THE CIVIL WAR, THE FEDERAL GOVERNMENT LED BY ABRAHAM LINCOLN HAD SOME TOUGH DECISIONS TO MAKE.
ALL PROPERTY CONFISCATED AND USED IN THE COMMISSION OF THE WAR WILL BE DEEMED CONTRABAND AND WILL NOT BE RETURNED TO THE ORIGINAL OWNER.

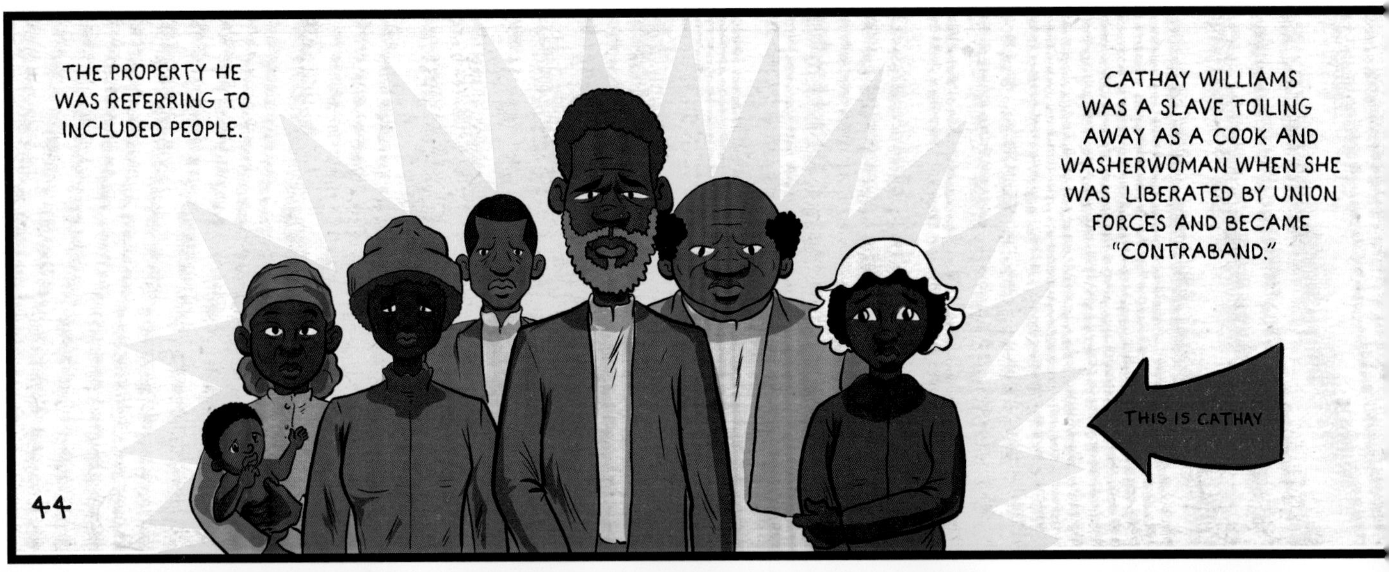
THE PROPERTY HE WAS REFERRING TO INCLUDED PEOPLE.
CATHAY WILLIAMS WAS A SLAVE TOILING AWAY AS A COOK AND WASHERWOMAN WHEN SHE WAS LIBERATED BY UNION FORCES AND BECAME "CONTRABAND."
THIS IS CATHAY

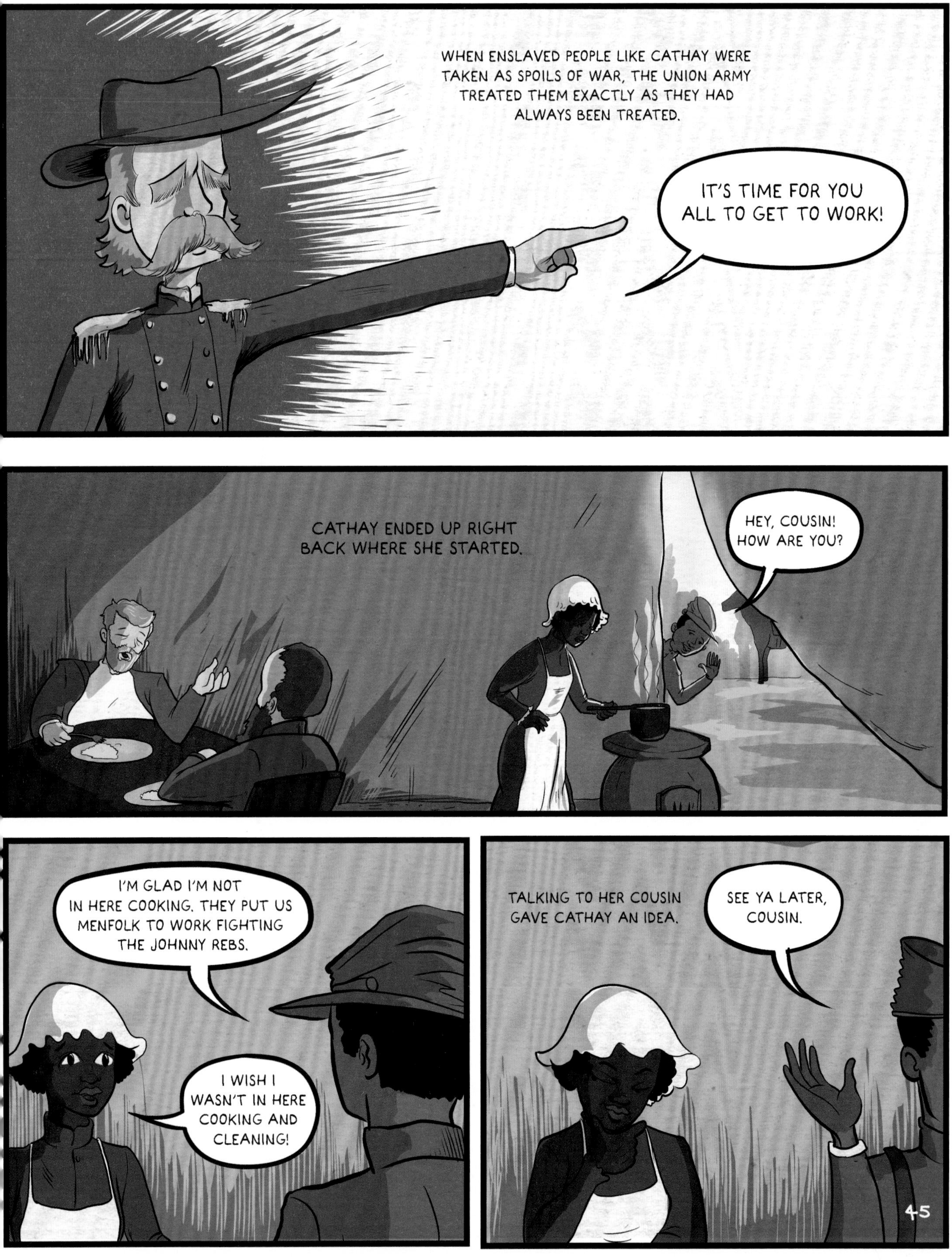
WHEN ENSLAVED PEOPLE LIKE CATHAY WERE TAKEN AS SPOILS OF WAR, THE UNION ARMY TREATED THEM EXACTLY AS THEY HAD ALWAYS BEEN TREATED.
IT'S TIME FOR YOU ALL TO GET TO WORK!
CATHAY ENDED UP RIGHT BACK WHERE SHE STARTED.
HEY, COUSIN! HOW ARE YOU?
I'M GLAD I'M NOT IN HERE COOKING. THEY PUT US MENFOLK TO WORK FIGHTING THE JOHNNY REBS.
I WISH I WASN'T IN HERE COOKING AND CLEANING!
TALKING TO HER COUSIN GAVE CATHAY AN IDEA.
SEE YA LATER, COUSIN.

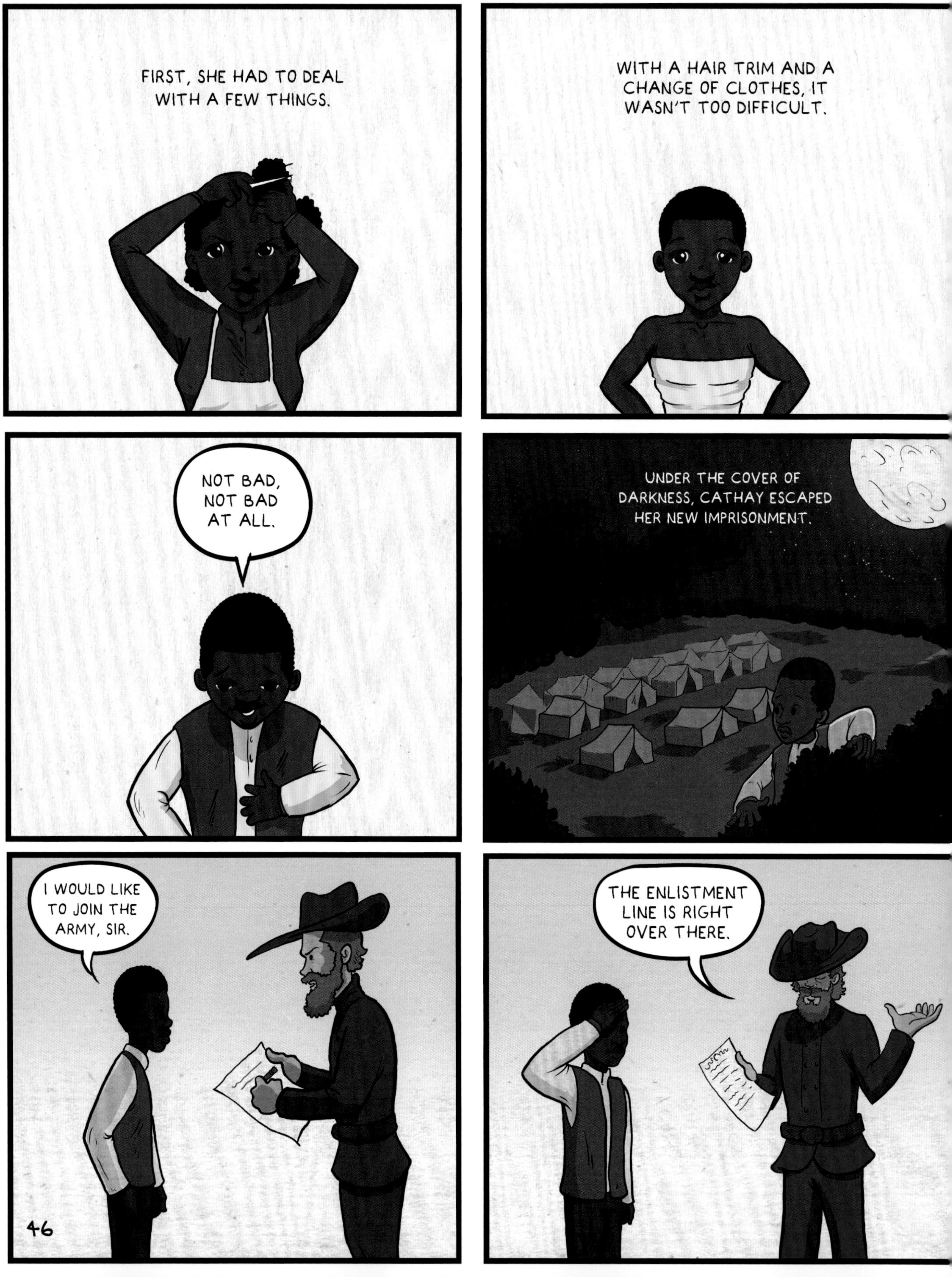
FIRST, SHE HAD TO DEAL WITH A FEW THINGS.
WITH A HAIR TRIM AND A CHANGE OF CLOTHES, IT WASN'T TOO DIFFICULT.
NOT BAD, NOT BAD AT ALL.
UNDER THE COVER OF DARKNESS, CATHAY ESCAPED HER NEW IMPRISONMENT.
I WOULD LIKE TO JOIN THE ARMY, SIR.
THE ENLISTMENT LINE IS RIGHT OVER THERE.

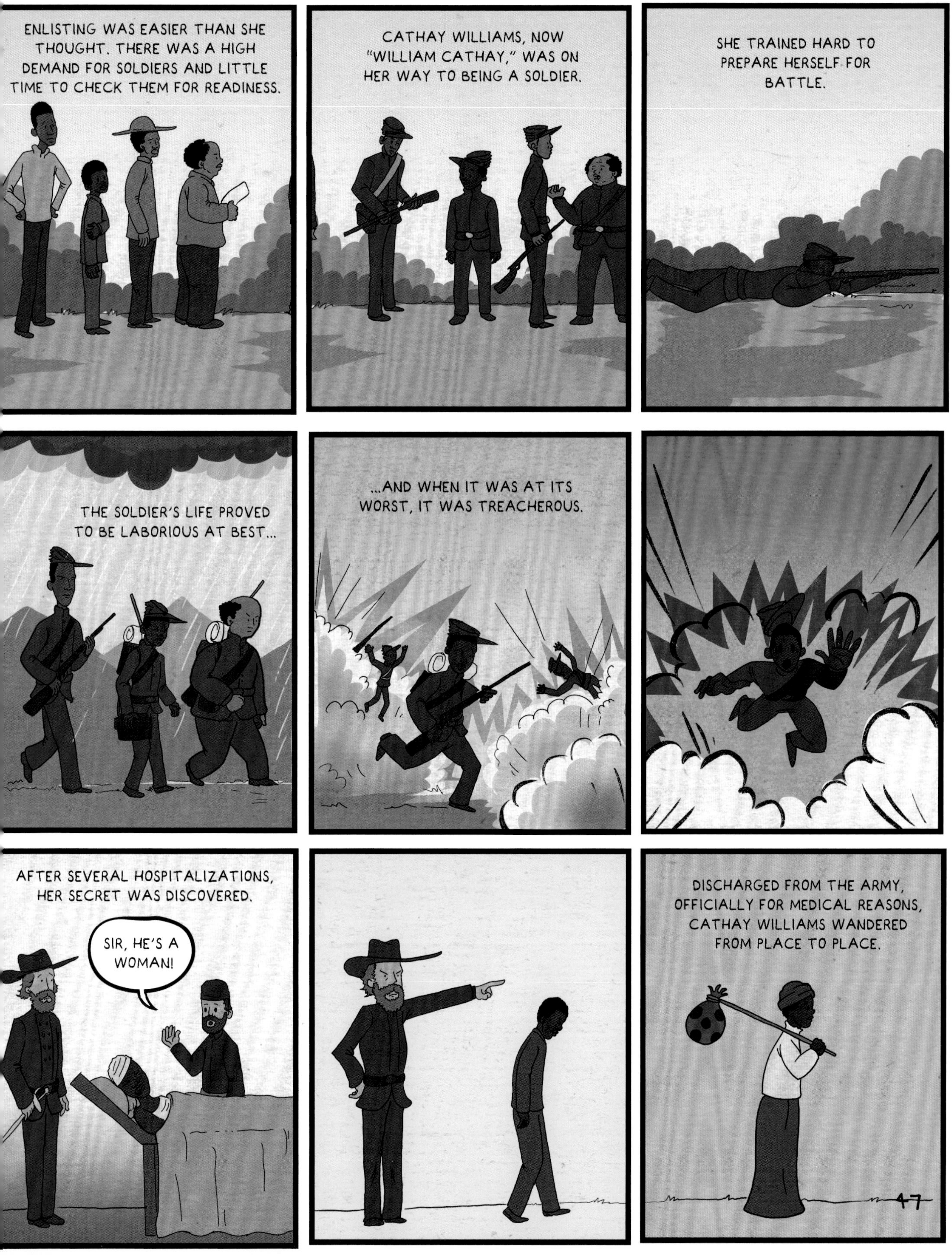

ENLISTING WAS EASIER THAN SHE THOUGHT. THERE WAS A HIGH DEMAND FOR SOLDIERS AND LITTLE TIME TO CHECK THEM FOR READINESS.
CATHAY WILLIAMS, NOW "WILLIAM CATHAY," WAS ON HER WAY TO BEING A SOLDIER.
SHE TRAINED HARD TO PREPARE HERSELF FOR BATTLE.
THE SOLDIER'S LIFE PROVED TO BE LABORIOUS AT BEST...
...AND WHEN IT WAS AT ITS WORST, IT WAS TREACHEROUS.
AFTER SEVERAL HOSPITALIZATIONS, HER SECRET WAS DISCOVERED.
SIR, HE'S A WOMAN!
DISCHARGED FROM THE ARMY, OFFICIALLY FOR MEDICAL REASONS, CATHAY WILLIAMS WANDERED FROM PLACE TO PLACE.

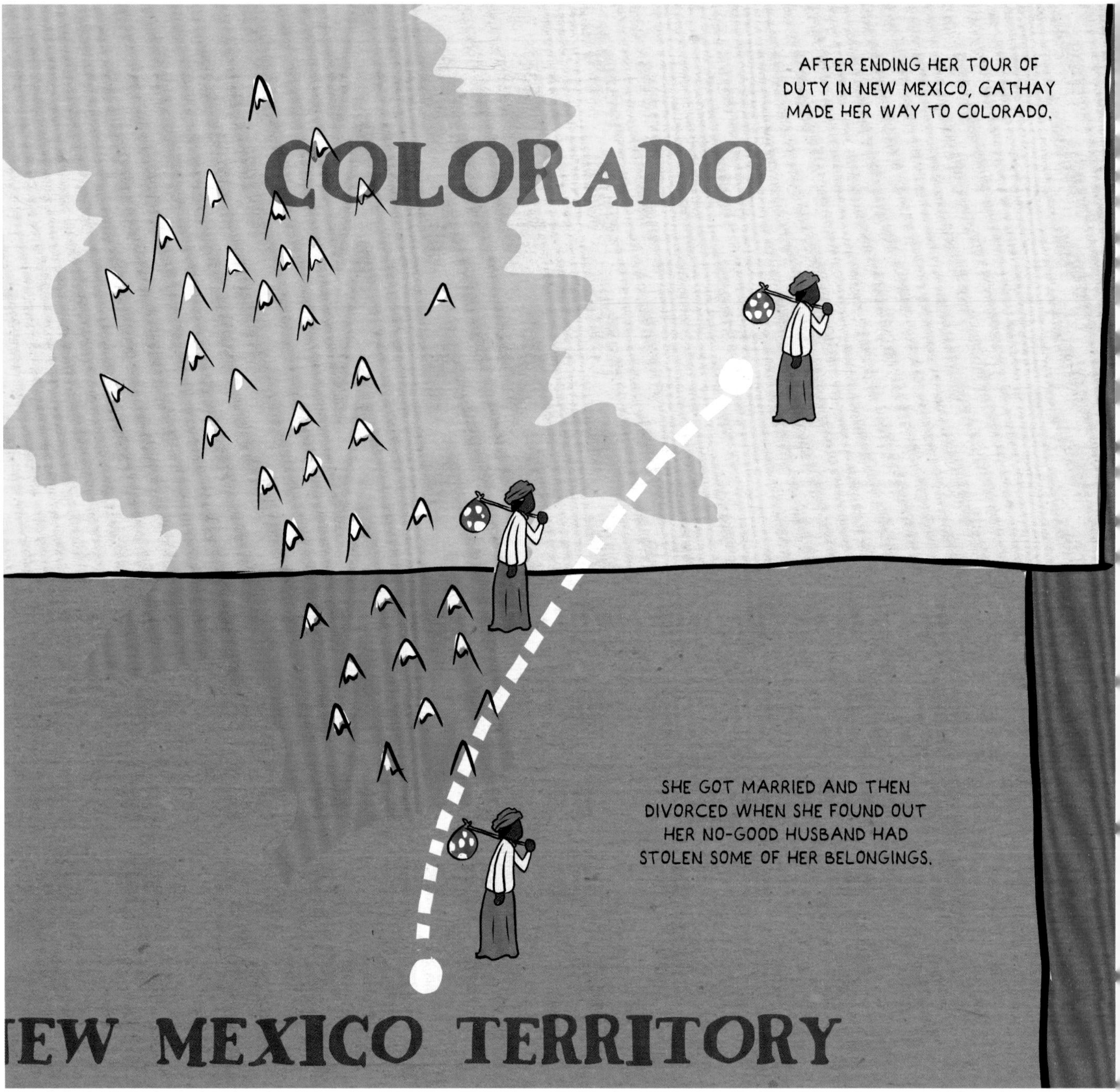
AFTER ENDING HER TOUR OF DUTY IN NEW MEXICO, CATHAY MADE HER WAY TO COLORADO.
COLORADO
SHE GOT MARRIED AND THEN DIVORCED WHEN SHE FOUND OUT HER NO-GOOD HUSBAND HAD STOLEN SOME OF HER BELONGINGS.
EW MEXICO TERRITORY

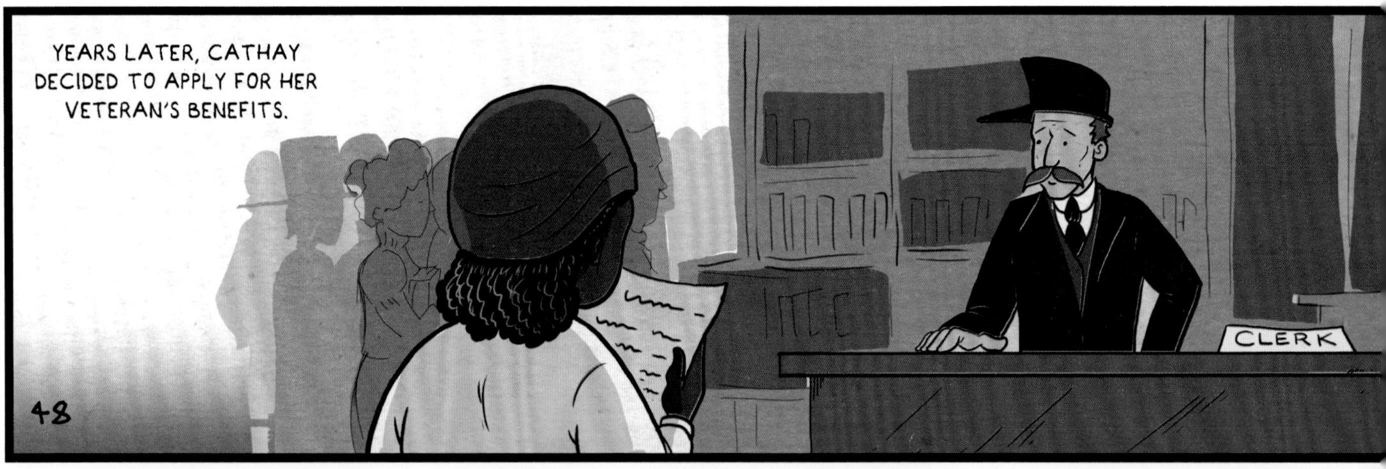
YEARS LATER, CATHAY DECIDED TO APPLY FOR HER VETERAN'S BENEFITS.
CLERK

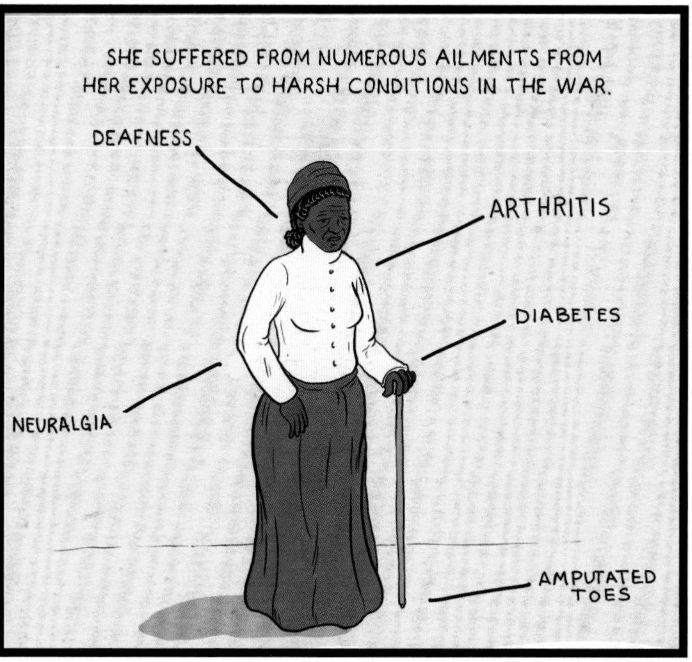
SHE SUFFERED FROM NUMEROUS AILMENTS FROM HER EXPOSURE TO HARSH CONDITIONS IN THE WAR.
DEAFNESS
ARTHRITIS
DIABETES
NEURALGIA
AMPUTATED TOES

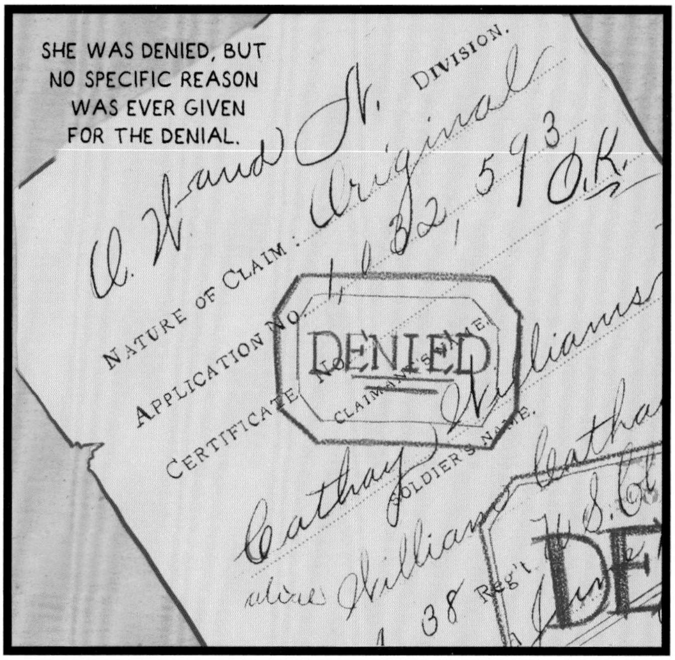
SHE WAS DENIED, BUT NO SPECIFIC REASON WAS EVER GIVEN FOR THE DENIAL.
DIVISION.
NATURE OF CLAIM: Original
APPLICATION NO. 1,032,593
CERTIFICATE NO.
DENIED
CLAIMANT'S NAME.
SOLDIER'S NAME.
Cathay Williams

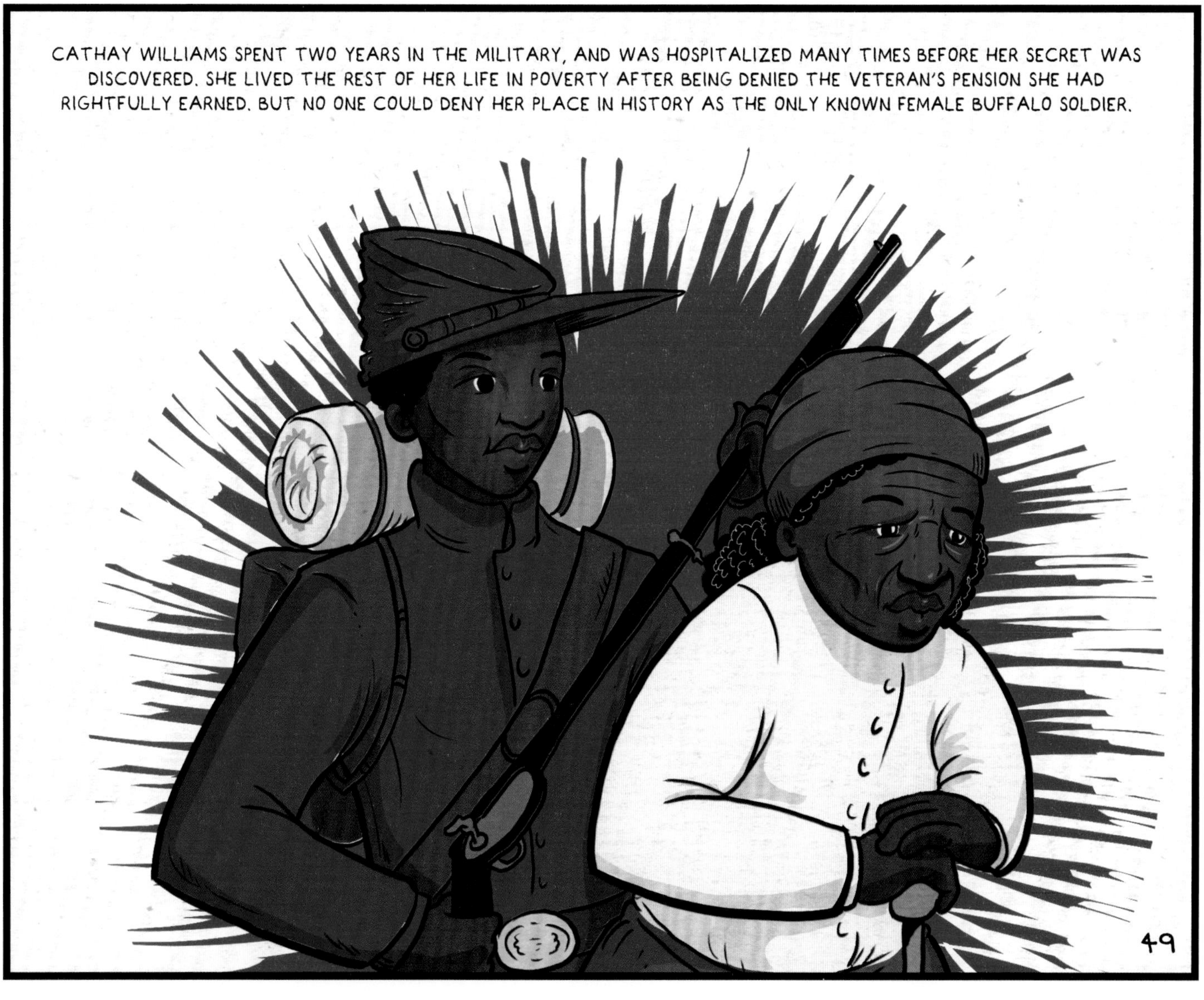
CATHAY WILLIAMS SPENT TWO YEARS IN THE MILITARY, AND WAS HOSPITALIZED MANY TIMES BEFORE HER SECRET WAS DISCOVERED. SHE LIVED THE REST OF HER LIFE IN POVERTY AFTER BEING DENIED THE VETERAN'S PENSION SHE HAD RIGHTFULLY EARNED. BUT NO ONE COULD DENY HER PLACE IN HISTORY AS THE ONLY KNOWN FEMALE BUFFALO SOLDIER.

BLIND TOM WIGGINS

ALL SOUND WAS MUSIC

ALL SOUND WAS MUSIC

THE STORY OF BLIND TOM WIGGINS

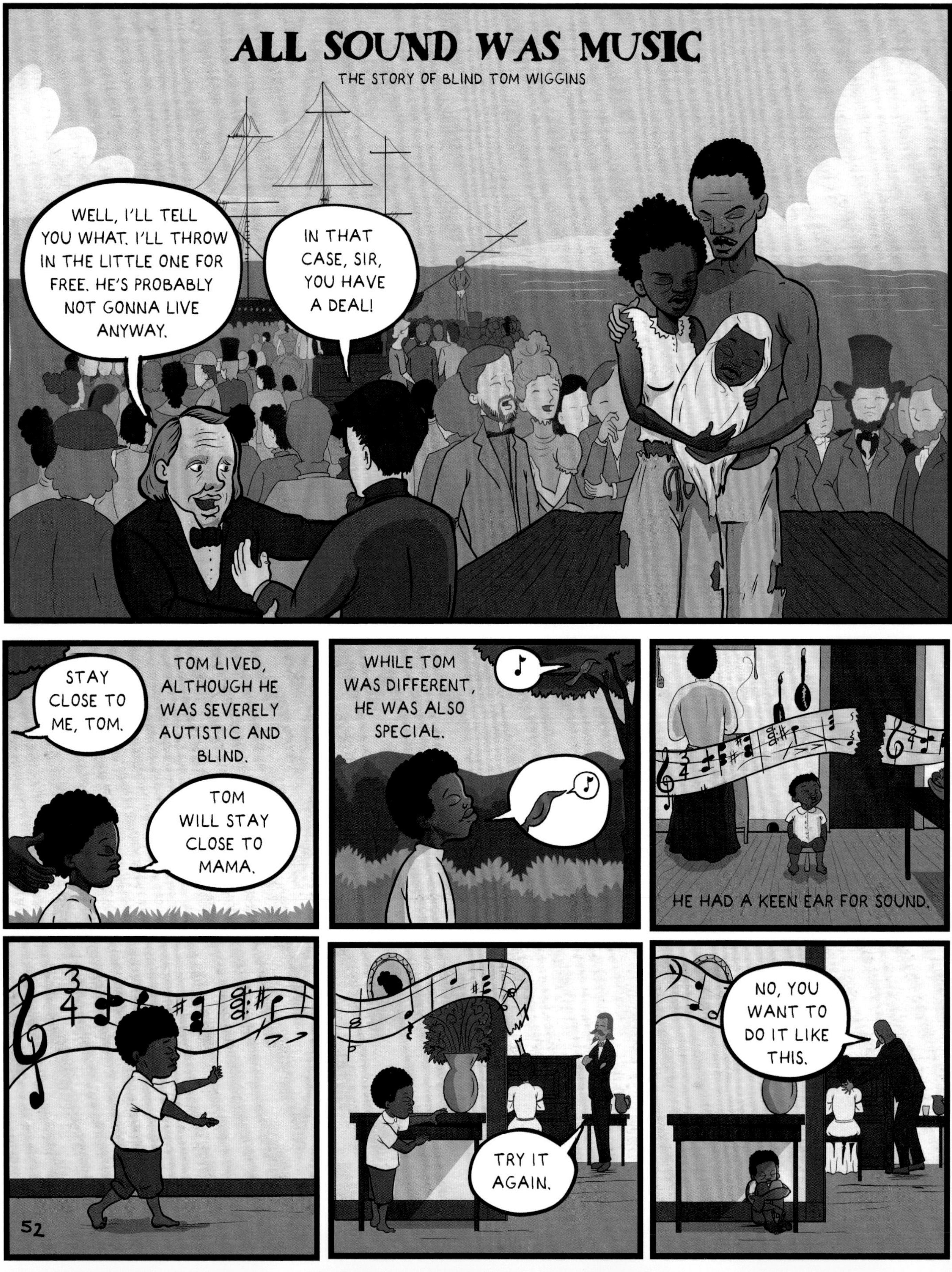
WELL, I'LL TELL YOU WHAT. I'LL THROW IN THE LITTLE ONE FOR FREE. HE'S PROBABLY NOT GONNA LIVE ANYWAY.
IN THAT CASE, SIR, YOU HAVE A DEAL!
STAY CLOSE TO ME, TOM.
TOM LIVED, ALTHOUGH HE WAS SEVERELY AUTISTIC AND BLIND.
TOM WILL STAY CLOSE TO MAMA.
WHILE TOM WAS DIFFERENT, HE WAS ALSO SPECIAL.
HE HAD A KEEN EAR FOR SOUND.
TRY IT AGAIN.
NO, YOU WANT TO DO IT LIKE THIS.

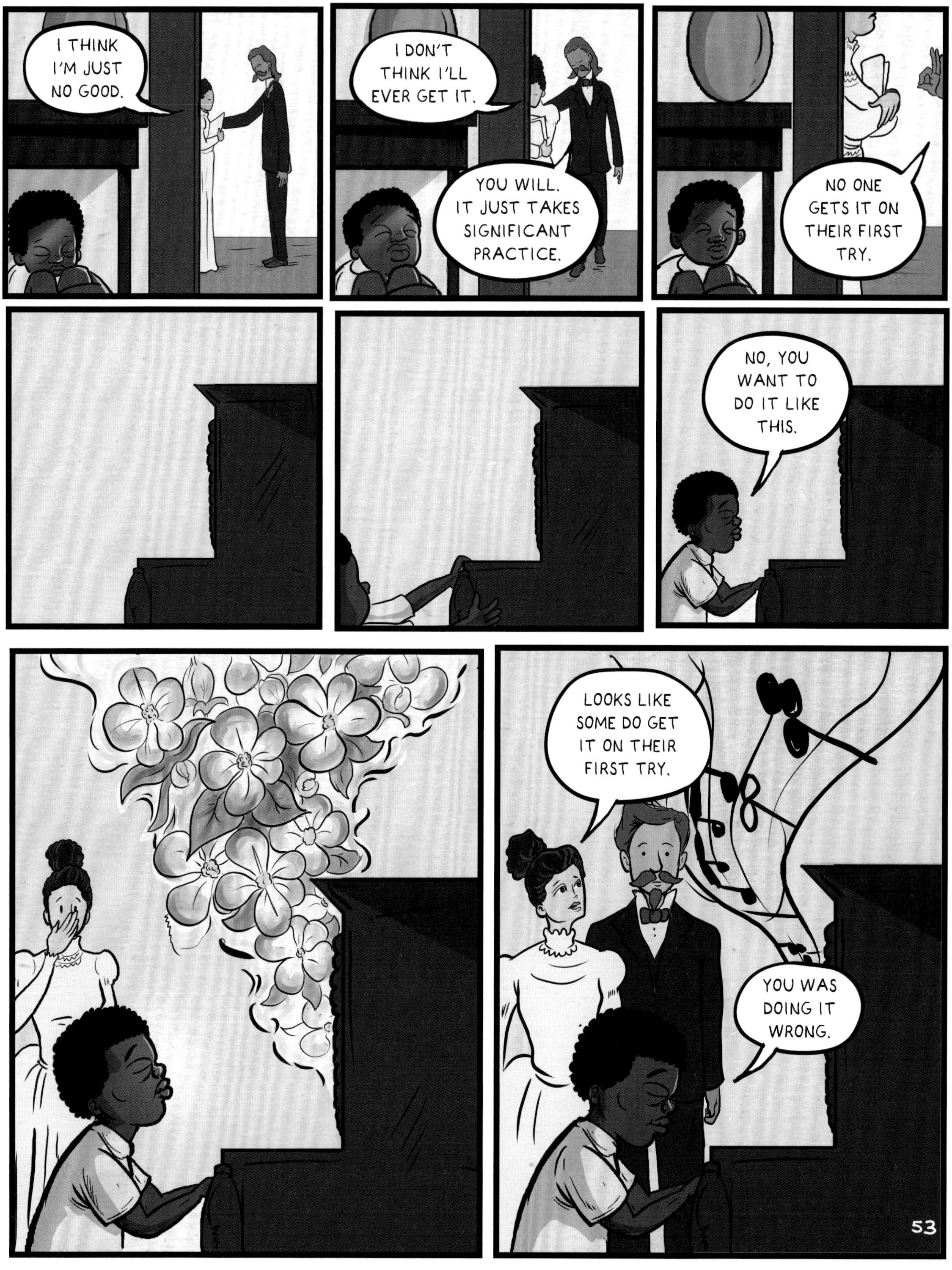
I THINK I'M JUST NO GOOD.
I DON'T THINK I'LL EVER GET IT.
YOU WILL. IT JUST TAKES SIGNIFICANT PRACTICE.
NO ONE GETS IT ON THEIR FIRST TRY.
NO, YOU WANT TO DO IT LIKE THIS.
LOOKS LIKE SOME DO GET IT ON THEIR FIRST TRY.
YOU WAS DOING IT WRONG.

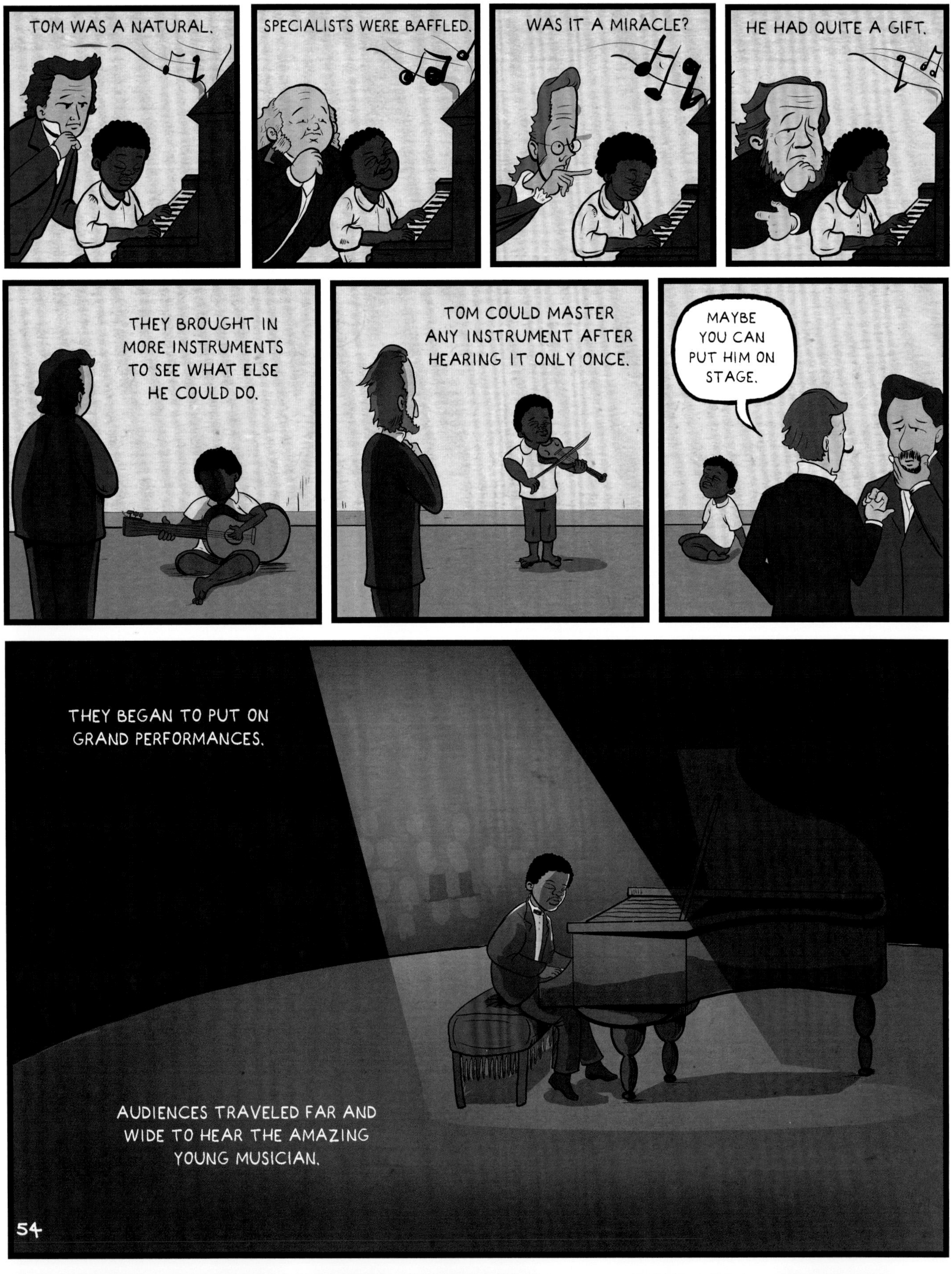
TOM WAS A NATURAL.
SPECIALISTS WERE BAFFLED.
WAS IT A MIRACLE?
HE HAD QUITE A GIFT.
THEY BROUGHT IN MORE INSTRUMENTS TO SEE WHAT ELSE HE COULD DO.
TOM COULD MASTER ANY INSTRUMENT AFTER HEARING IT ONLY ONCE.
MAYBE YOU CAN PUT HIM ON STAGE.
THEY BEGAN TO PUT ON GRAND PERFORMANCES.
AUDIENCES TRAVELED FAR AND WIDE TO HEAR THE AMAZING YOUNG MUSICIAN.

TOM WAS INDEED GIFTED, BUT HIS MIND WAS FILLED WITH SO MUCH SOUND THAT THERE WAS NO ROOM FOR OTHER THINGS.

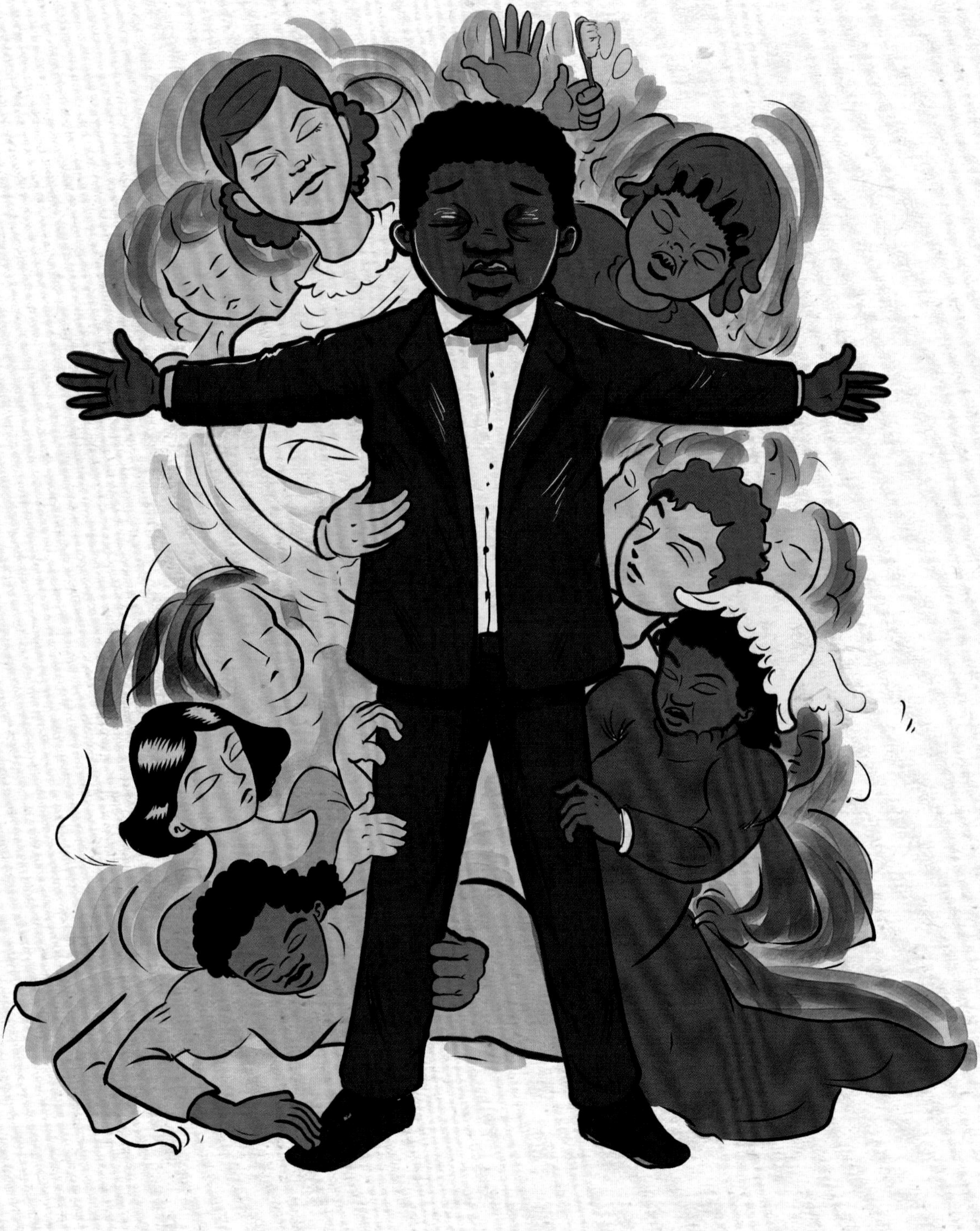

HE NEEDED HELP WITH PUTTING ON HIS CLOTHES, BATHING HIMSELF, AND BRUSHING HIS HAIR.

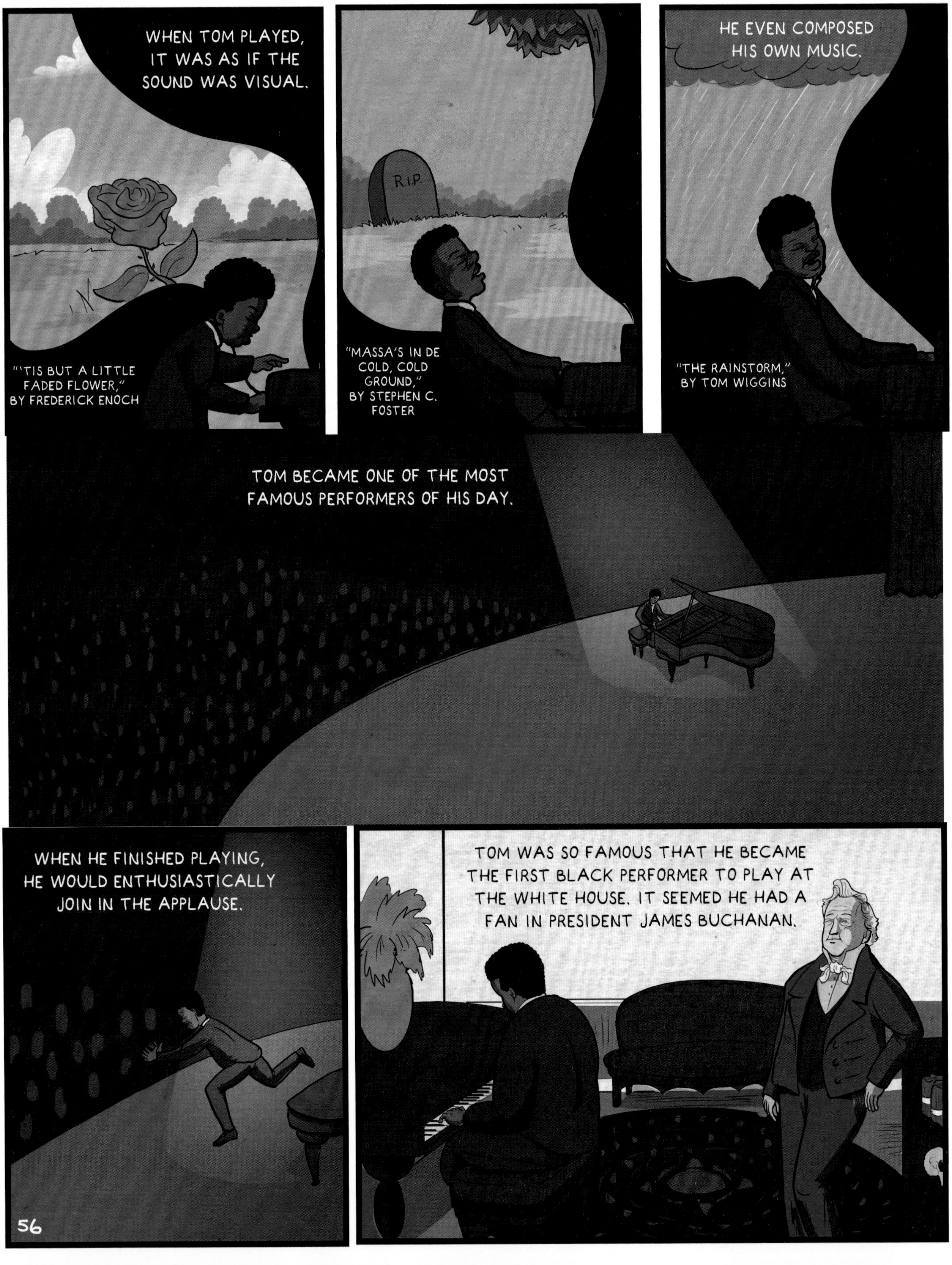
WHEN TOM PLAYED, IT WAS AS IF THE SOUND WAS VISUAL.
"'TIS BUT A LITTLE FADED FLOWER," BY FREDERICK ENOCH
R.I.P.
"MASSA'S IN DE COLD, COLD GROUND," BY STEPHEN C. FOSTER
HE EVEN COMPOSED HIS OWN MUSIC.
"THE RAINSTORM," BY TOM WIGGINS
TOM BECAME ONE OF THE MOST FAMOUS PERFORMERS OF HIS DAY.
WHEN HE FINISHED PLAYING, HE WOULD ENTHUSIASTICALLY JOIN IN THE APPLAUSE.
TOM WAS SO FAMOUS THAT HE BECAME THE FIRST BLACK PERFORMER TO PLAY AT THE WHITE HOUSE. IT SEEMED HE HAD A FAN IN PRESIDENT JAMES BUCHANAN.

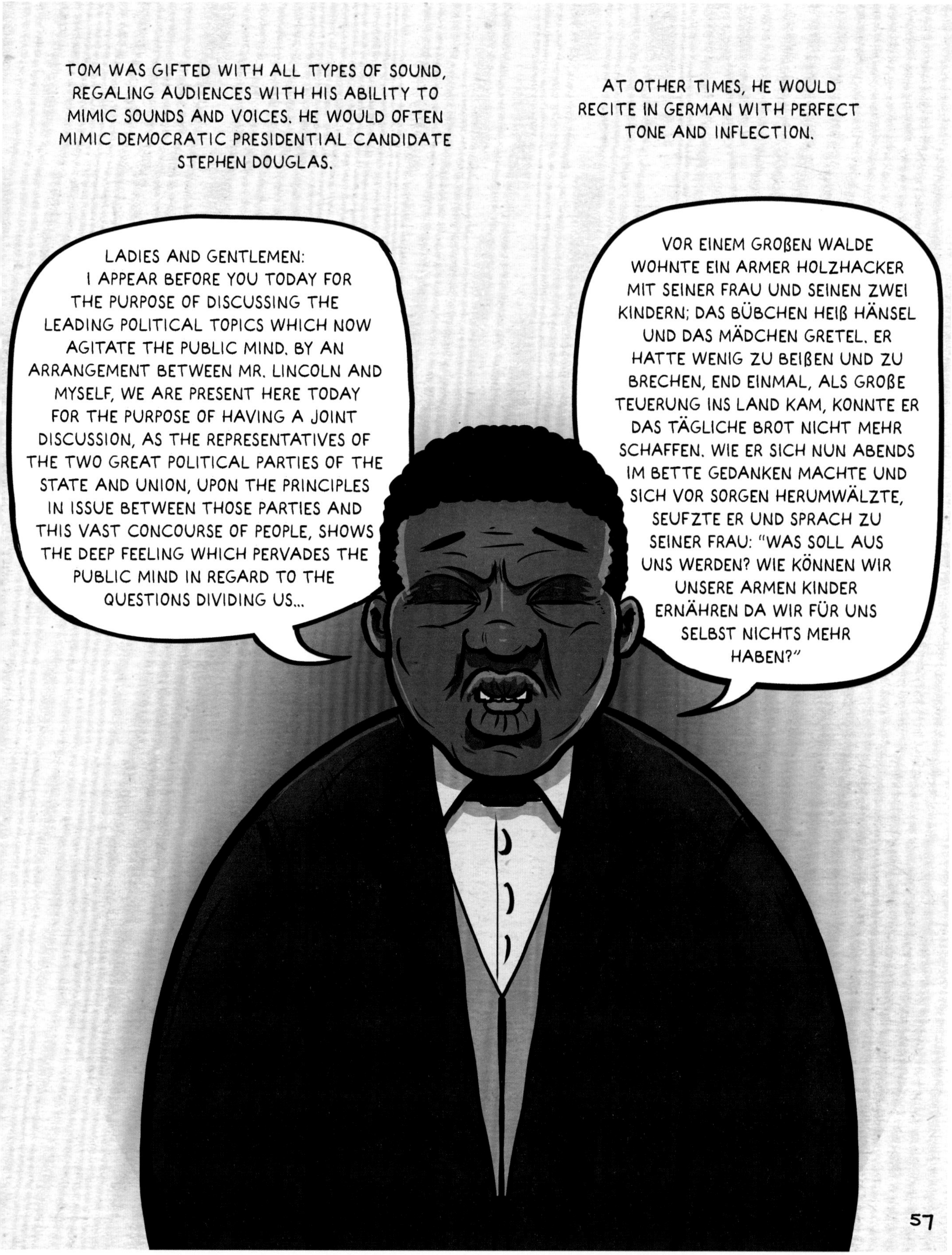
TOM WAS GIFTED WITH ALL TYPES OF SOUND, REGALING AUDIENCES WITH HIS ABILITY TO MIMIC SOUNDS AND VOICES. HE WOULD OFTEN MIMIC DEMOCRATIC PRESIDENTIAL CANDIDATE STEPHEN DOUGLAS.
AT OTHER TIMES, HE WOULD RECITE IN GERMAN WITH PERFECT TONE AND INFLECTION.
LADIES AND GENTLEMEN: I APPEAR BEFORE YOU TODAY FOR THE PURPOSE OF DISCUSSING THE LEADING POLITICAL TOPICS WHICH NOW AGITATE THE PUBLIC MIND. BY AN ARRANGEMENT BETWEEN MR. LINCOLN AND MYSELF, WE ARE PRESENT HERE TODAY FOR THE PURPOSE OF HAVING A JOINT DISCUSSION, AS THE REPRESENTATIVES OF THE TWO GREAT POLITICAL PARTIES OF THE STATE AND UNION, UPON THE PRINCIPLES IN ISSUE BETWEEN THOSE PARTIES AND THIS VAST CONCOURSE OF PEOPLE, SHOWS THE DEEP FEELING WHICH PERVADES THE PUBLIC MIND IN REGARD TO THE QUESTIONS DIVIDING US...
VOR EINEM GROßEN WALDE WOHNTE EIN ARMER HOLZHACKER MIT SEINER FRAU UND SEINEN ZWEI KINDERN; DAS BÜBCHEN HEIß HÄNSEL UND DAS MÄDCHEN GRETEL. ER HATTE WENIG ZU BEIßEN UND ZU BRECHEN, END EINMAL, ALS GROßE TEUERUNG INS LAND KAM, KONNTE ER DAS TÄGLICHE BROT NICHT MEHR SCHAFFEN. WIE ER SICH NUN ABENDS IM BETTE GEDANKEN MACHTE UND SICH VOR SORGEN HERUMWÄLZTE, SEUFZTE ER UND SPRACH ZU SEINER FRAU: "WAS SOLL AUS UNS WERDEN? WIE KÖNNEN WIR UNSERE ARMEN KINDER ERNÄHREN DA WIR FÜR UNS SELBST NICHTS MEHR HABEN?"

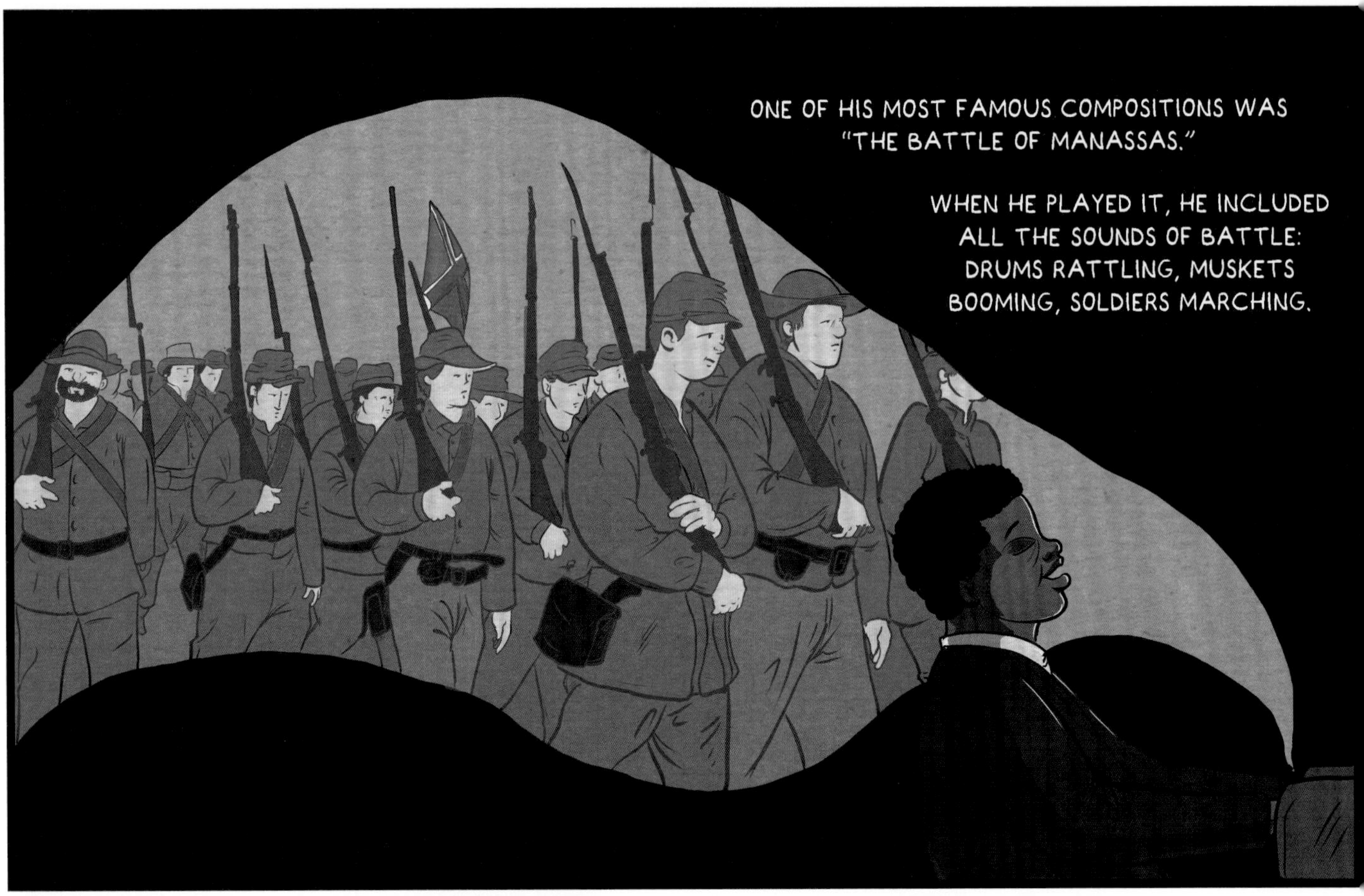
ONE OF HIS MOST FAMOUS COMPOSITIONS WAS "THE BATTLE OF MANASSAS."
WHEN HE PLAYED IT, HE INCLUDED ALL THE SOUNDS OF BATTLE: DRUMS RATTLING, MUSKETS BOOMING, SOLDIERS MARCHING.

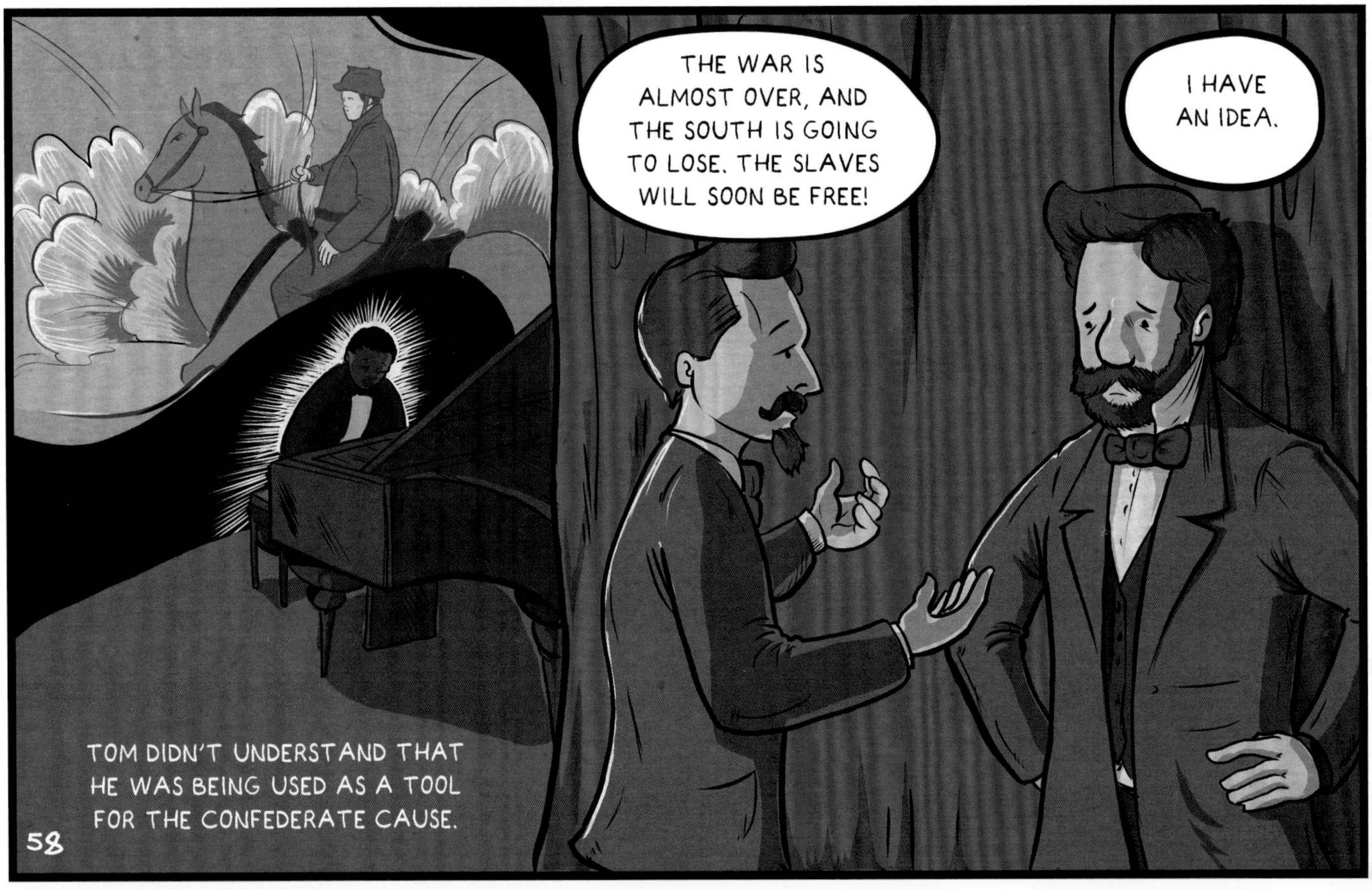
THE WAR IS ALMOST OVER, AND THE SOUTH IS GOING TO LOSE. THE SLAVES WILL SOON BE FREE!
I HAVE AN IDEA.
TOM DIDN'T UNDERSTAND THAT HE WAS BEING USED AS A TOOL FOR THE CONFEDERATE CAUSE.

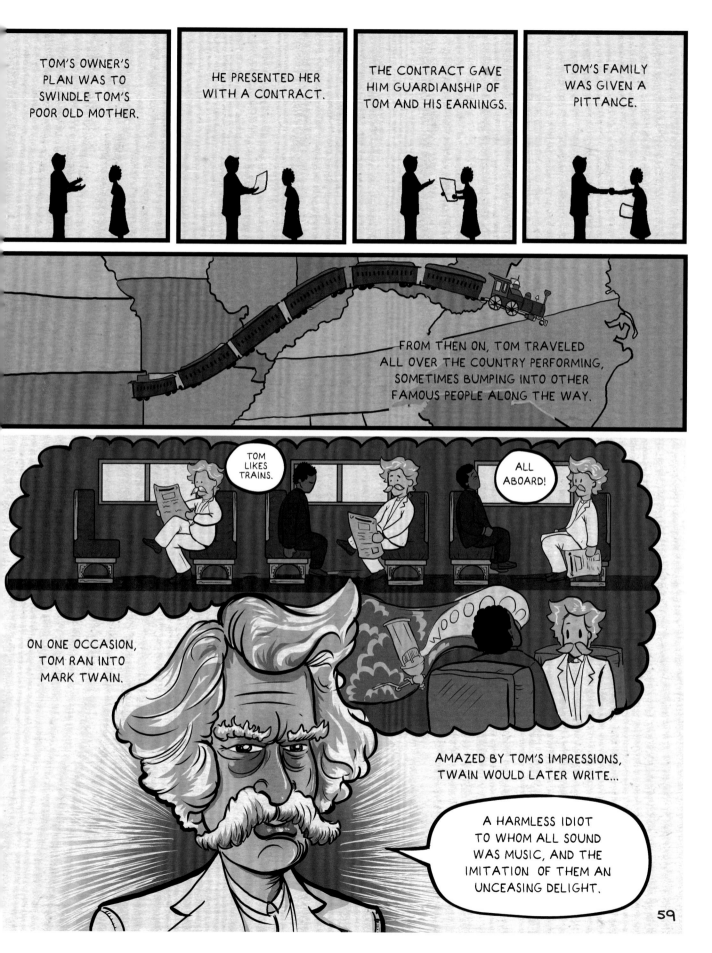

TOM'S OWNER'S PLAN WAS TO SWINDLE TOM'S POOR OLD MOTHER.

HE PRESENTED HER WITH A CONTRACT.

THE CONTRACT GAVE HIM GUARDIANSHIP OF TOM AND HIS EARNINGS.

TOM'S FAMILY WAS GIVEN A PITTANCE.

FROM THEN ON, TOM TRAVELED ALL OVER THE COUNTRY PERFORMING, SOMETIMES BUMPING INTO OTHER FAMOUS PEOPLE ALONG THE WAY.

TOM LIKES TRAINS.

ALL ABOARD!

ON ONE OCCASION, TOM RAN INTO MARK TWAIN.

AMAZED BY TOM'S IMPRESSIONS, TWAIN WOULD LATER WRITE...

A HARMLESS IDIOT TO WHOM ALL SOUND WAS MUSIC, AND THE IMITATION OF THEM AN UNCEASING DELIGHT.

59

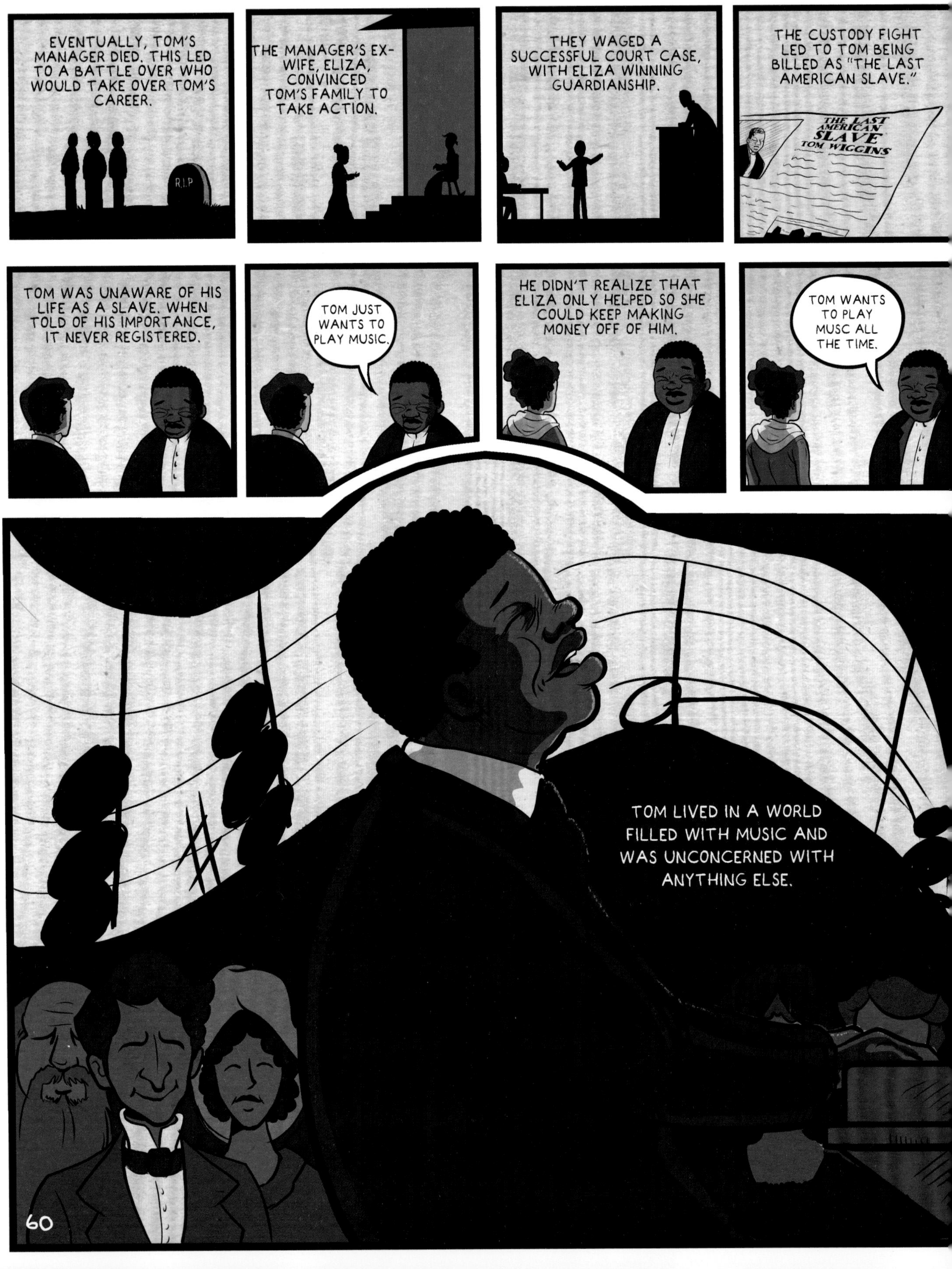
EVENTUALLY, TOM'S MANAGER DIED. THIS LED TO A BATTLE OVER WHO WOULD TAKE OVER TOM'S CAREER.
R.I.P
THE MANAGER'S EX-WIFE, ELIZA, CONVINCED TOM'S FAMILY TO TAKE ACTION.
THEY WAGED A SUCCESSFUL COURT CASE, WITH ELIZA WINNING GUARDIANSHIP.
THE CUSTODY FIGHT LED TO TOM BEING BILLED AS "THE LAST AMERICAN SLAVE."
THE LAST AMERICAN SLAVE
TOM WIGGINS
TOM WAS UNAWARE OF HIS LIFE AS A SLAVE. WHEN TOLD OF HIS IMPORTANCE, IT NEVER REGISTERED.
TOM JUST WANTS TO PLAY MUSIC.
HE DIDN'T REALIZE THAT ELIZA ONLY HELPED SO SHE COULD KEEP MAKING MONEY OFF OF HIM.
TOM WANTS TO PLAY MUSC ALL THE TIME.
TOM LIVED IN A WORLD FILLED WITH MUSIC AND WAS UNCONCERNED WITH ANYTHING ELSE.

TOM SPENT HIS FINAL DAYS DOING WHAT HE LOVED:
PLAYING MUSIC. SADLY, THERE ARE NO ORIGINAL
RECORDINGS OF HIS CONCERTS OR COMPOSITIONS.
WE ARE LEFT ONLY WITH PHOTOGRAPHS AND SHEET MUSIC,
THE REMNANTS OF A LIFE LIVED THROUGH SOUND.

NOTHING ELSE MATTERED TO TOM. TO HIM,
THE WORLD WAS FULL OF BEAUTIFUL NOISE,
AND ALL SOUND WAS MUSIC.

MILLIE AND CHRISTINE McCOY

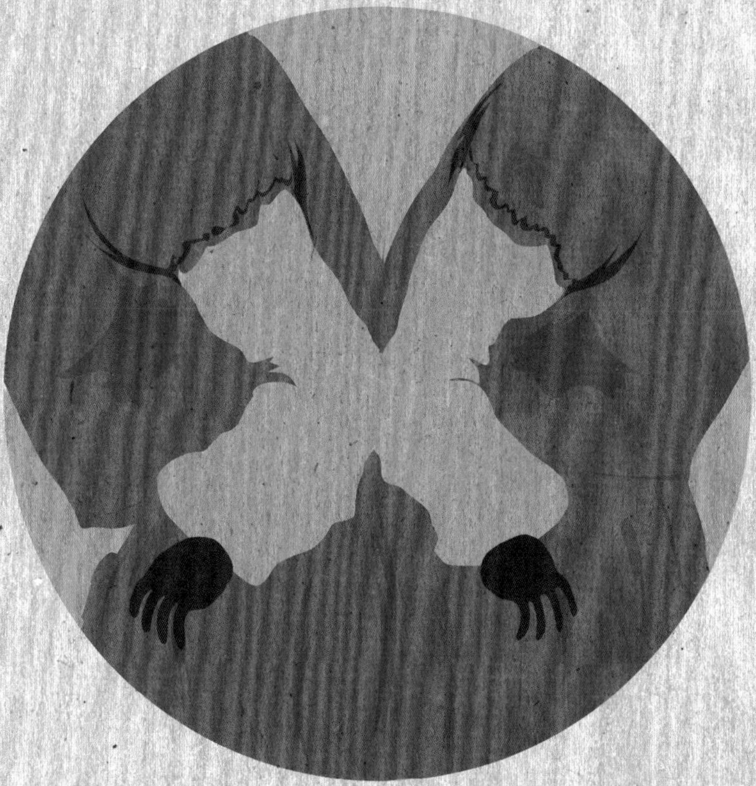

STRONGER TOGETHER

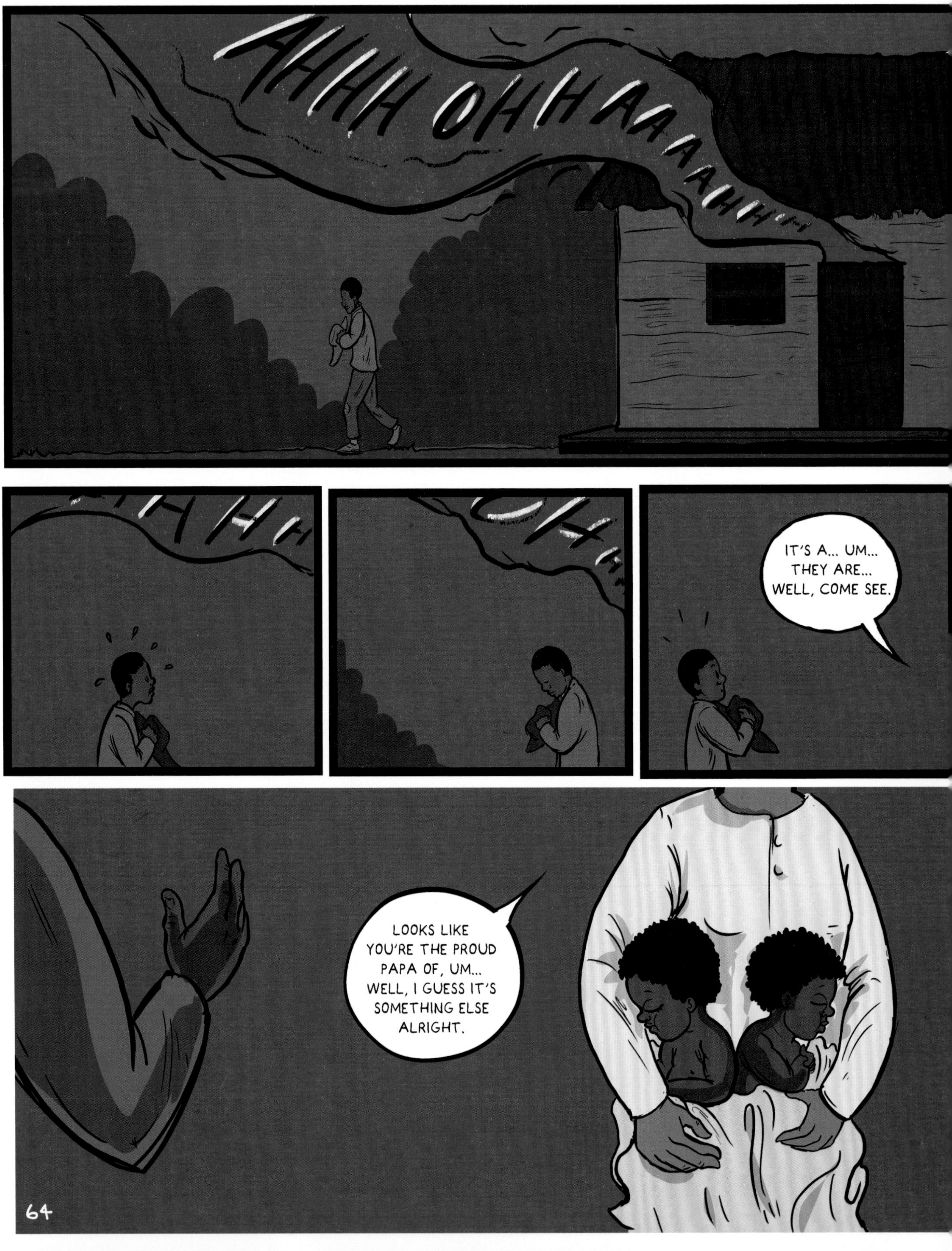
AHHH OHHAAAAAHHH
IT'S A... UM... THEY ARE... WELL, COME SEE.
LOOKS LIKE YOU'RE THE PROUD PAPA OF, UM... WELL, I GUESS IT'S SOMETHING ELSE ALRIGHT.

STRONGER TOGETHER

THE STORY OF MILLIE AND CHRISTINE McCOY, THE TWO-HEADED NIGHTINGALE

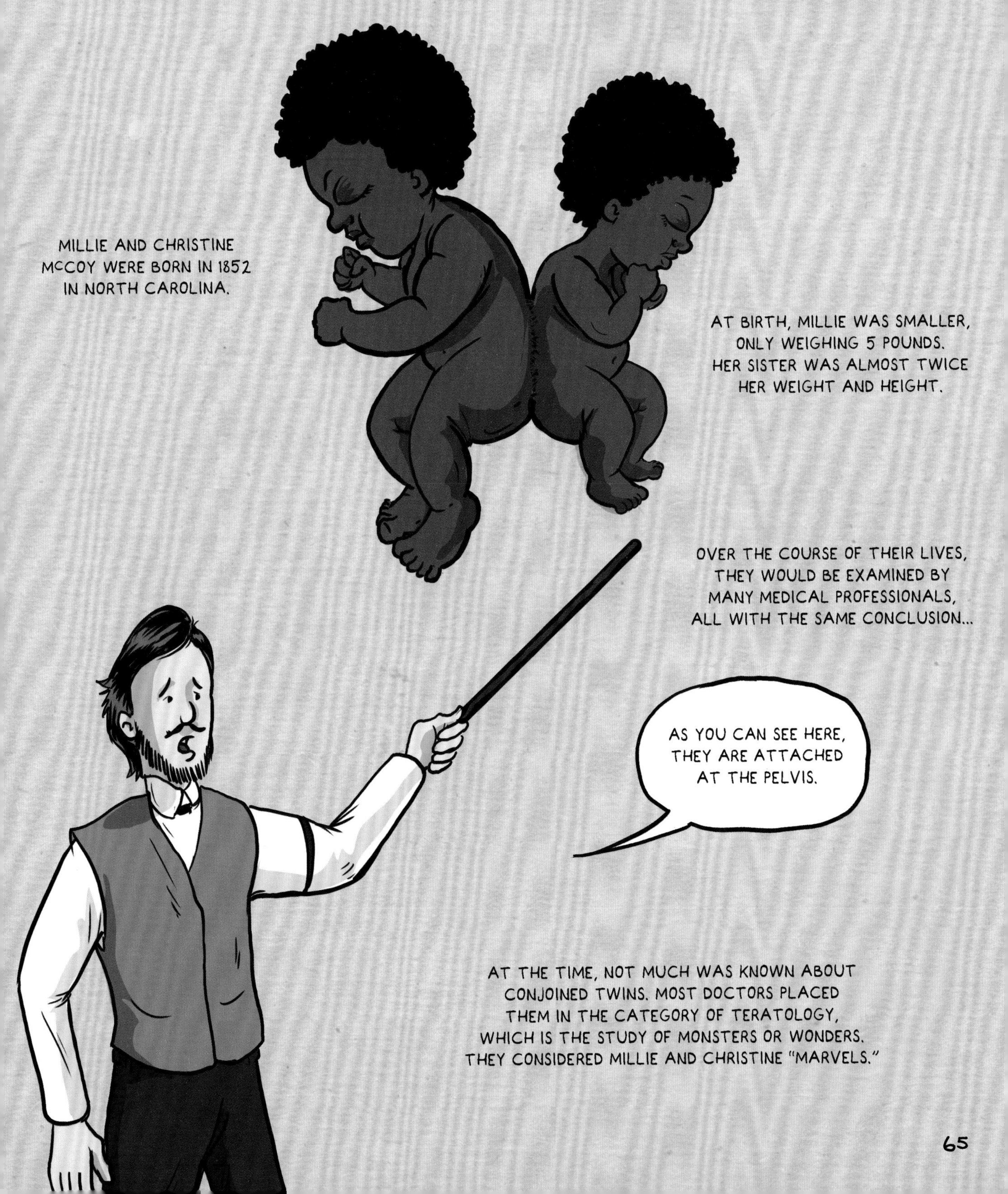
MILLIE AND CHRISTINE McCOY WERE BORN IN 1852 IN NORTH CAROLINA.
AT BIRTH, MILLIE WAS SMALLER, ONLY WEIGHING 5 POUNDS. HER SISTER WAS ALMOST TWICE HER WEIGHT AND HEIGHT.
OVER THE COURSE OF THEIR LIVES, THEY WOULD BE EXAMINED BY MANY MEDICAL PROFESSIONALS, ALL WITH THE SAME CONCLUSION...
AS YOU CAN SEE HERE, THEY ARE ATTACHED AT THE PELVIS.
AT THE TIME, NOT MUCH WAS KNOWN ABOUT CONJOINED TWINS. MOST DOCTORS PLACED THEM IN THE CATEGORY OF TERATOLOGY, WHICH IS THE STUDY OF MONSTERS OR WONDERS. THEY CONSIDERED MILLIE AND CHRISTINE "MARVELS."

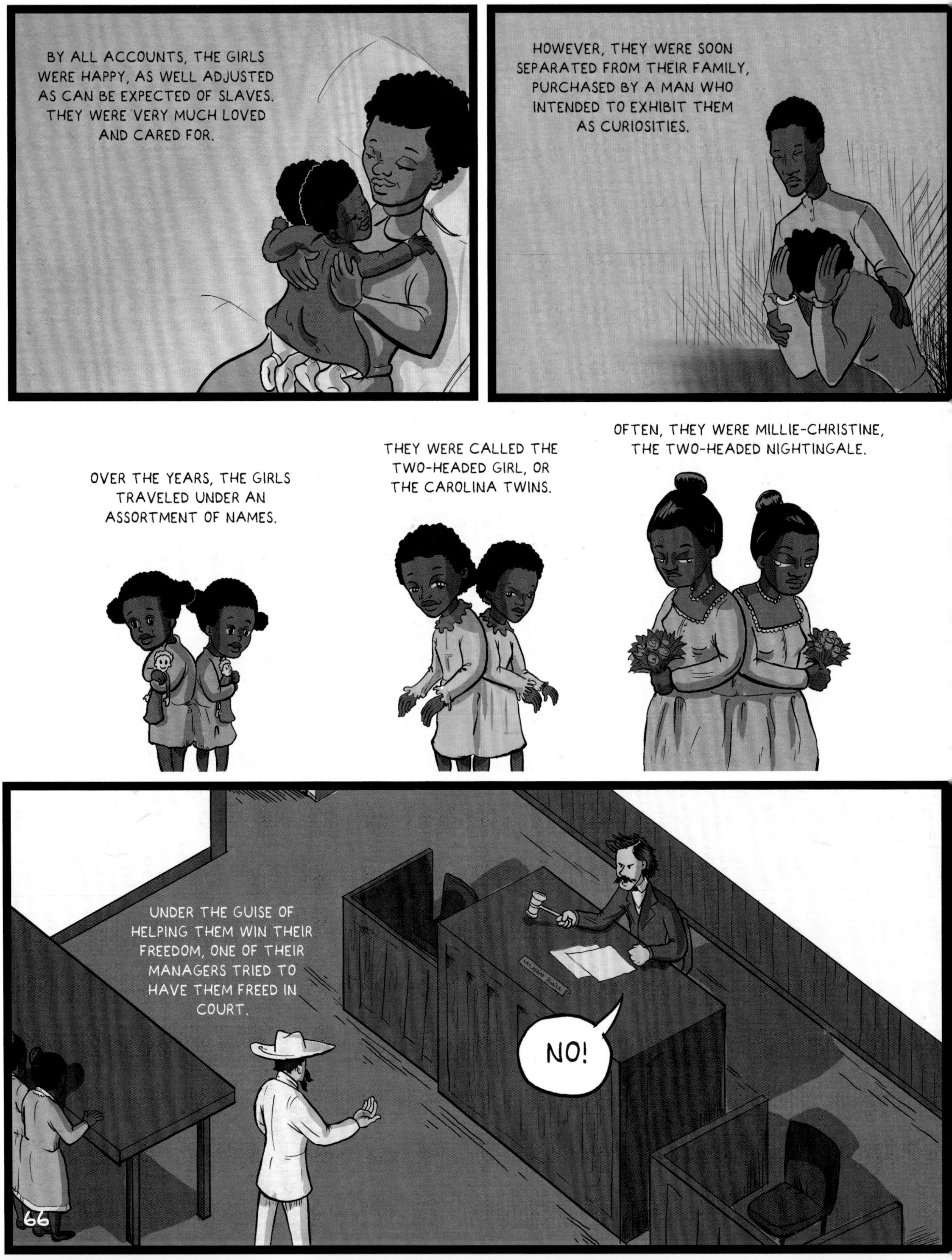
BY ALL ACCOUNTS, THE GIRLS WERE HAPPY, AS WELL ADJUSTED AS CAN BE EXPECTED OF SLAVES. THEY WERE VERY MUCH LOVED AND CARED FOR.
HOWEVER, THEY WERE SOON SEPARATED FROM THEIR FAMILY, PURCHASED BY A MAN WHO INTENDED TO EXHIBIT THEM AS CURIOSITIES.
OVER THE YEARS, THE GIRLS TRAVELED UNDER AN ASSORTMENT OF NAMES.
THEY WERE CALLED THE TWO-HEADED GIRL, OR THE CAROLINA TWINS.
OFTEN, THEY WERE MILLIE-CHRISTINE, THE TWO-HEADED NIGHTINGALE.
UNDER THE GUISE OF HELPING THEM WIN THEIR FREEDOM, ONE OF THEIR MANAGERS TRIED TO HAVE THEM FREED IN COURT.
NO!

WHEN HIS PLAN FAILED, HE DECIDED TO TAKE A DIFFERENT APPROACH.

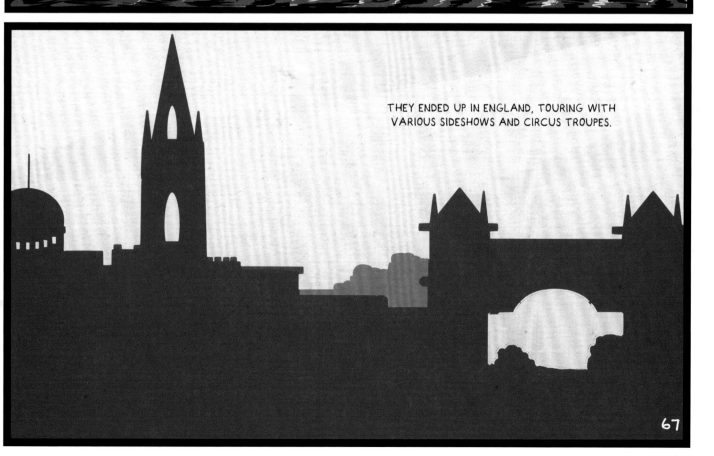

HE KIDNAPPED THE GIRLS AND HIGHTAILED IT TO EUROPE, WHERE THEY TOURED FOR A FEW YEARS.

THEY ENDED UP IN ENGLAND, TOURING WITH VARIOUS SIDESHOWS AND CIRCUS TROUPES.

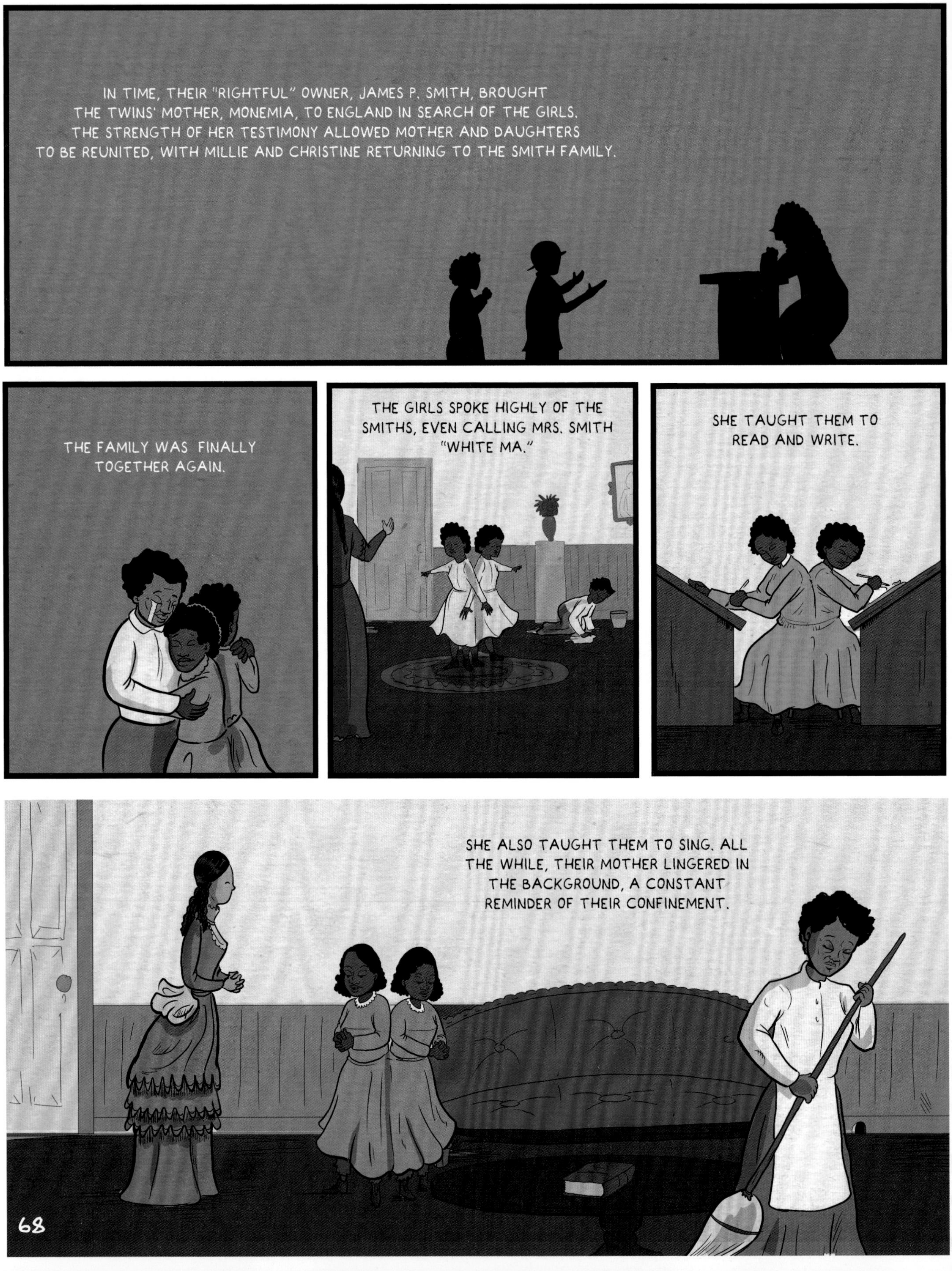
IN TIME, THEIR "RIGHTFUL" OWNER, JAMES P. SMITH, BROUGHT THE TWINS' MOTHER, MONEMIA, TO ENGLAND IN SEARCH OF THE GIRLS. THE STRENGTH OF HER TESTIMONY ALLOWED MOTHER AND DAUGHTERS TO BE REUNITED, WITH MILLIE AND CHRISTINE RETURNING TO THE SMITH FAMILY.
THE FAMILY WAS FINALLY TOGETHER AGAIN.
THE GIRLS SPOKE HIGHLY OF THE SMITHS, EVEN CALLING MRS. SMITH "WHITE MA."
SHE TAUGHT THEM TO READ AND WRITE.
SHE ALSO TAUGHT THEM TO SING. ALL THE WHILE, THEIR MOTHER LINGERED IN THE BACKGROUND, A CONSTANT REMINDER OF THEIR CONFINEMENT.

YOU MIGHT NOT THINK THAT WOMEN OF SUCH A BACKGROUND WOULD BE ABLE TO ASSERT CONTROL OVER THEIR LIVES, BUT MILLIE AND CHRISTINE DID. BEGINNING AT AGE 15, THEY REFUSED TO LET DOCTORS POKE AND PROD AT THEM, ENDING THE EMBARRASSING PUBLIC MEDICAL EXAMINATIONS THAT HAD BEEN PART OF THEIR PERFORMANCES. ACCORDING TO PROFESSOR ELLEN SAMUELS, IN HER PAPER "WHERE ENSLAVEMENT AND ENFREAKMENT MEET," THIS SHOWED THAT THEY EXHIBITED SOME MEASURE OF CONTROL OVER THEIR LIVES. YOU CAN SEE IT IN THE FIRST FEW LINES OF THE BIOGRAPHY PAMPHLET THEY SOLD AT THEIR SHOWS:

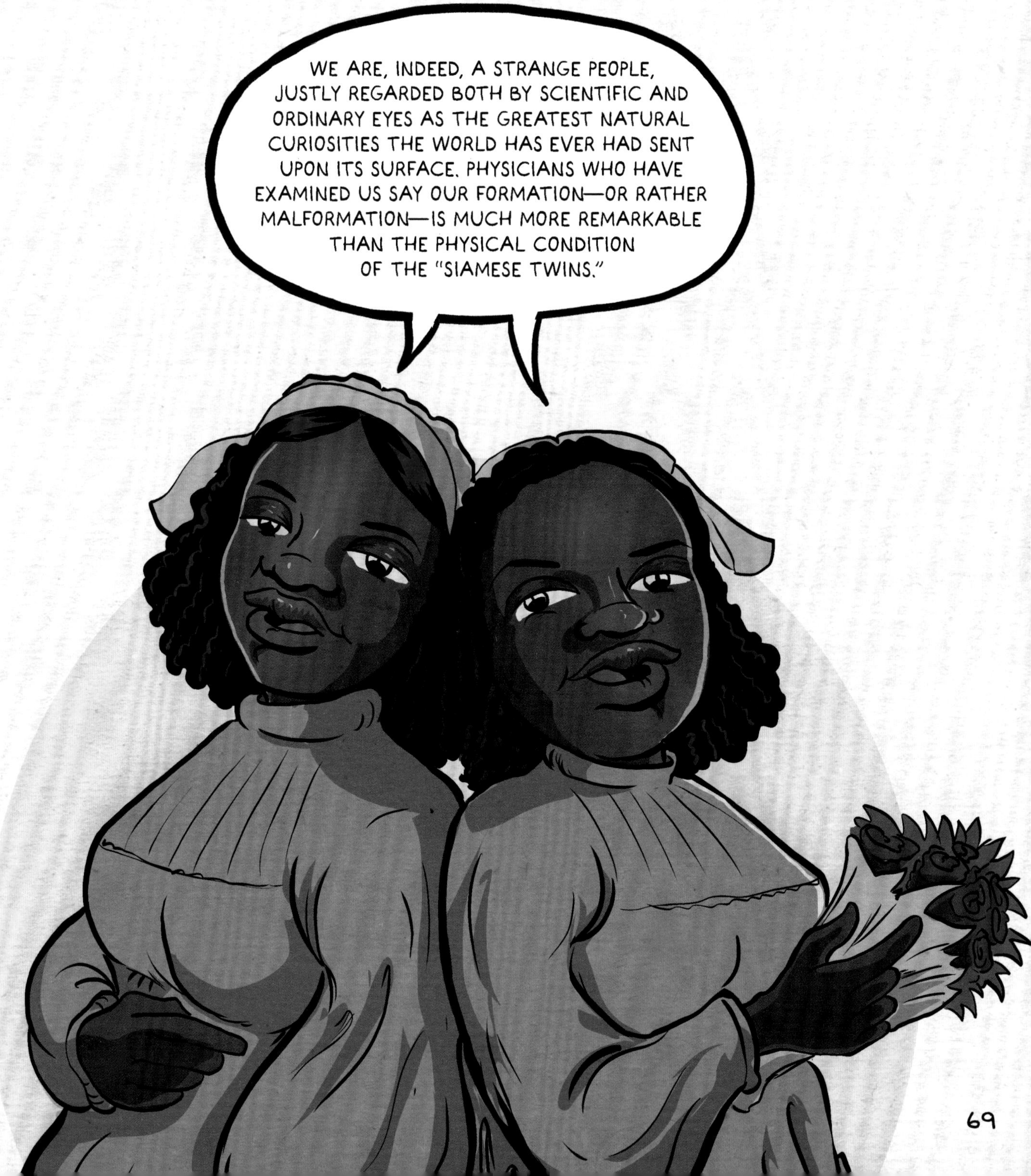
WE ARE, INDEED, A STRANGE PEOPLE, JUSTLY REGARDED BOTH BY SCIENTIFIC AND ORDINARY EYES AS THE GREATEST NATURAL CURIOSITIES THE WORLD HAS EVER HAD SENT UPON ITS SURFACE. PHYSICIANS WHO HAVE EXAMINED US SAY OUR FORMATION—OR RATHER MALFORMATION—IS MUCH MORE REMARKABLE THAN THE PHYSICAL CONDITION OF THE "SIAMESE TWINS."

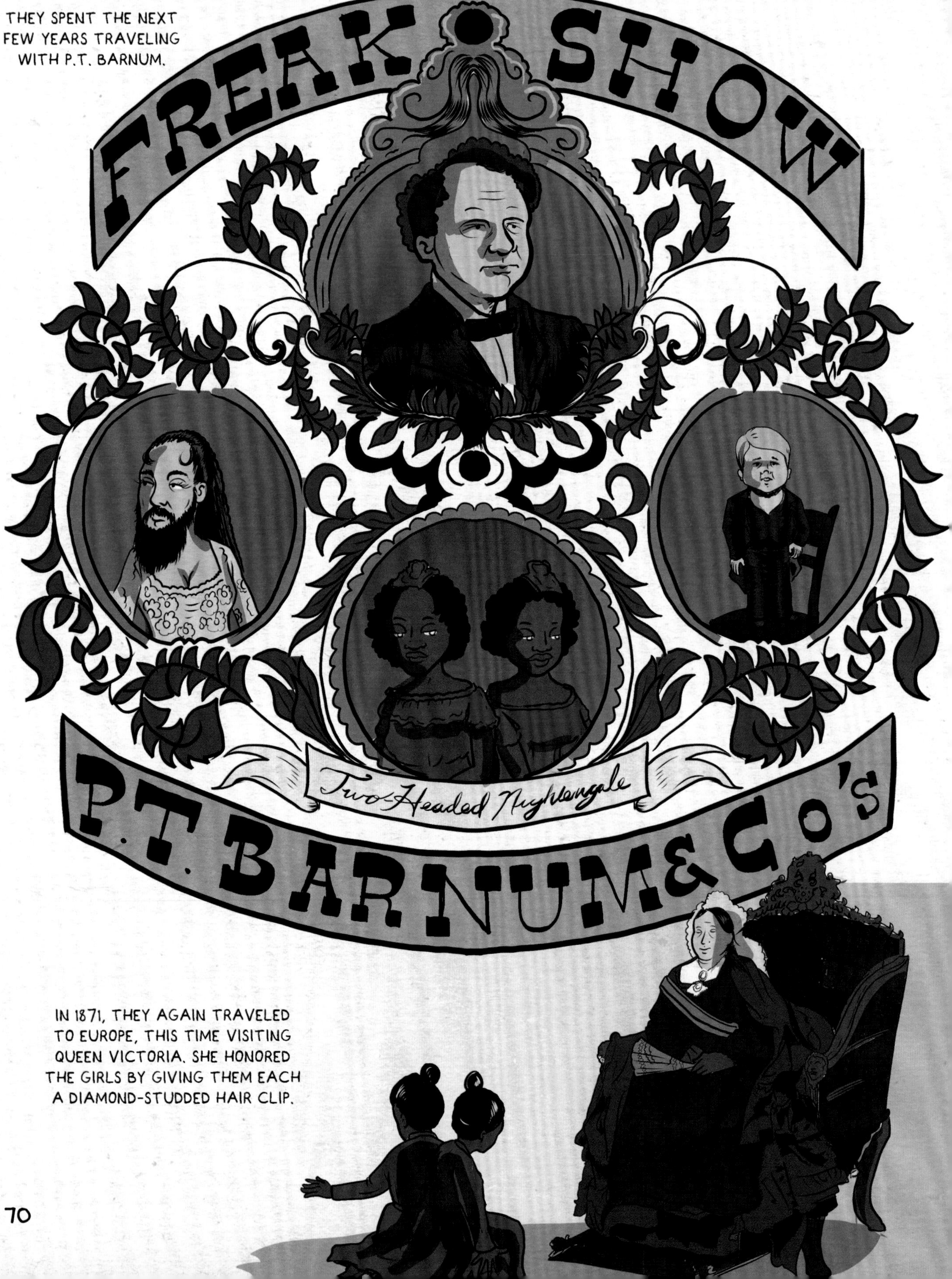
THEY SPENT THE NEXT FEW YEARS TRAVELING WITH P.T. BARNUM.
FREAK SHOW
Two-Headed Nightingale
P.T. BARNUM & Co's
IN 1871, THEY AGAIN TRAVELED TO EUROPE, THIS TIME VISITING QUEEN VICTORIA. SHE HONORED THE GIRLS BY GIVING THEM EACH A DIAMOND-STUDDED HAIR CLIP.

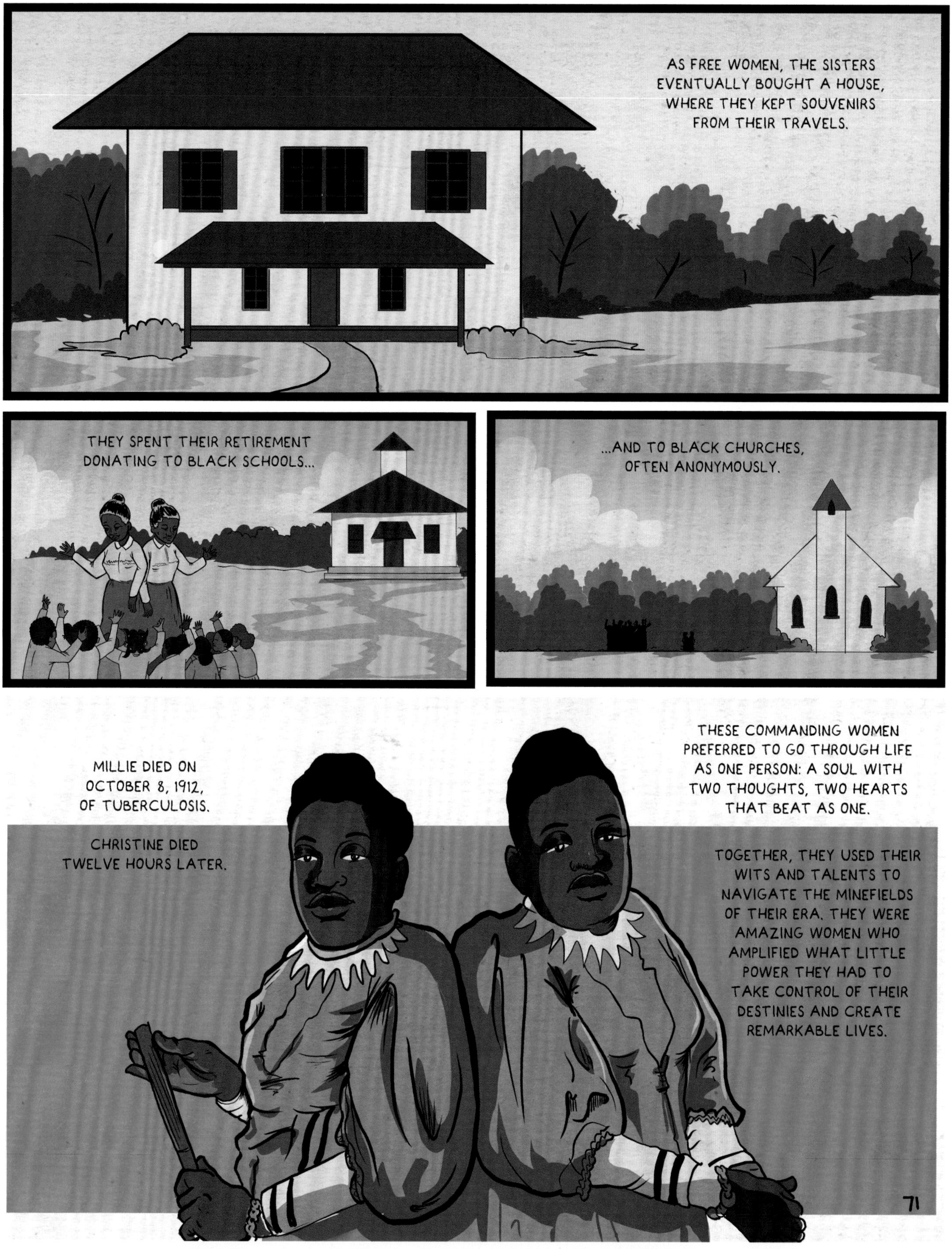
AS FREE WOMEN, THE SISTERS EVENTUALLY BOUGHT A HOUSE, WHERE THEY KEPT SOUVENIRS FROM THEIR TRAVELS.
THEY SPENT THEIR RETIREMENT DONATING TO BLACK SCHOOLS...
...AND TO BLACK CHURCHES, OFTEN ANONYMOUSLY.
MILLIE DIED ON OCTOBER 8, 1912, OF TUBERCULOSIS.
CHRISTINE DIED TWELVE HOURS LATER.
THESE COMMANDING WOMEN PREFERRED TO GO THROUGH LIFE AS ONE PERSON: A SOUL WITH TWO THOUGHTS, TWO HEARTS THAT BEAT AS ONE.
TOGETHER, THEY USED THEIR WITS AND TALENTS TO NAVIGATE THE MINEFIELDS OF THEIR ERA. THEY WERE AMAZING WOMEN WHO AMPLIFIED WHAT LITTLE POWER THEY HAD TO TAKE CONTROL OF THEIR DESTINIES AND CREATE REMARKABLE LIVES.

VICTOR GREEN

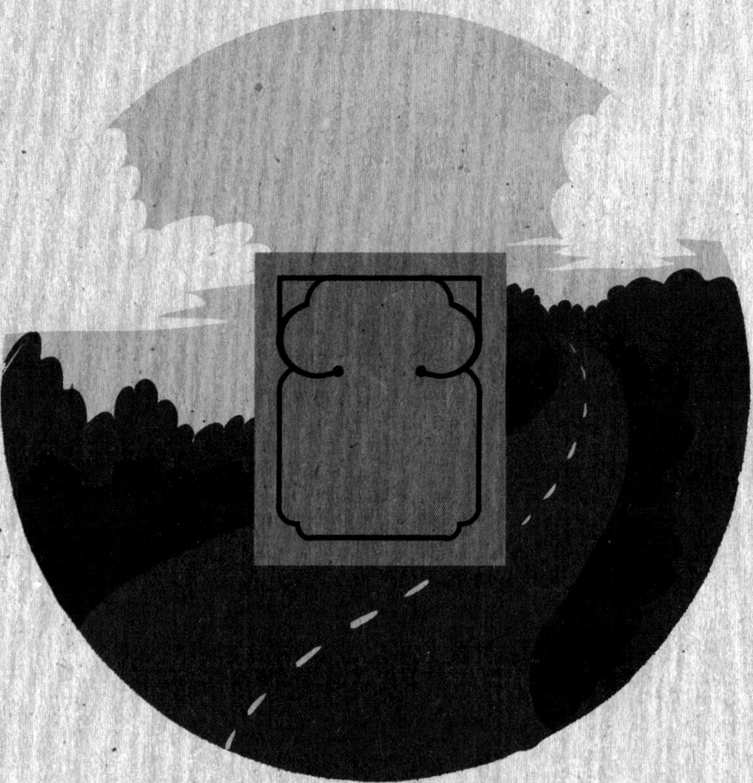

THE GREEN BOOK FOR THE NEGRO MOTORIST

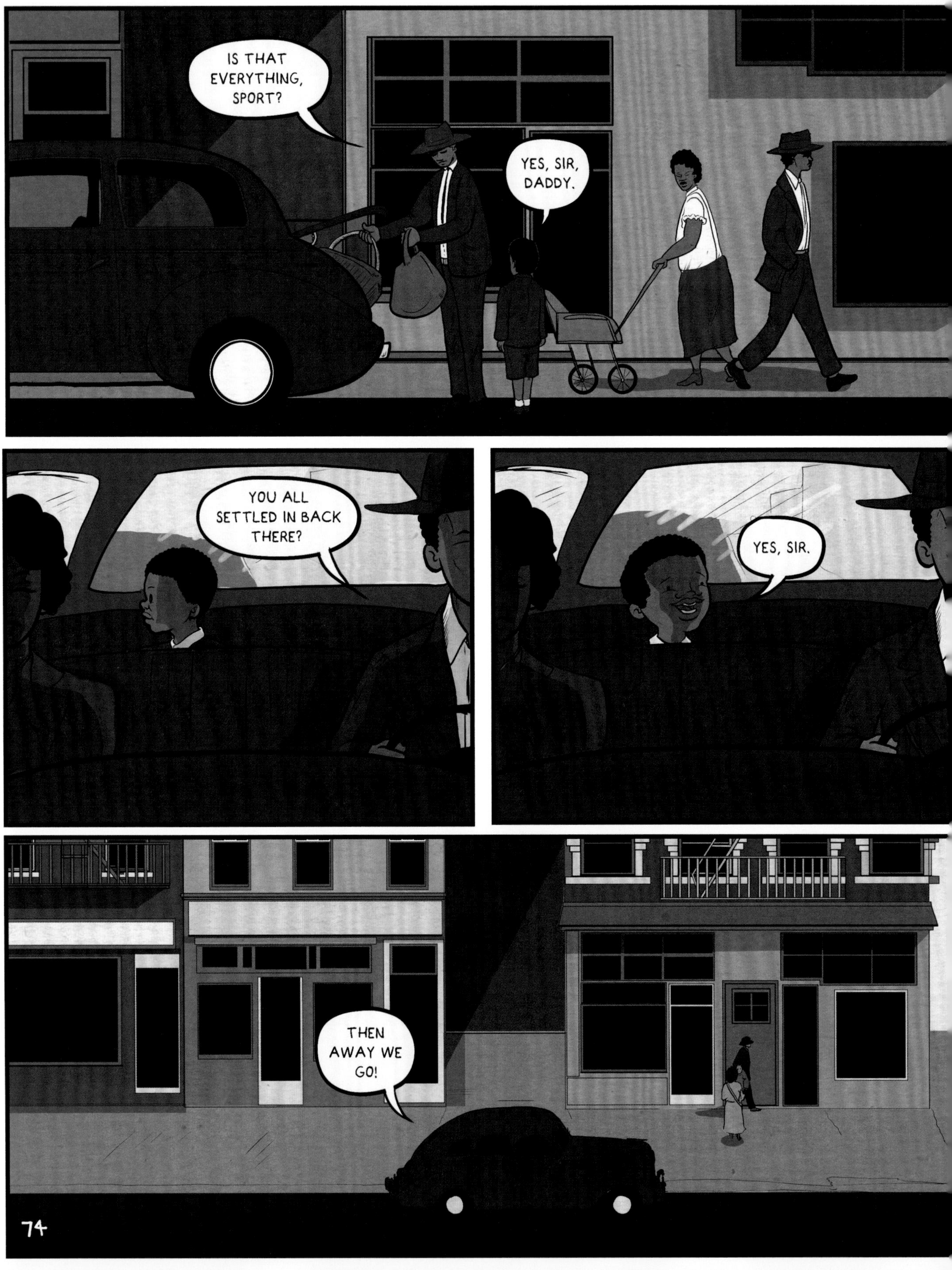
IS THAT EVERYTHING, SPORT?
YES, SIR, DADDY.
YOU ALL SETTLED IN BACK THERE?
YES, SIR.
THEN AWAY WE GO!

THE STORY OF THE GREEN BOOK

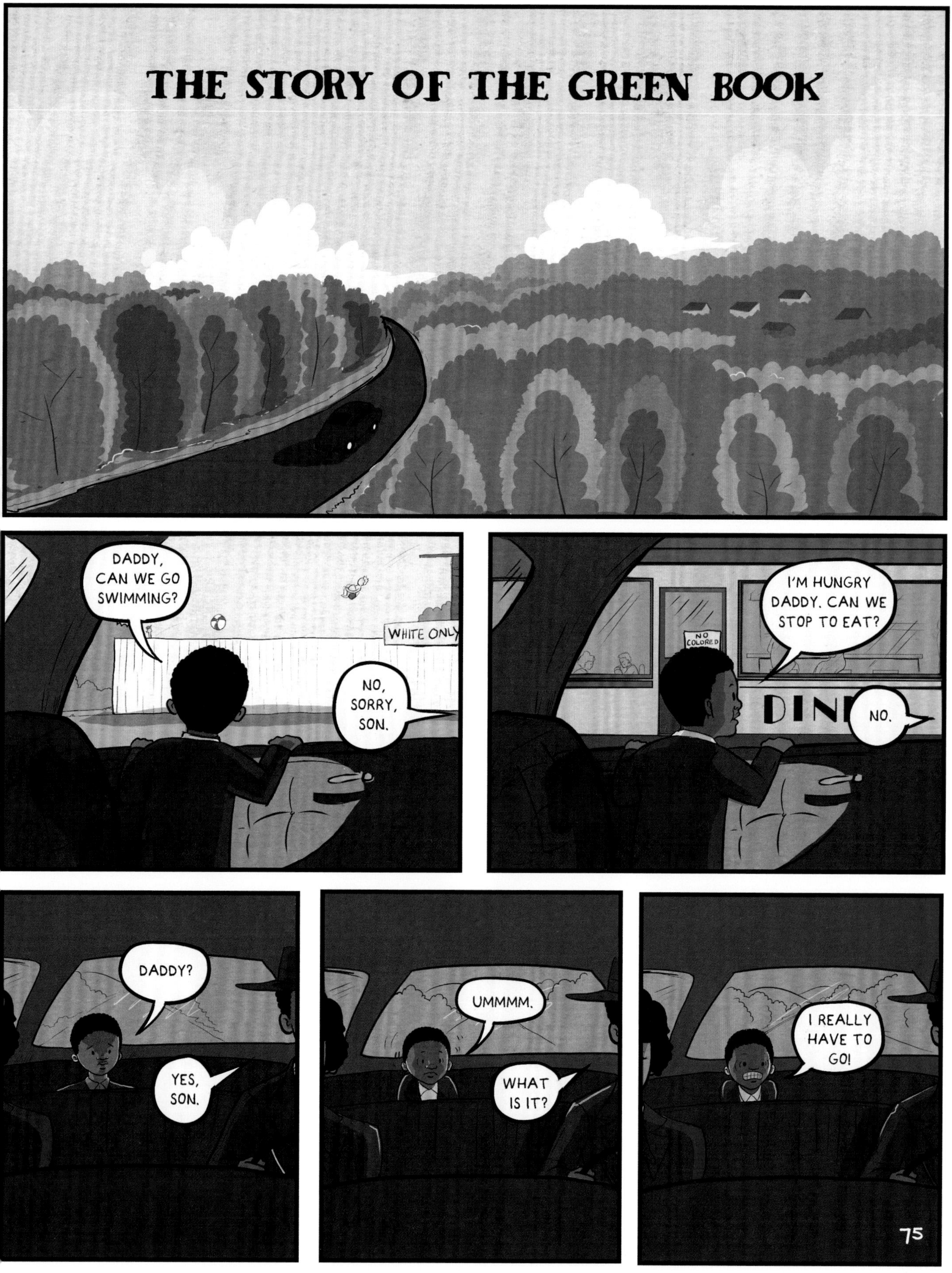
DADDY, CAN WE GO SWIMMING?
WHITE ONLY
NO, SORRY, SON.
I'M HUNGRY DADDY. CAN WE STOP TO EAT?
NO COLORED
NO.
DADDY?
YES, SON.
UMMMM.
WHAT IS IT?
I REALLY HAVE TO GO!

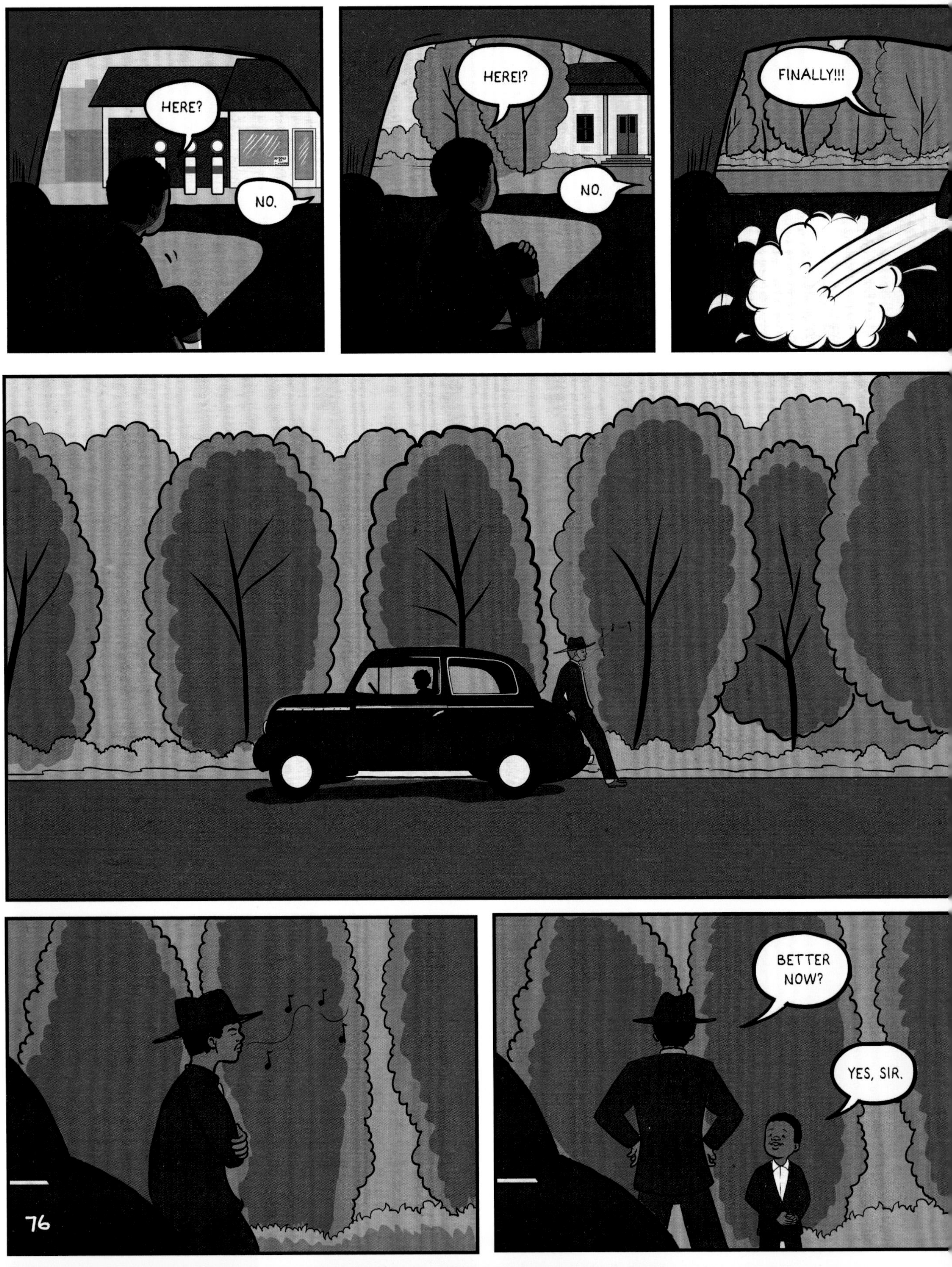
HERE?
NO.
HERE!?
NO.
FINALLY!!!
BETTER NOW?
YES, SIR.

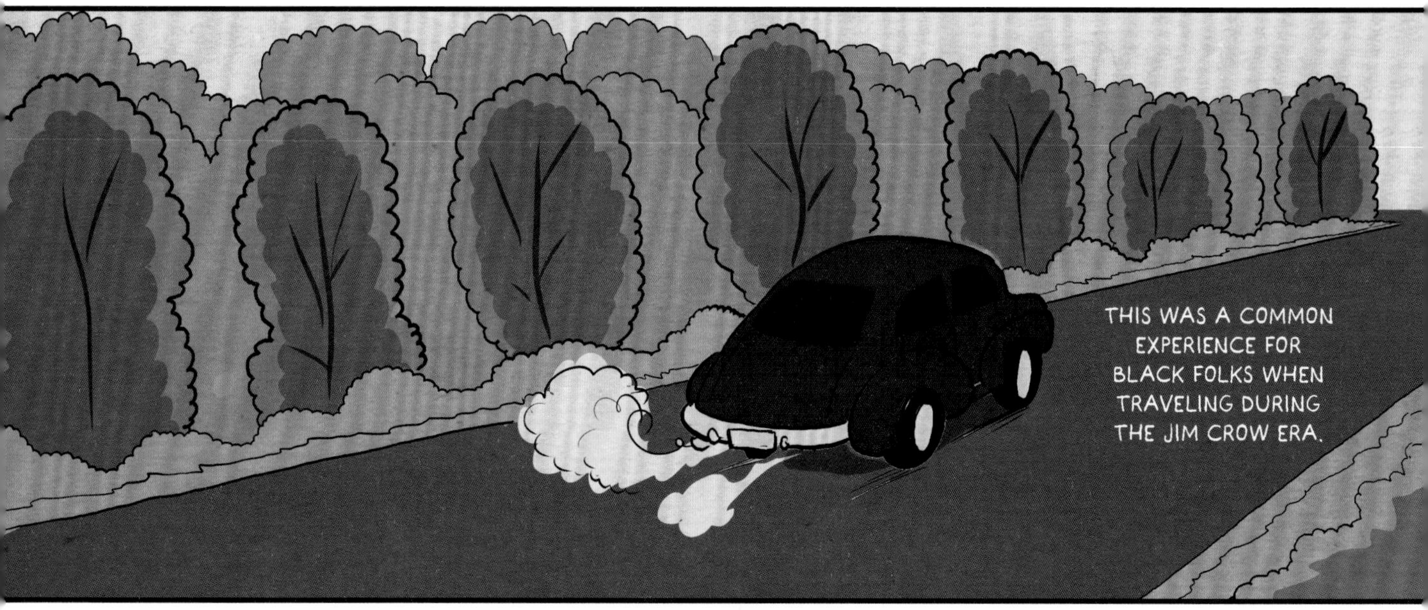
THIS WAS A COMMON EXPERIENCE FOR BLACK FOLKS WHEN TRAVELING DURING THE JIM CROW ERA.

AT LEAST UNTIL A MAN NAMED VICTOR GREEN HAD AN IDEA.

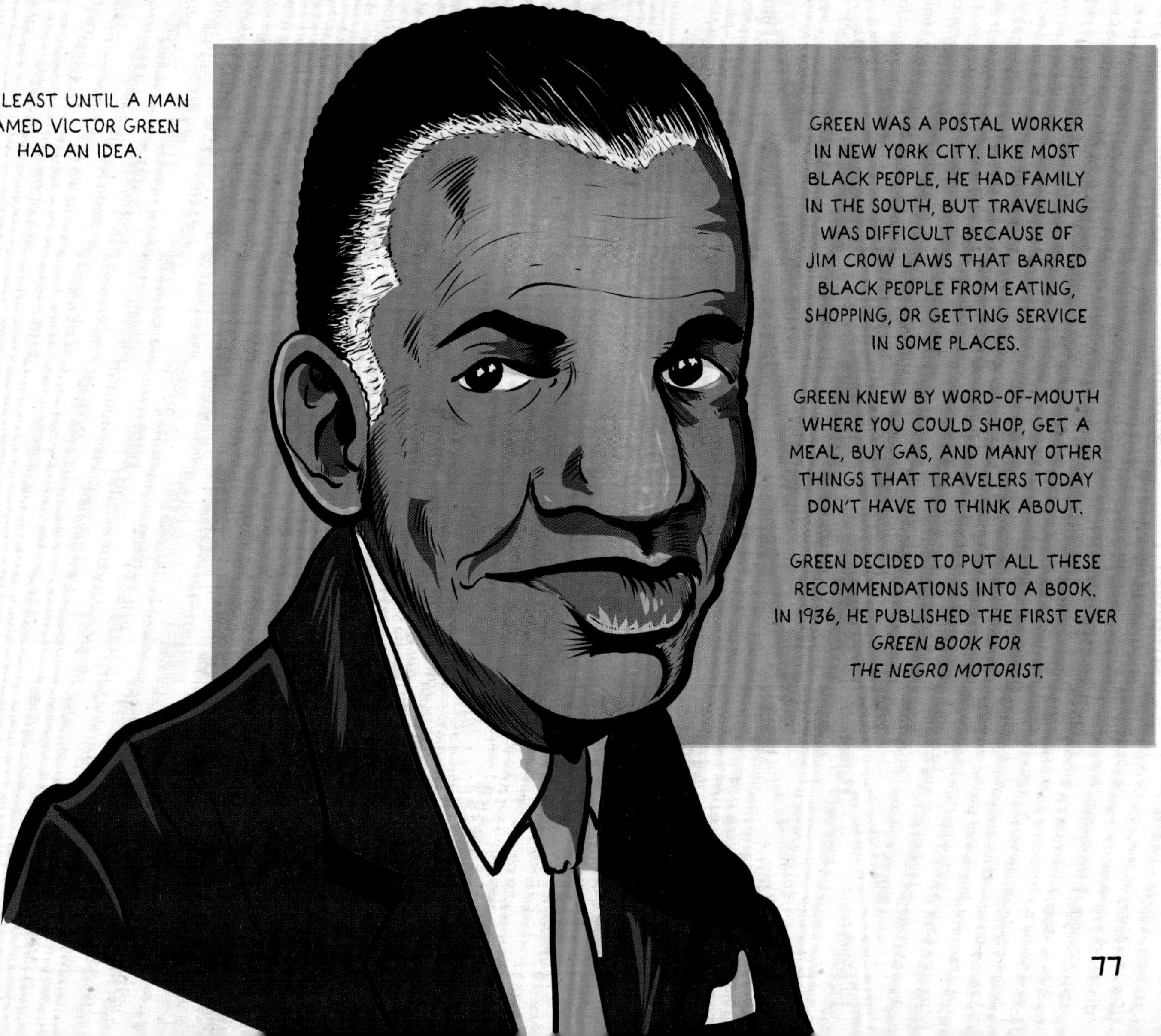
GREEN WAS A POSTAL WORKER IN NEW YORK CITY. LIKE MOST BLACK PEOPLE, HE HAD FAMILY IN THE SOUTH, BUT TRAVELING WAS DIFFICULT BECAUSE OF JIM CROW LAWS THAT BARRED BLACK PEOPLE FROM EATING, SHOPPING, OR GETTING SERVICE IN SOME PLACES.
GREEN KNEW BY WORD-OF-MOUTH WHERE YOU COULD SHOP, GET A MEAL, BUY GAS, AND MANY OTHER THINGS THAT TRAVELERS TODAY DON'T HAVE TO THINK ABOUT.
GREEN DECIDED TO PUT ALL THESE RECOMMENDATIONS INTO A BOOK. IN 1936, HE PUBLISHED THE FIRST EVER *GREEN BOOK FOR THE NEGRO MOTORIST.*

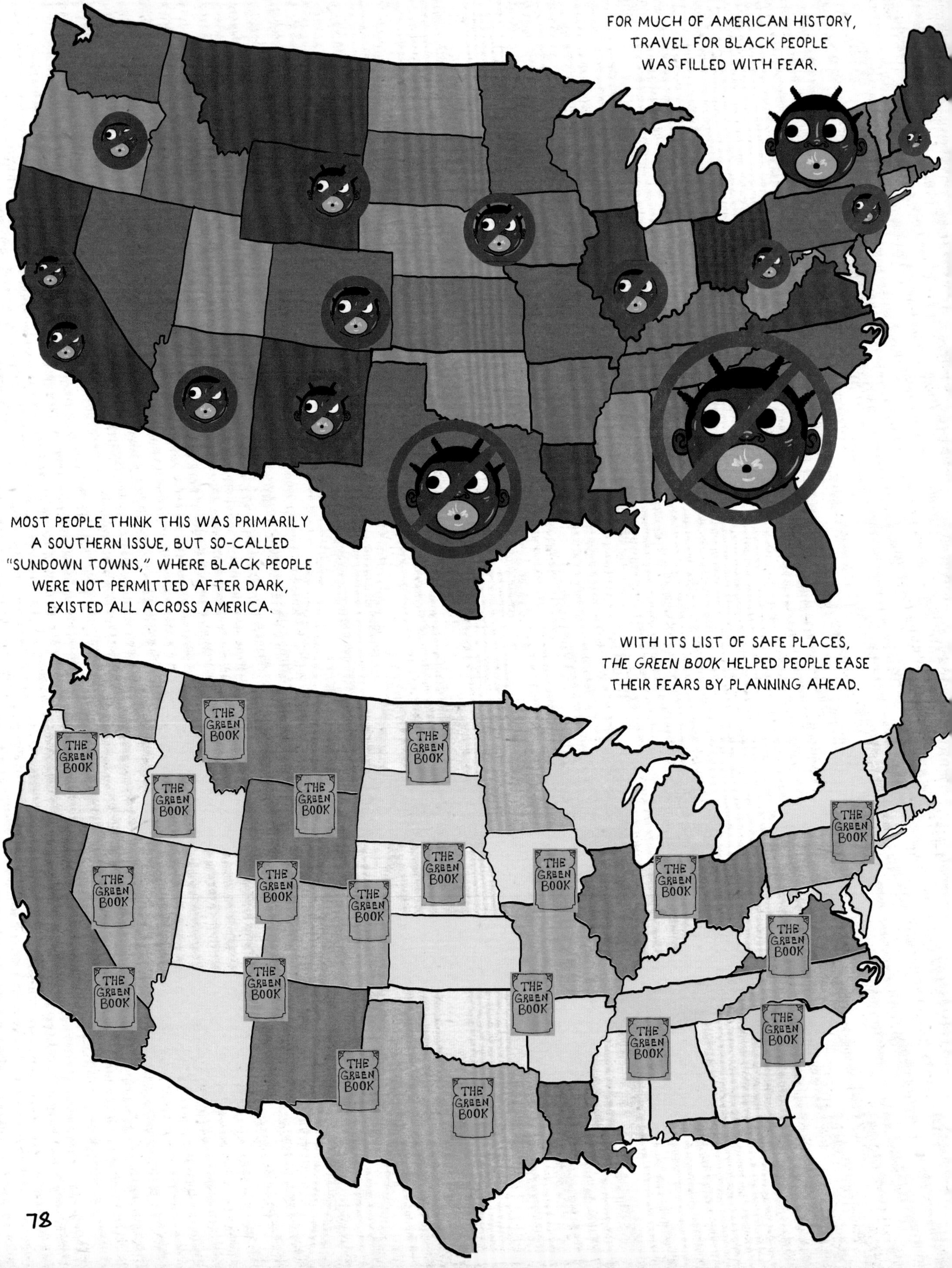
FOR MUCH OF AMERICAN HISTORY, TRAVEL FOR BLACK PEOPLE WAS FILLED WITH FEAR.
MOST PEOPLE THINK THIS WAS PRIMARILY A SOUTHERN ISSUE, BUT SO-CALLED "SUNDOWN TOWNS," WHERE BLACK PEOPLE WERE NOT PERMITTED AFTER DARK, EXISTED ALL ACROSS AMERICA.
WITH ITS LIST OF SAFE PLACES, *THE GREEN BOOK* HELPED PEOPLE EASE THEIR FEARS BY PLANNING AHEAD.
THE GREEN BOOK

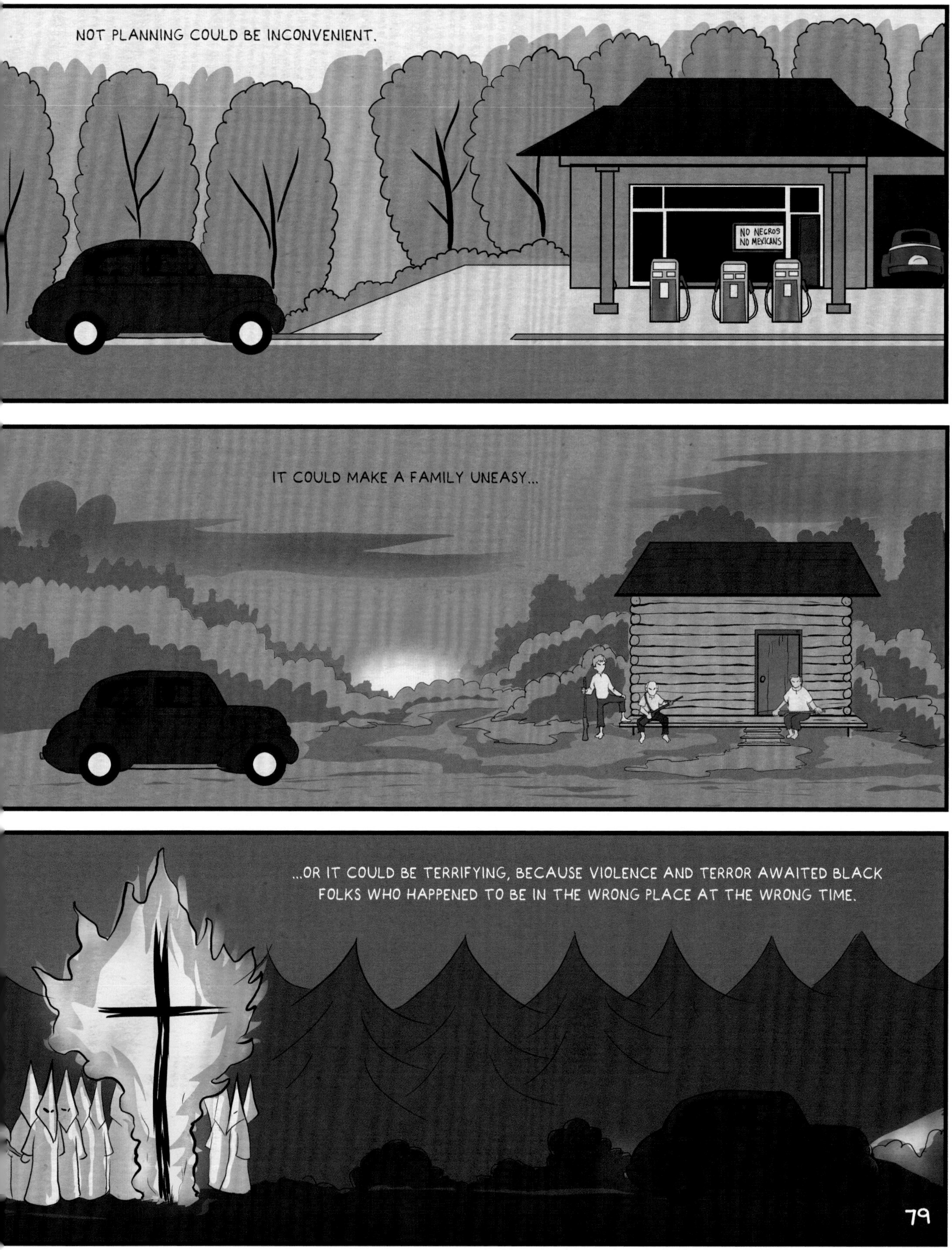
NOT PLANNING COULD BE INCONVENIENT.
NO NEGROS
NO MEXICANS
IT COULD MAKE A FAMILY UNEASY...
...OR IT COULD BE TERRIFYING, BECAUSE VIOLENCE AND TERROR AWAITED BLACK FOLKS WHO HAPPENED TO BE IN THE WRONG PLACE AT THE WRONG TIME.

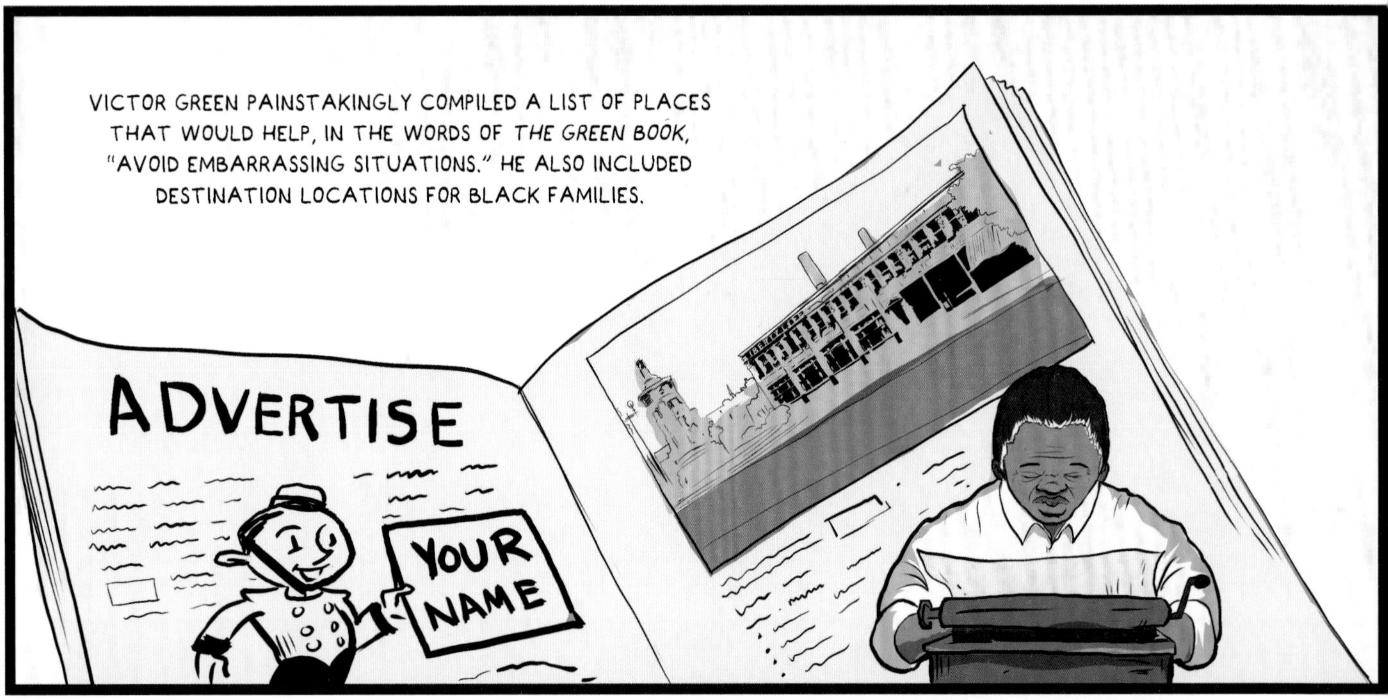
VICTOR GREEN PAINSTAKINGLY COMPILED A LIST OF PLACES THAT WOULD HELP, IN THE WORDS OF *THE GREEN BOOK*, "AVOID EMBARRASSING SITUATIONS." HE ALSO INCLUDED DESTINATION LOCATIONS FOR BLACK FAMILIES.
ADVERTISE
YOUR NAME

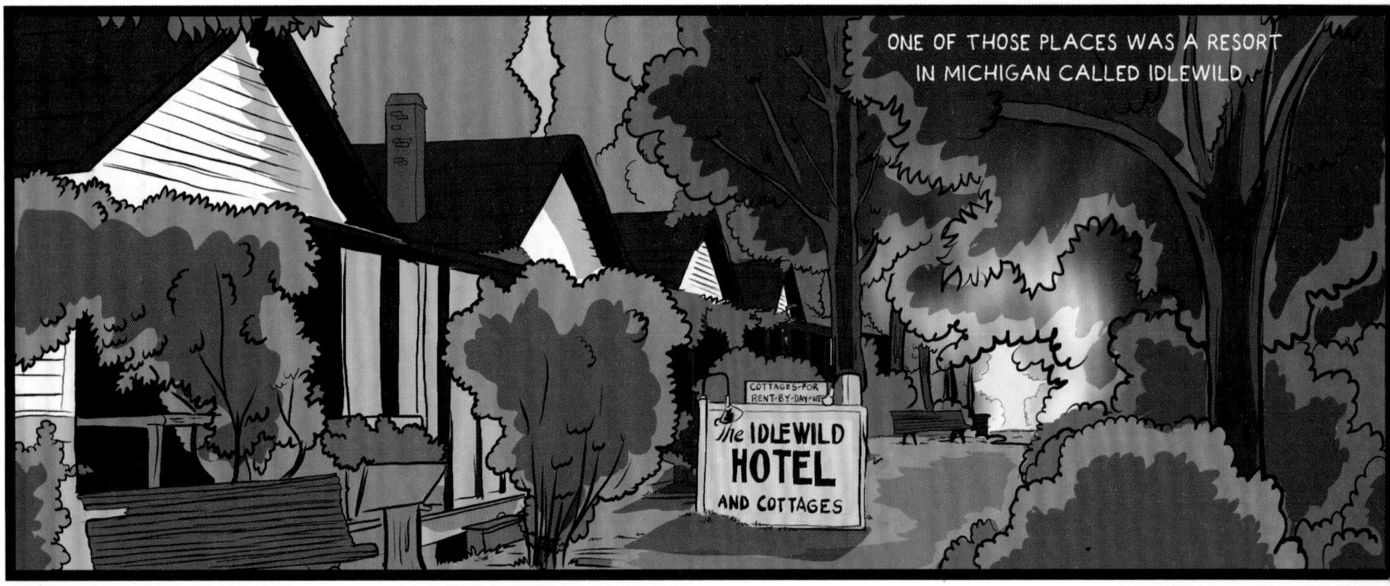
ONE OF THOSE PLACES WAS A RESORT IN MICHIGAN CALLED IDLEWILD.
COTTAGES FOR RENT BY DAY
The IDLEWILD HOTEL AND COTTAGES

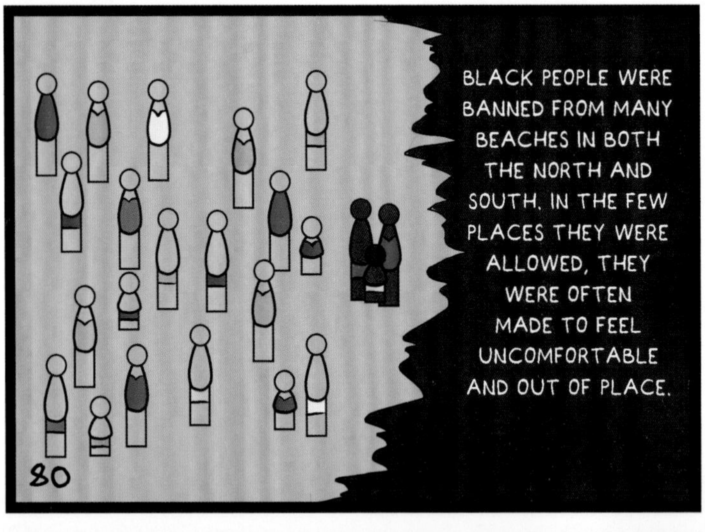
BLACK PEOPLE WERE BANNED FROM MANY BEACHES IN BOTH THE NORTH AND SOUTH. IN THE FEW PLACES THEY WERE ALLOWED, THEY WERE OFTEN MADE TO FEEL UNCOMFORTABLE AND OUT OF PLACE.

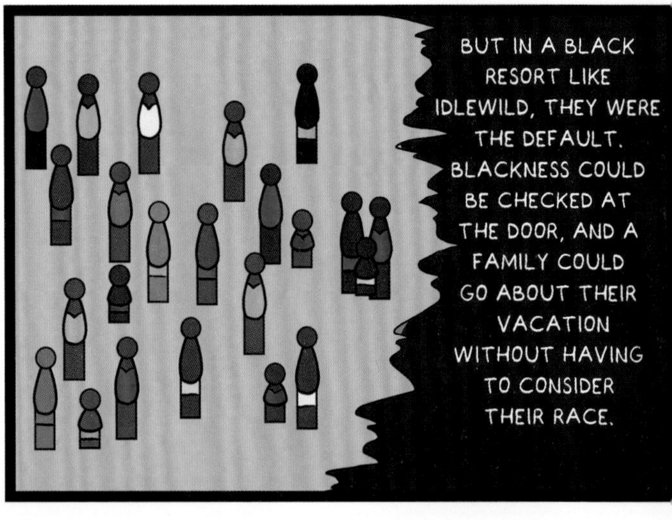
BUT IN A BLACK RESORT LIKE IDLEWILD, THEY WERE THE DEFAULT. BLACKNESS COULD BE CHECKED AT THE DOOR, AND A FAMILY COULD GO ABOUT THEIR VACATION WITHOUT HAVING TO CONSIDER THEIR RACE.

IDLEWILD WAS ONE OF THE FEW PLACES WHERE
BLACK PEOPLE COULD GO TO BE FREE OF THE OUTSIDE WORLD.

IT'S NO WONDER THAT IDLEWILD WAS CALLED "THE BLACK EDEN."

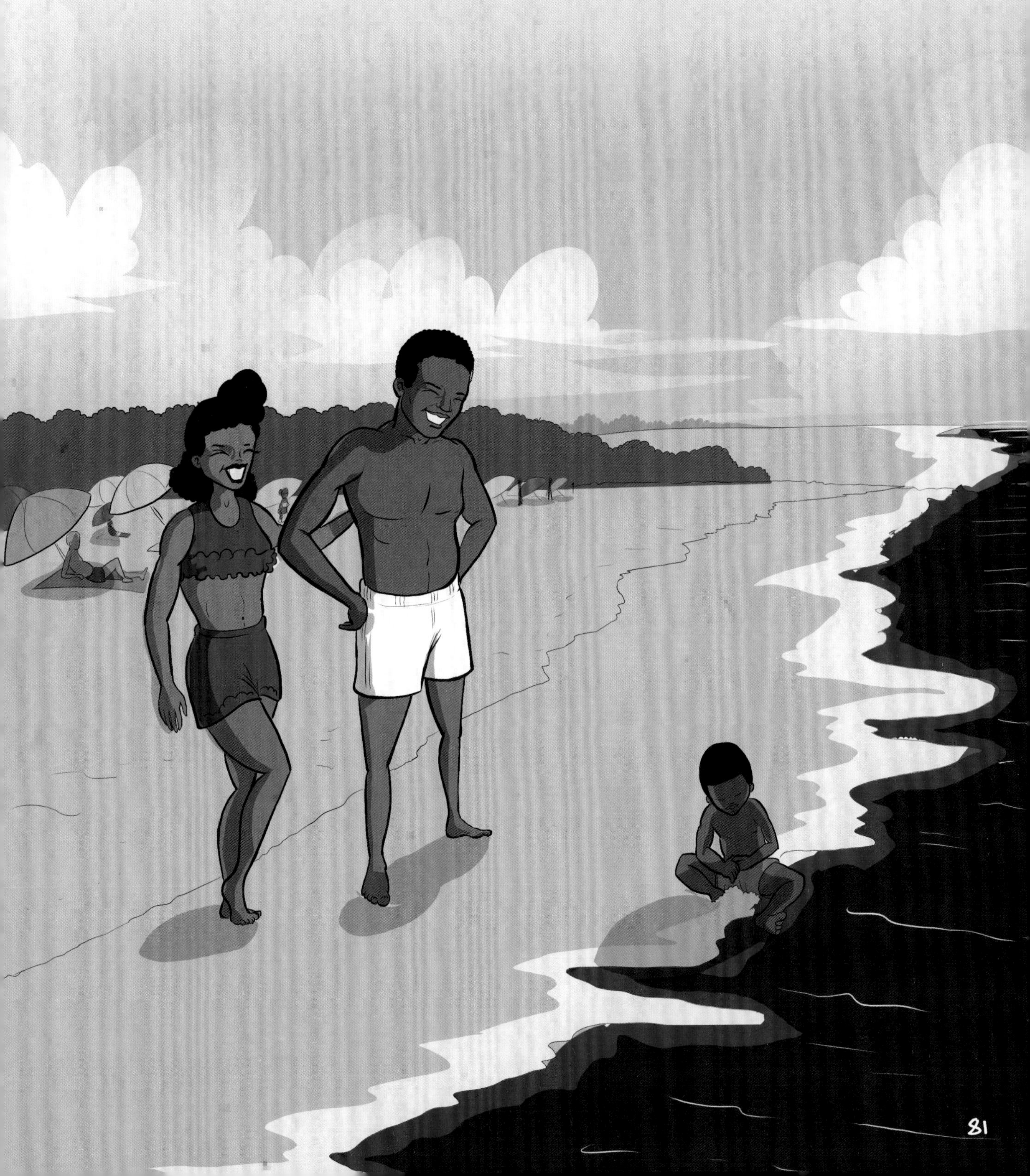

WITH THE CIVIL RIGHTS ACT OF 1964, DISCRIMINATION OF THE KIND THAT REQUIRED PEOPLE OF COLOR TO CARRY A BOOK OF BLACK-FRIENDLY ESTABLISHMENTS WOULD END.

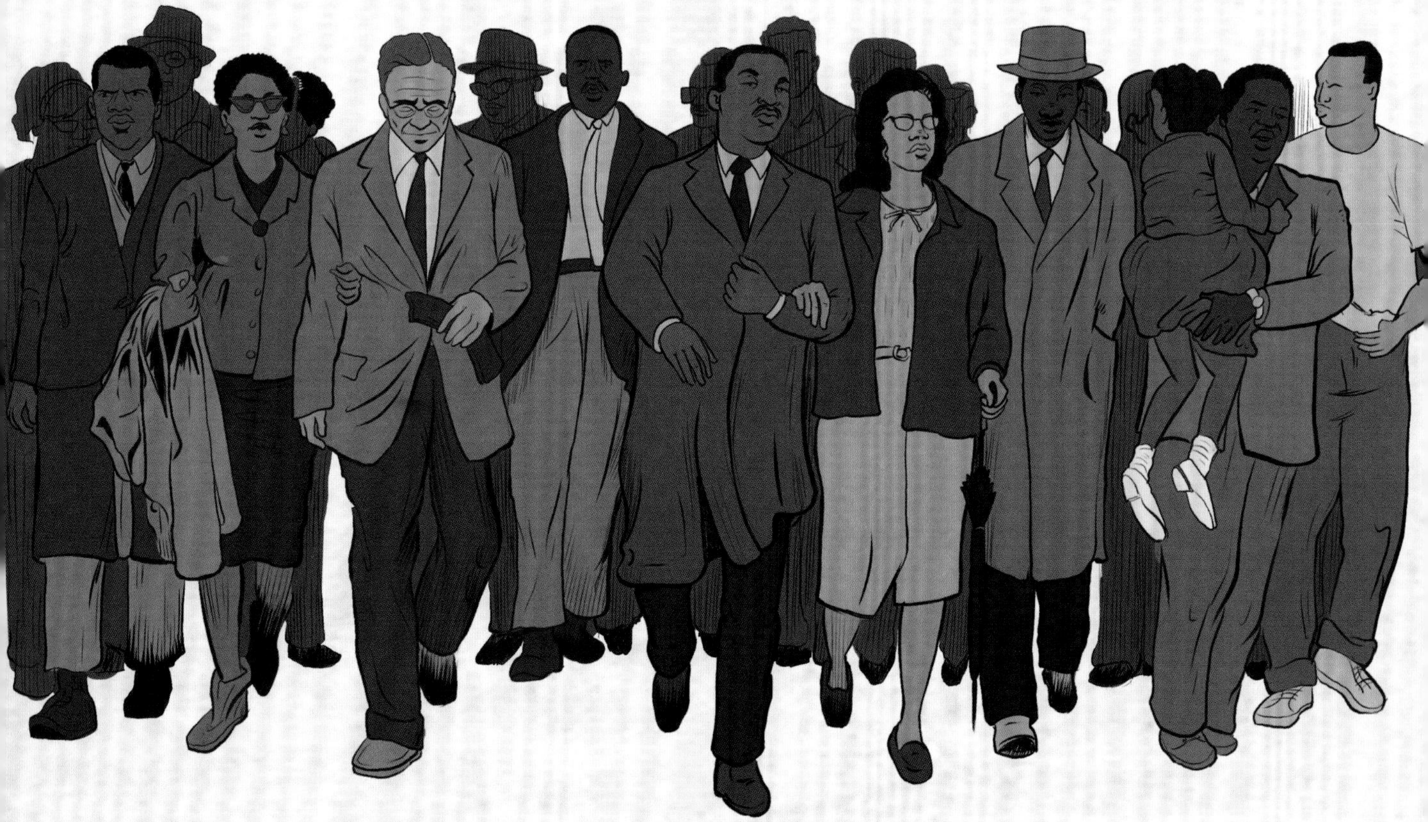

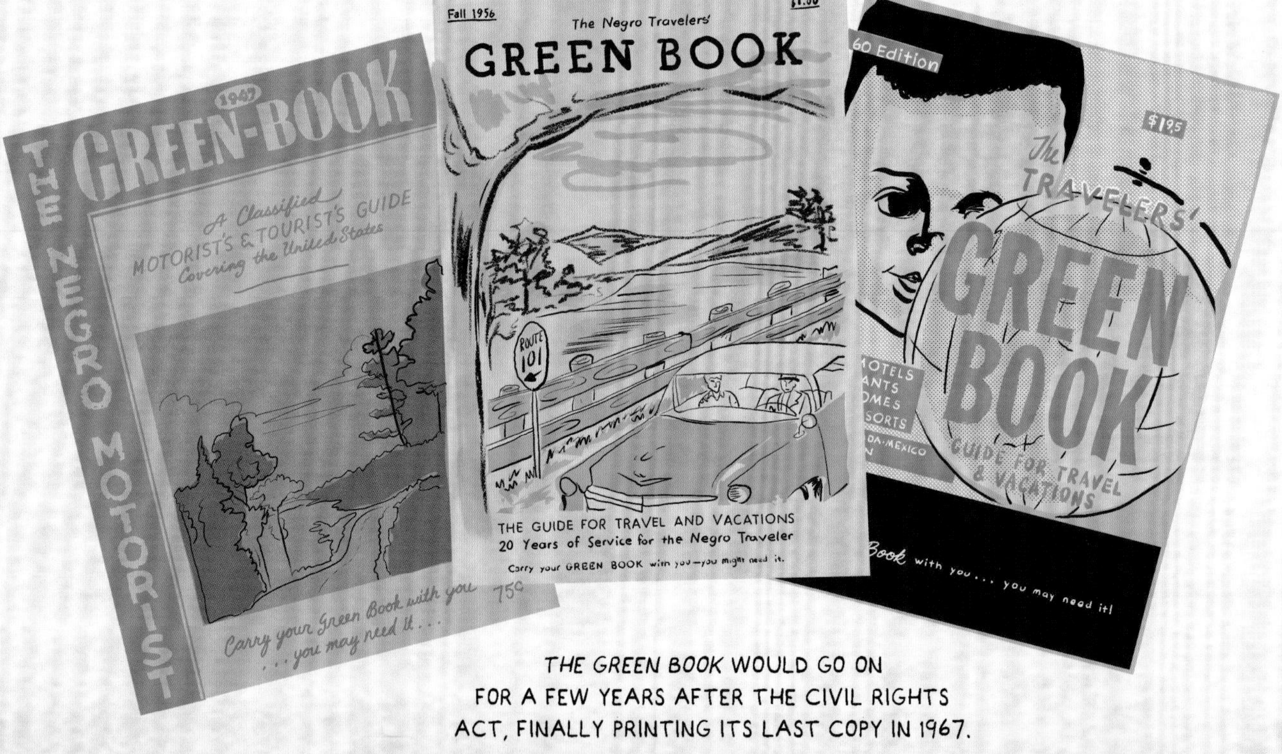
1947
GREEN-BOOK
THE NEGRO MOTORIST
A Classified MOTORIST'S & TOURIST'S GUIDE Covering the United States
Carry your Green Book with you . . . you may need it . . .
75¢
Fall 1956
$1.00
The Negro Travelers'
GREEN BOOK
ROUTE 101
THE GUIDE FOR TRAVEL AND VACATIONS
20 Years of Service for the Negro Traveler
Carry your GREEN BOOK with you—you might need it.
60 Edition
$1.95
The TRAVELERS' GREEN BOOK
GUIDE FOR TRAVEL & VACATIONS
Book with you . . . you may need it!

THE GREEN BOOK WOULD GO ON FOR A FEW YEARS AFTER THE CIVIL RIGHTS ACT, FINALLY PRINTING ITS LAST COPY IN 1967.

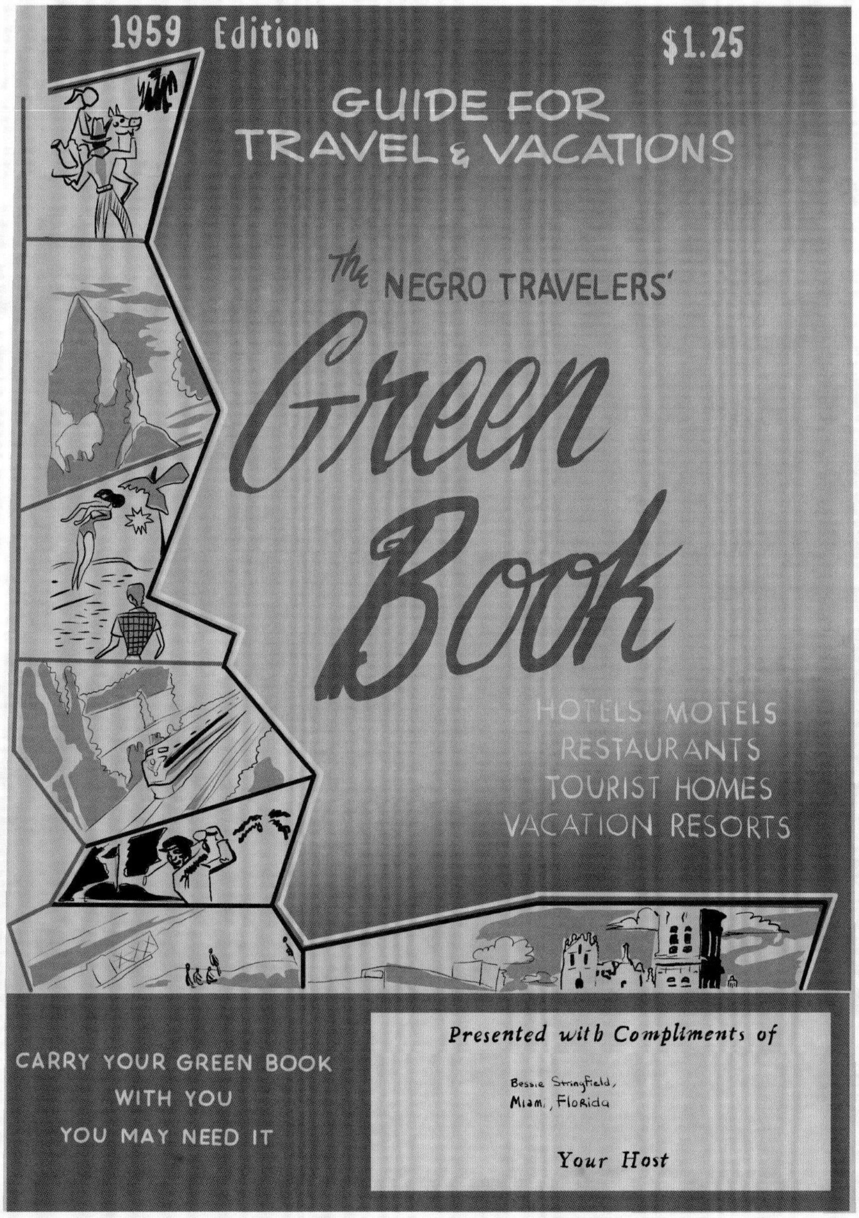

1959 Edition
$1.25
GUIDE FOR TRAVEL & VACATIONS
the NEGRO TRAVELERS'
Green Book
HOTELS MOTELS
RESTAURANTS
TOURIST HOMES
VACATION RESORTS
CARRY YOUR GREEN BOOK
WITH YOU
YOU MAY NEED IT
Presented with Compliments of
Bessie Stringfield,
Miami, Florida
Your Host

VICTOR GREEN DREAMED OF A WORLD THAT WOULD NO LONGER NEED A GUIDE LIKE HIS. IN 1948, HE WROTE,

"THERE WILL BE A DAY SOMETIME IN THE NEAR FUTURE WHEN THIS GUIDE WILL NOT HAVE TO BE PUBLISHED. THAT IS WHEN WE AS A RACE WILL HAVE EQUAL OPPORTUNITIES AND PRIVILEGES IN THE UNITED STATES. IT WILL BE A GREAT DAY FOR US TO SUSPEND THIS PUBLICATION, FOR THEN WE CAN GO WHEREVER WE PLEASE, AND WITHOUT EMBARRASSMENT."

FOR THE MOST PART, THIS IS REALITY. WE HAVE DRIVEN A LONG ROAD WITH GUIDES LIKE *THE GREEN BOOK*, AND WE DON'T NEED A BOOK TO TELL US WHERE WE CAN SHOP, RELAX, OR EAT. BUT WE STILL HAVE SOME DRIVING TO DO BEFORE WE REACH THE WORLD THAT VICTOR GREEN ENVISIONED.

EUGENE BULLARD

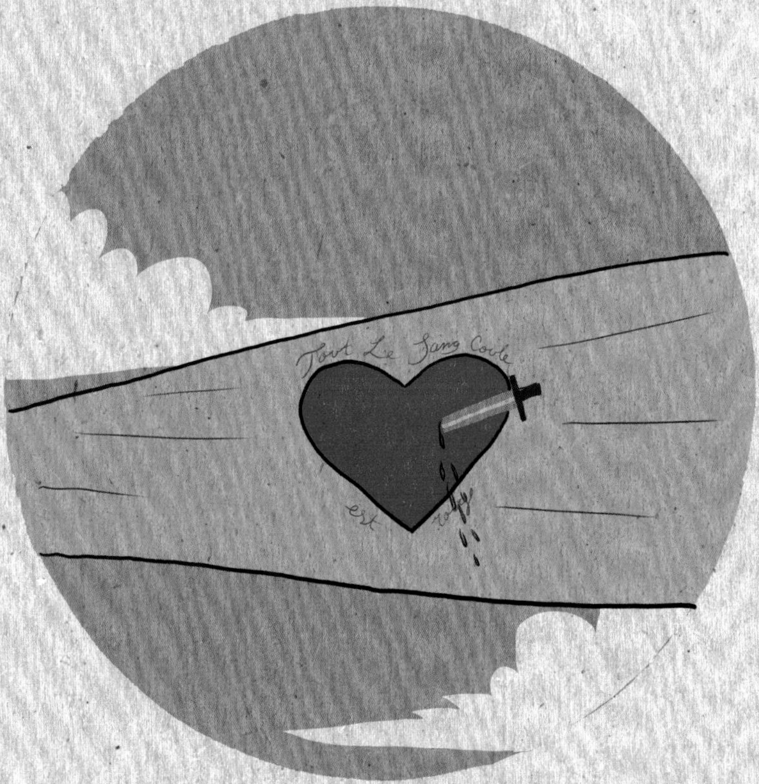
Tout Le Sang Coule
est

ALL BLOOD RUNS RED

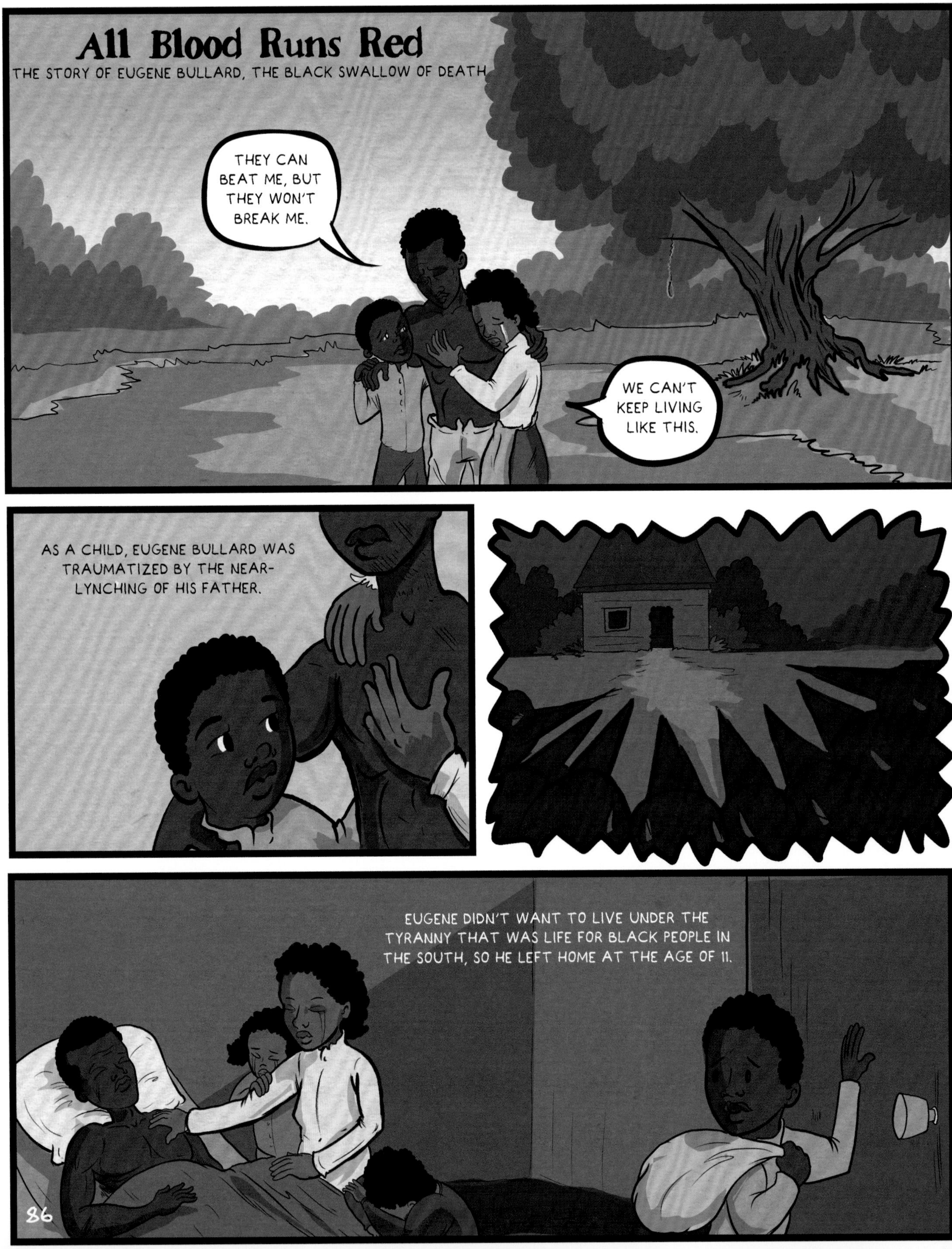
All Blood Runs Red
THE STORY OF EUGENE BULLARD, THE BLACK SWALLOW OF DEATH
THEY CAN BEAT ME, BUT THEY WON'T BREAK ME.
WE CAN'T KEEP LIVING LIKE THIS.
AS A CHILD, EUGENE BULLARD WAS TRAUMATIZED BY THE NEAR-LYNCHING OF HIS FATHER.
EUGENE DIDN'T WANT TO LIVE UNDER THE TYRANNY THAT WAS LIFE FOR BLACK PEOPLE IN THE SOUTH, SO HE LEFT HOME AT THE AGE OF 11.

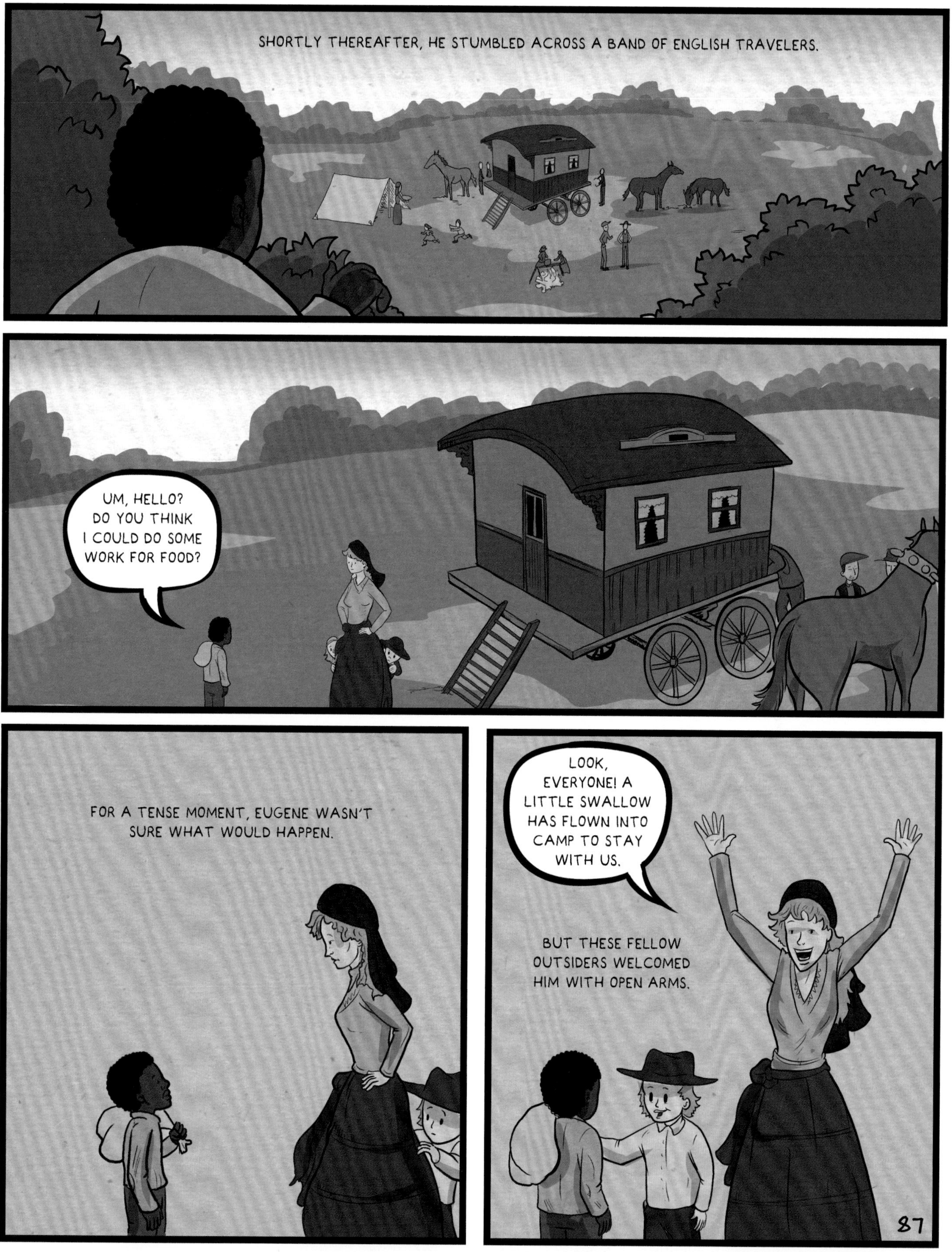

SHORTLY THEREAFTER, HE STUMBLED ACROSS A BAND OF ENGLISH TRAVELERS.
UM, HELLO? DO YOU THINK I COULD DO SOME WORK FOR FOOD?
FOR A TENSE MOMENT, EUGENE WASN'T SURE WHAT WOULD HAPPEN.
LOOK, EVERYONE! A LITTLE SWALLOW HAS FLOWN INTO CAMP TO STAY WITH US.
BUT THESE FELLOW OUTSIDERS WELCOMED HIM WITH OPEN ARMS.

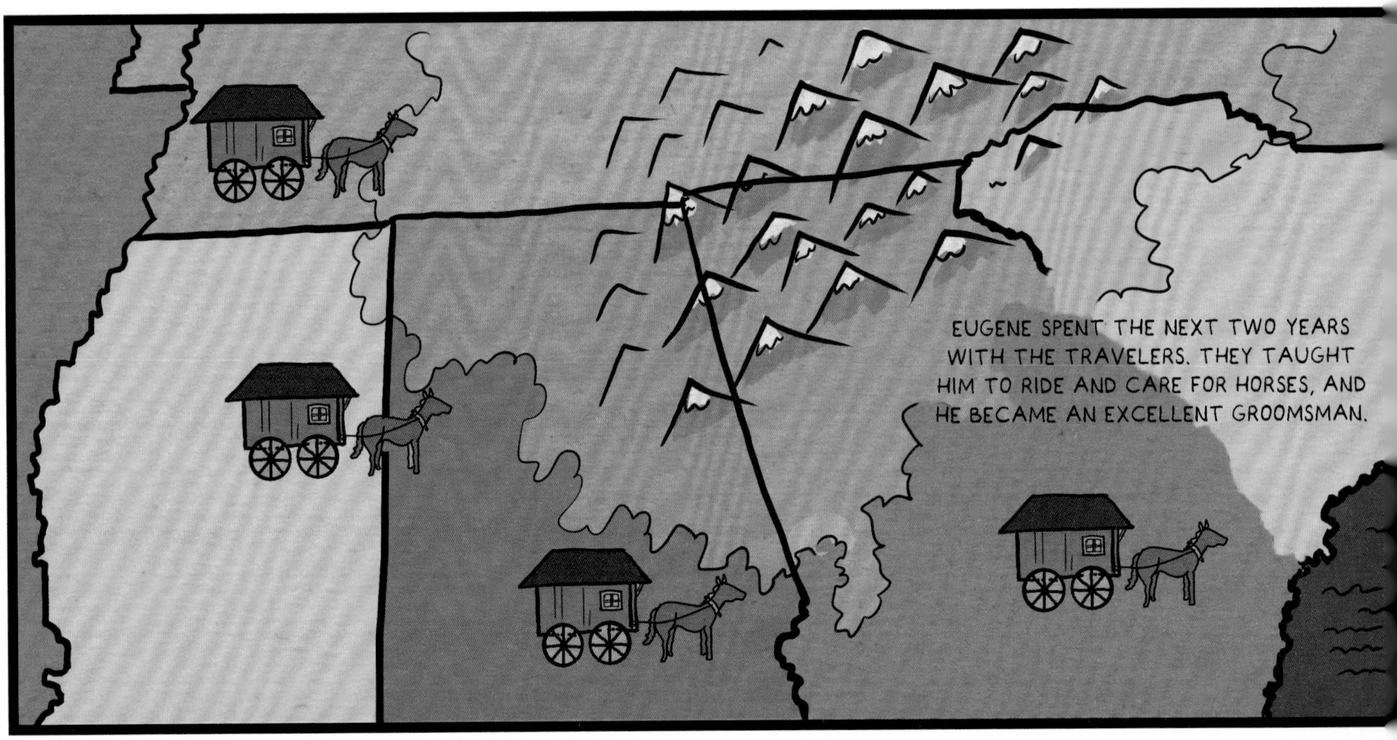
EUGENE SPENT THE NEXT TWO YEARS WITH THE TRAVELERS. THEY TAUGHT HIM TO RIDE AND CARE FOR HORSES, AND HE BECAME AN EXCELLENT GROOMSMAN.

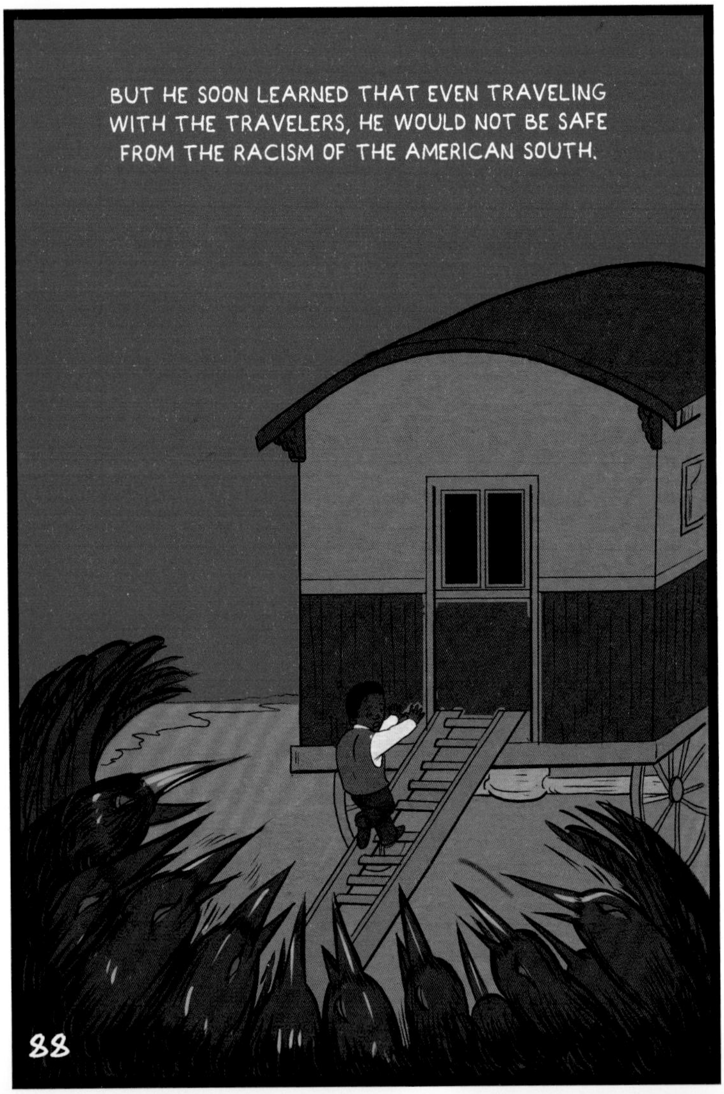
BUT HE SOON LEARNED THAT EVEN TRAVELING WITH THE TRAVELERS, HE WOULD NOT BE SAFE FROM THE RACISM OF THE AMERICAN SOUTH.

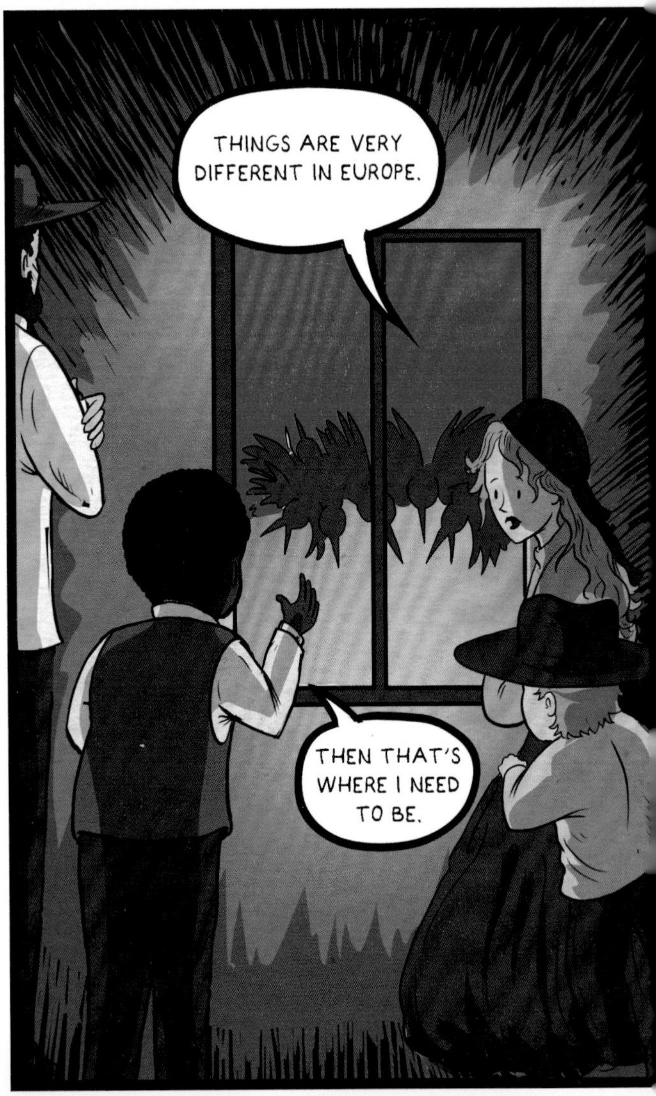
THINGS ARE VERY DIFFERENT IN EUROPE.
THEN THAT'S WHERE I NEED TO BE.

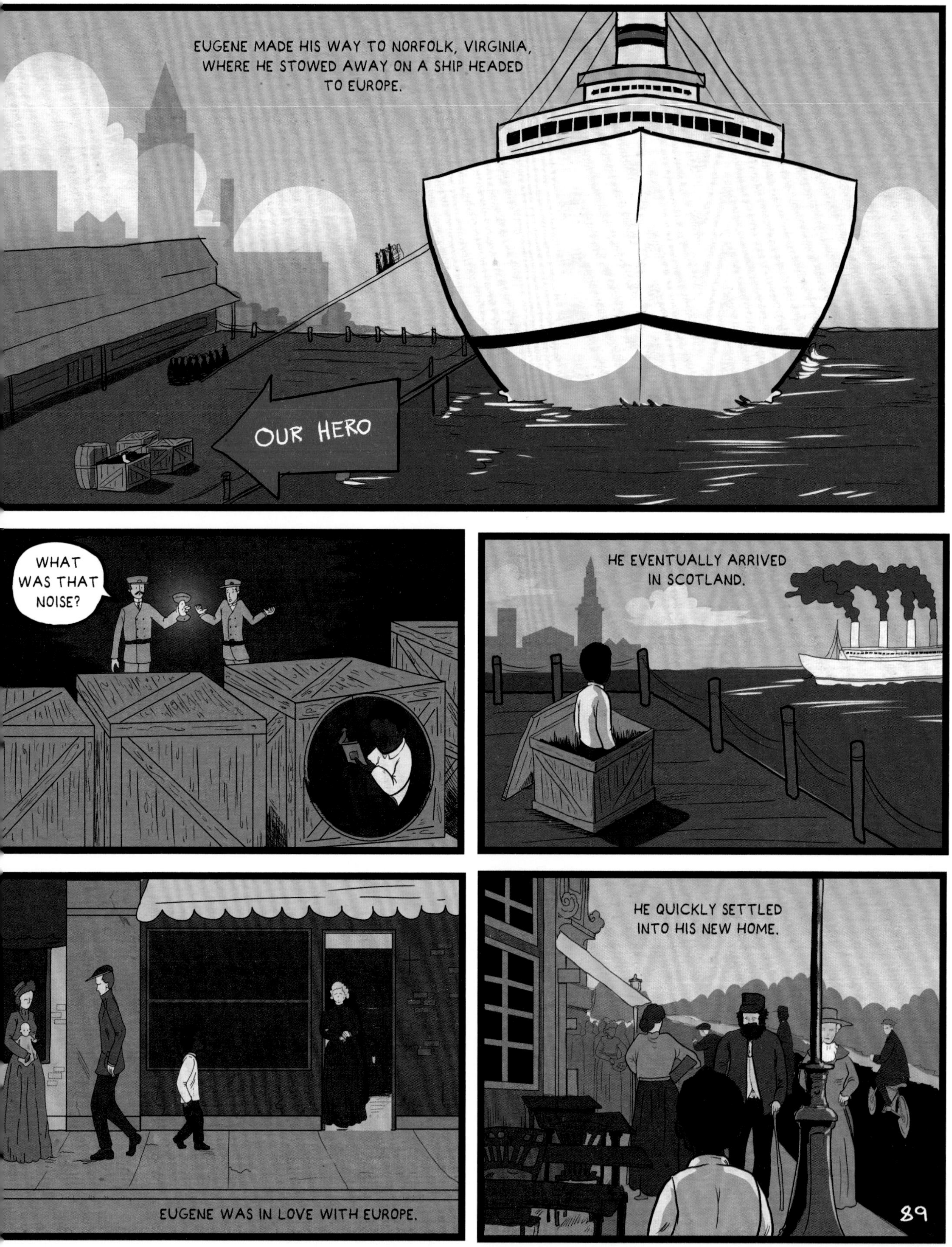
EUGENE MADE HIS WAY TO NORFOLK, VIRGINIA, WHERE HE STOWED AWAY ON A SHIP HEADED TO EUROPE.
OUR HERO
WHAT WAS THAT NOISE?
HE EVENTUALLY ARRIVED IN SCOTLAND.
EUGENE WAS IN LOVE WITH EUROPE.
HE QUICKLY SETTLED INTO HIS NEW HOME.

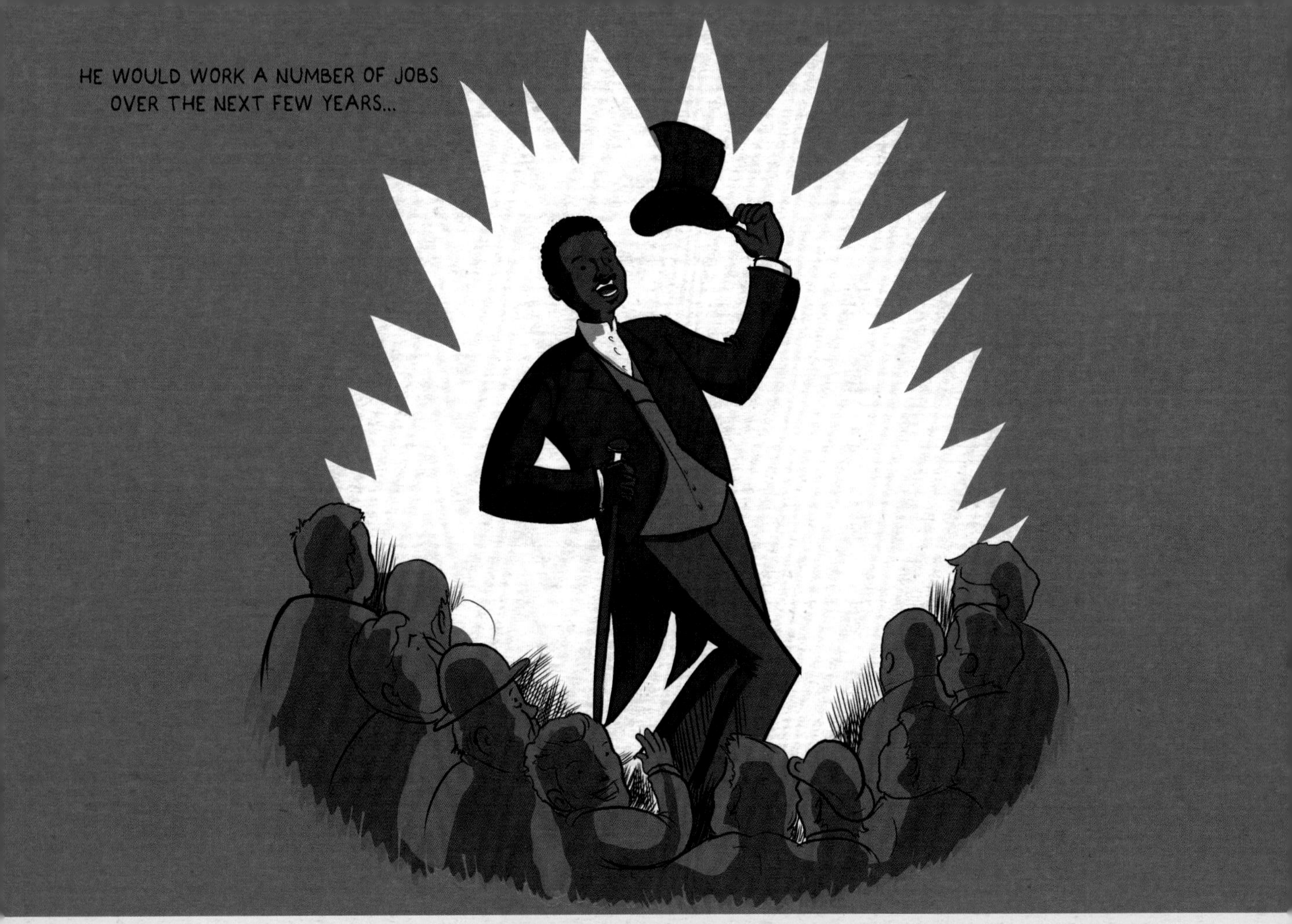
HE WOULD WORK A NUMBER OF JOBS
OVER THE NEXT FEW YEARS...

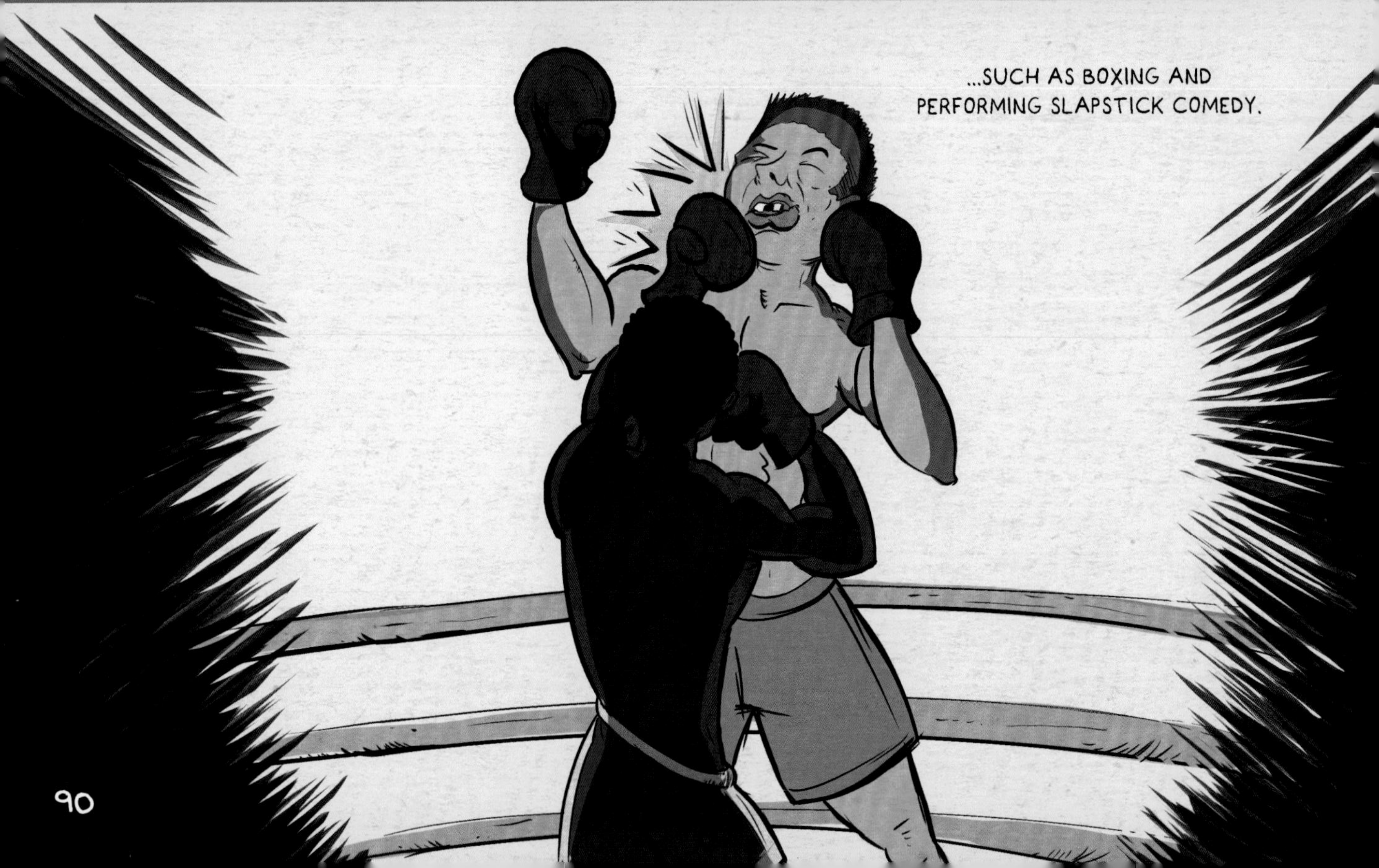
...SUCH AS BOXING AND
PERFORMING SLAPSTICK COMEDY.

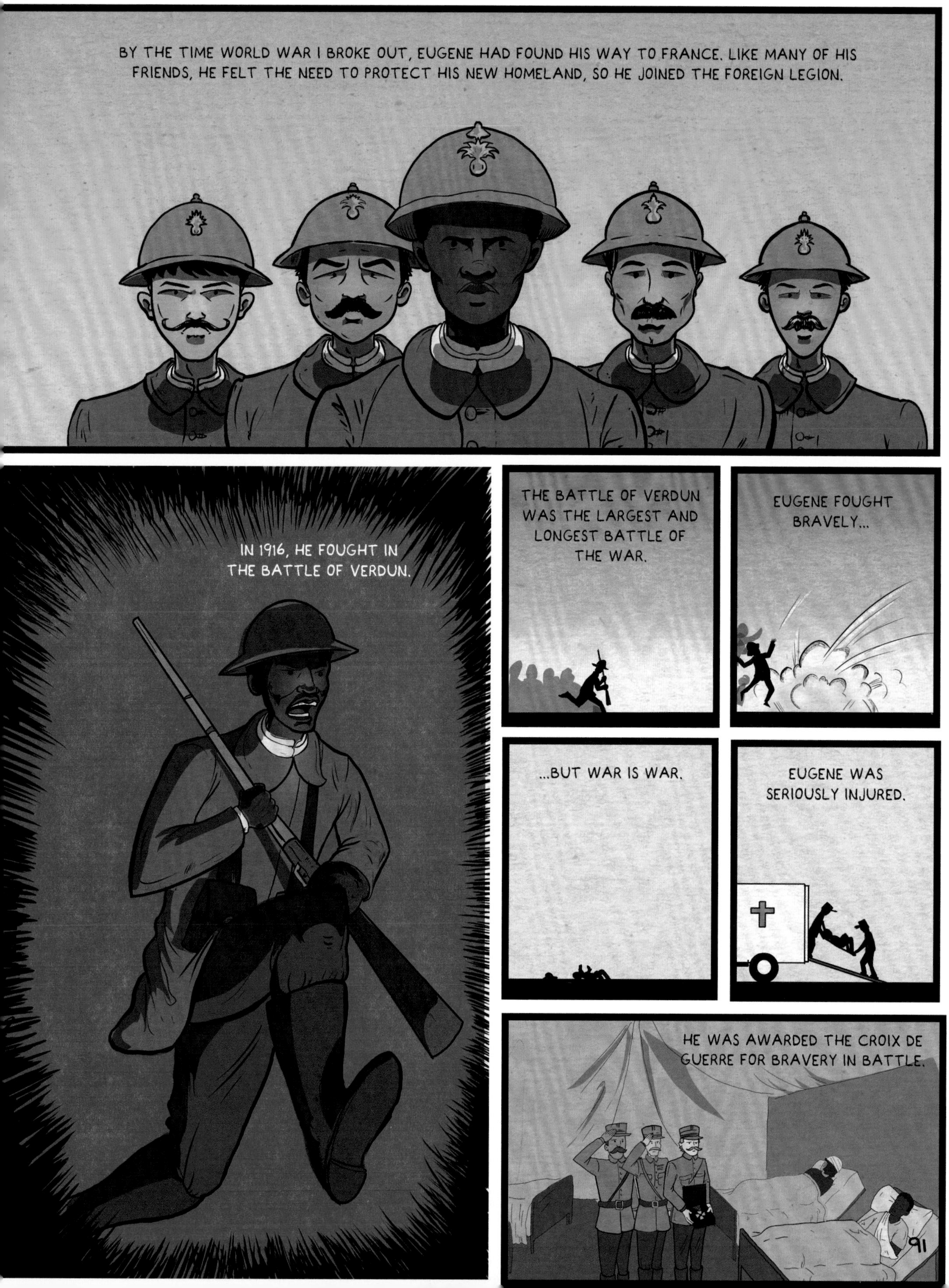
BY THE TIME WORLD WAR I BROKE OUT, EUGENE HAD FOUND HIS WAY TO FRANCE. LIKE MANY OF HIS FRIENDS, HE FELT THE NEED TO PROTECT HIS NEW HOMELAND, SO HE JOINED THE FOREIGN LEGION.
IN 1916, HE FOUGHT IN THE BATTLE OF VERDUN.
THE BATTLE OF VERDUN WAS THE LARGEST AND LONGEST BATTLE OF THE WAR.
EUGENE FOUGHT BRAVELY...
...BUT WAR IS WAR.
EUGENE WAS SERIOUSLY INJURED.
HE WAS AWARDED THE CROIX DE GUERRE FOR BRAVERY IN BATTLE.

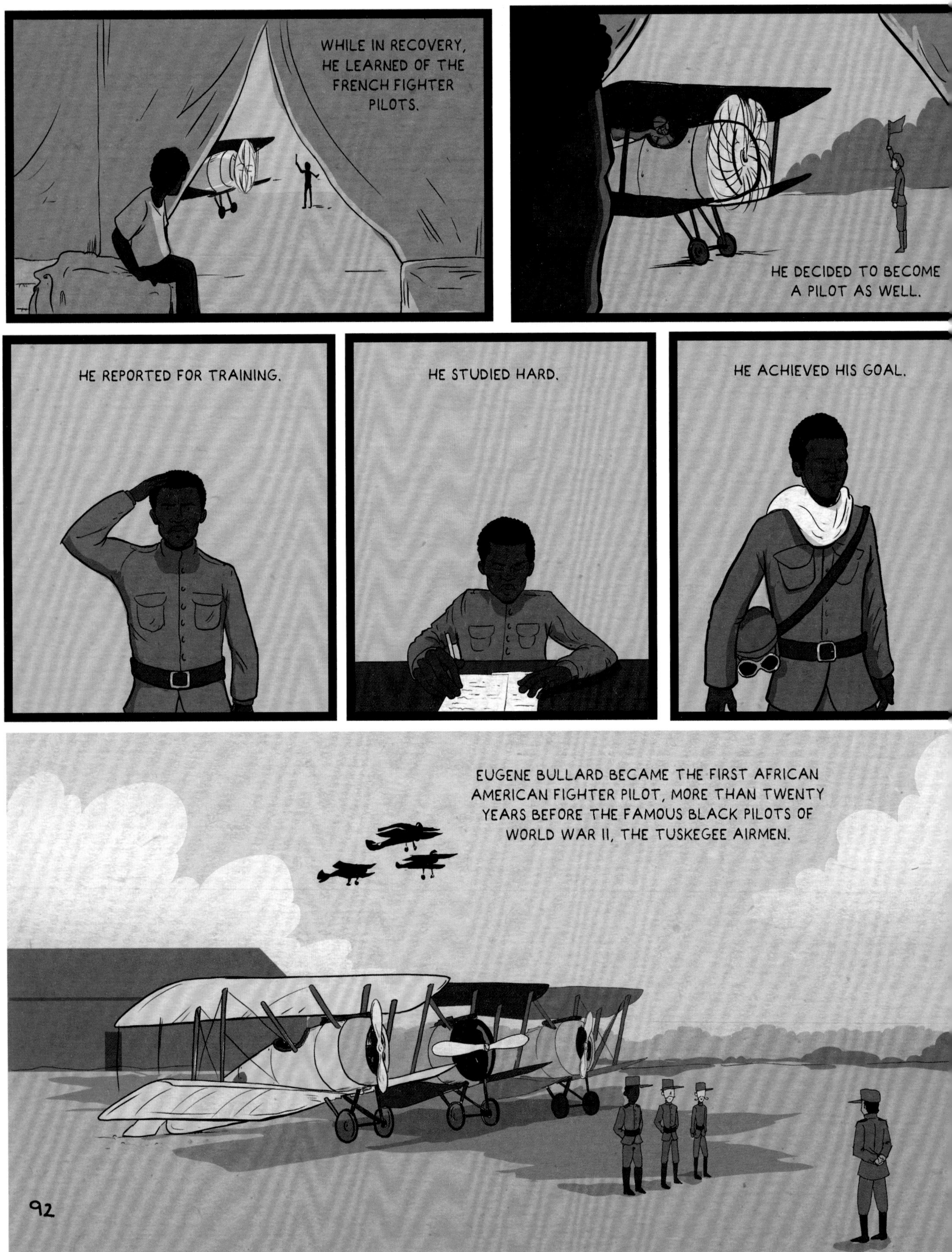

WHILE IN RECOVERY, HE LEARNED OF THE FRENCH FIGHTER PILOTS.
HE DECIDED TO BECOME A PILOT AS WELL.
HE REPORTED FOR TRAINING.
HE STUDIED HARD.
HE ACHIEVED HIS GOAL.
EUGENE BULLARD BECAME THE FIRST AFRICAN AMERICAN FIGHTER PILOT, MORE THAN TWENTY YEARS BEFORE THE FAMOUS BLACK PILOTS OF WORLD WAR II, THE TUSKEGEE AIRMEN.

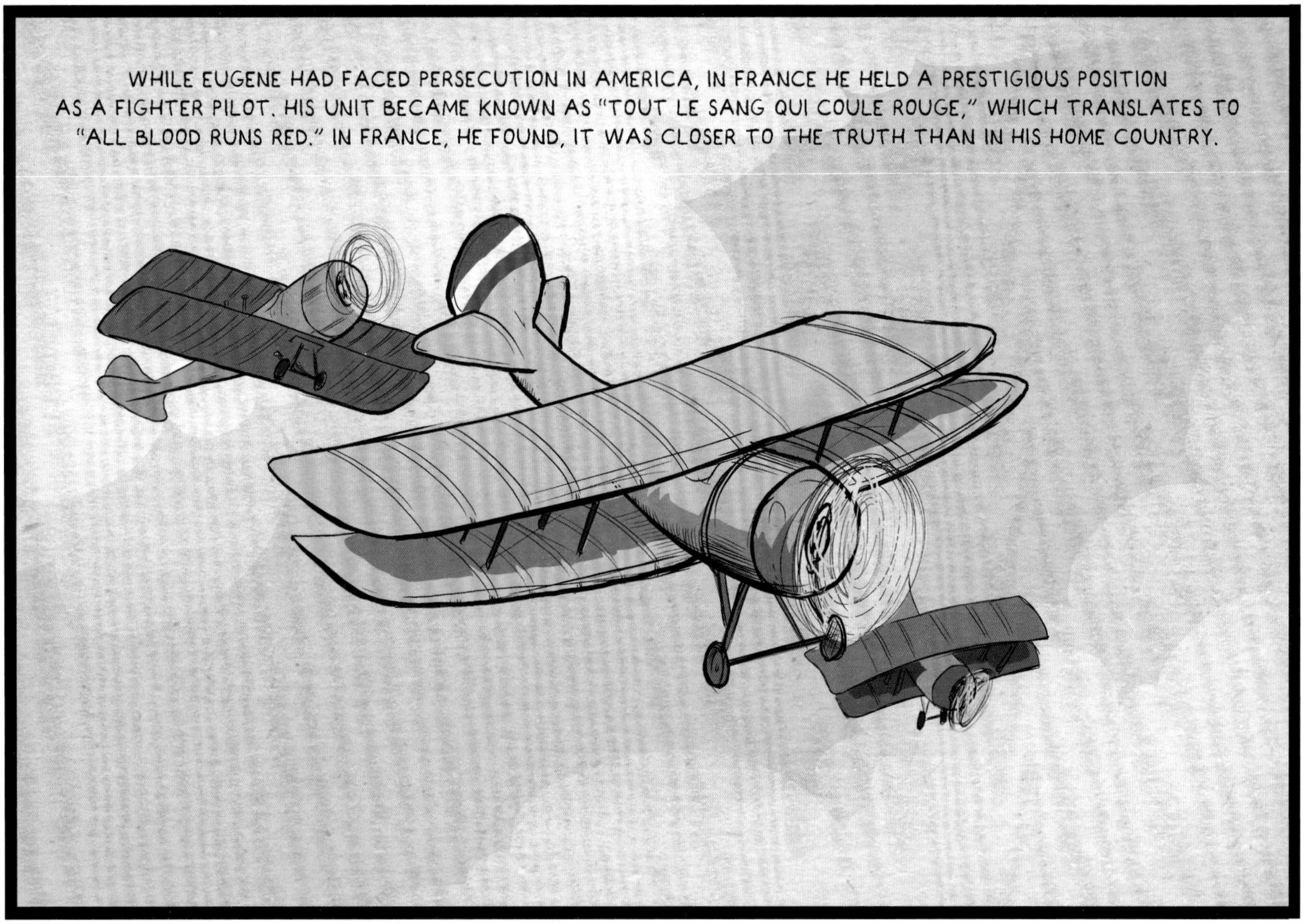
WHILE EUGENE HAD FACED PERSECUTION IN AMERICA, IN FRANCE HE HELD A PRESTIGIOUS POSITION AS A FIGHTER PILOT. HIS UNIT BECAME KNOWN AS "TOUT LE SANG QUI COULE ROUGE," WHICH TRANSLATES TO "ALL BLOOD RUNS RED." IN FRANCE, HE FOUND, IT WAS CLOSER TO THE TRUTH THAN IN HIS HOME COUNTRY.

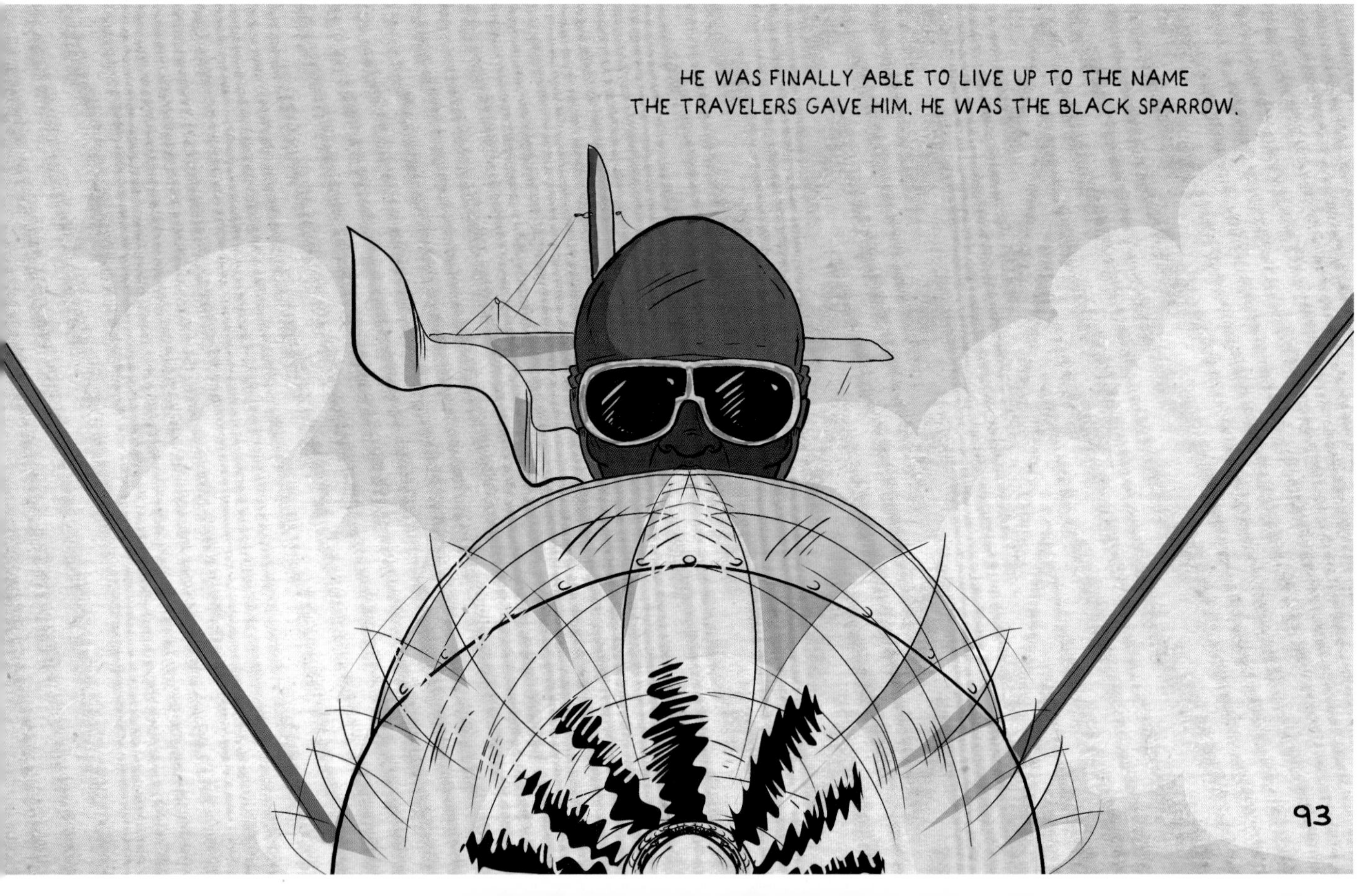
HE WAS FINALLY ABLE TO LIVE UP TO THE NAME THE TRAVELERS GAVE HIM. HE WAS THE BLACK SPARROW.

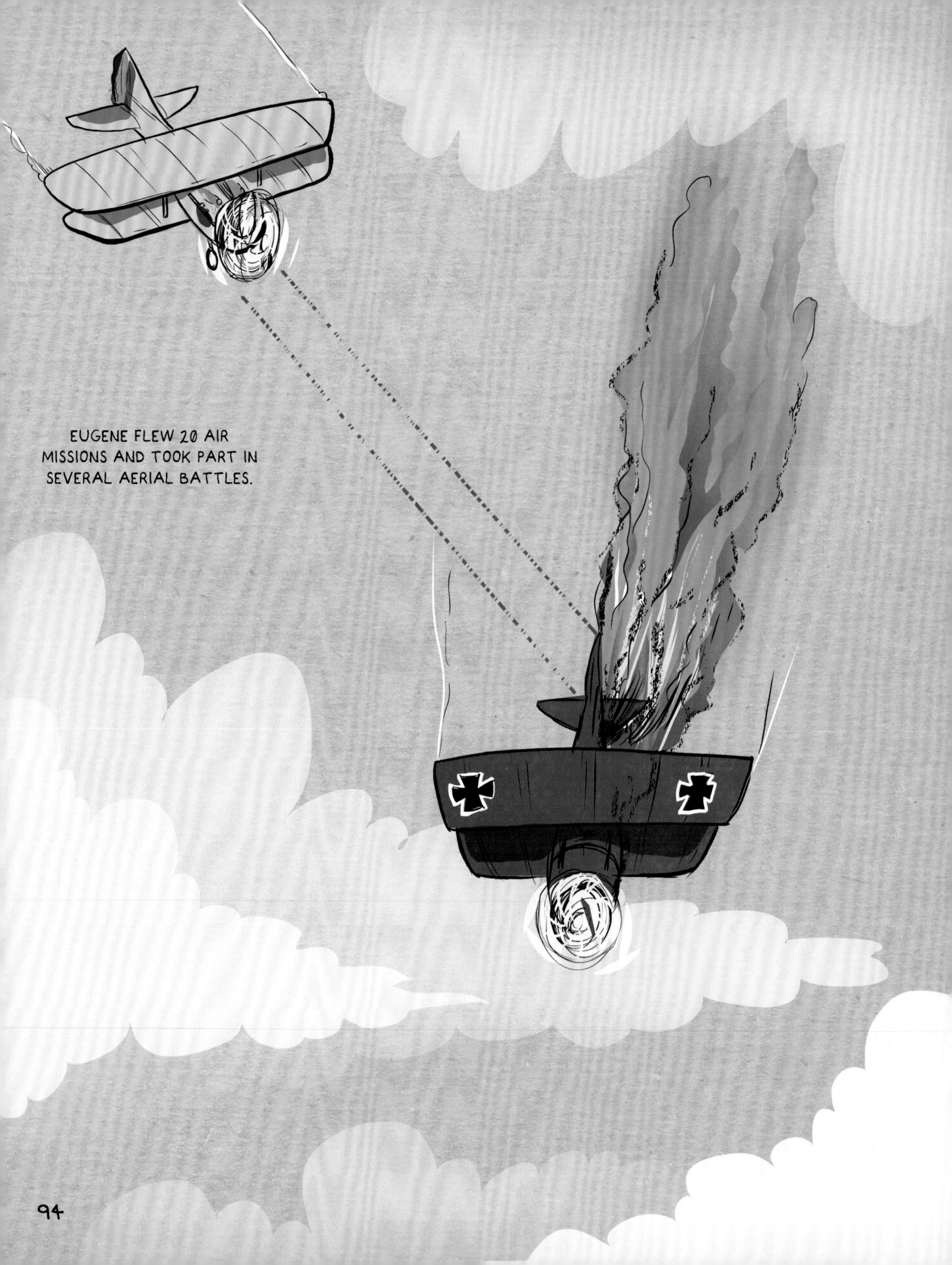
EUGENE FLEW 20 AIR MISSIONS AND TOOK PART IN SEVERAL AERIAL BATTLES.

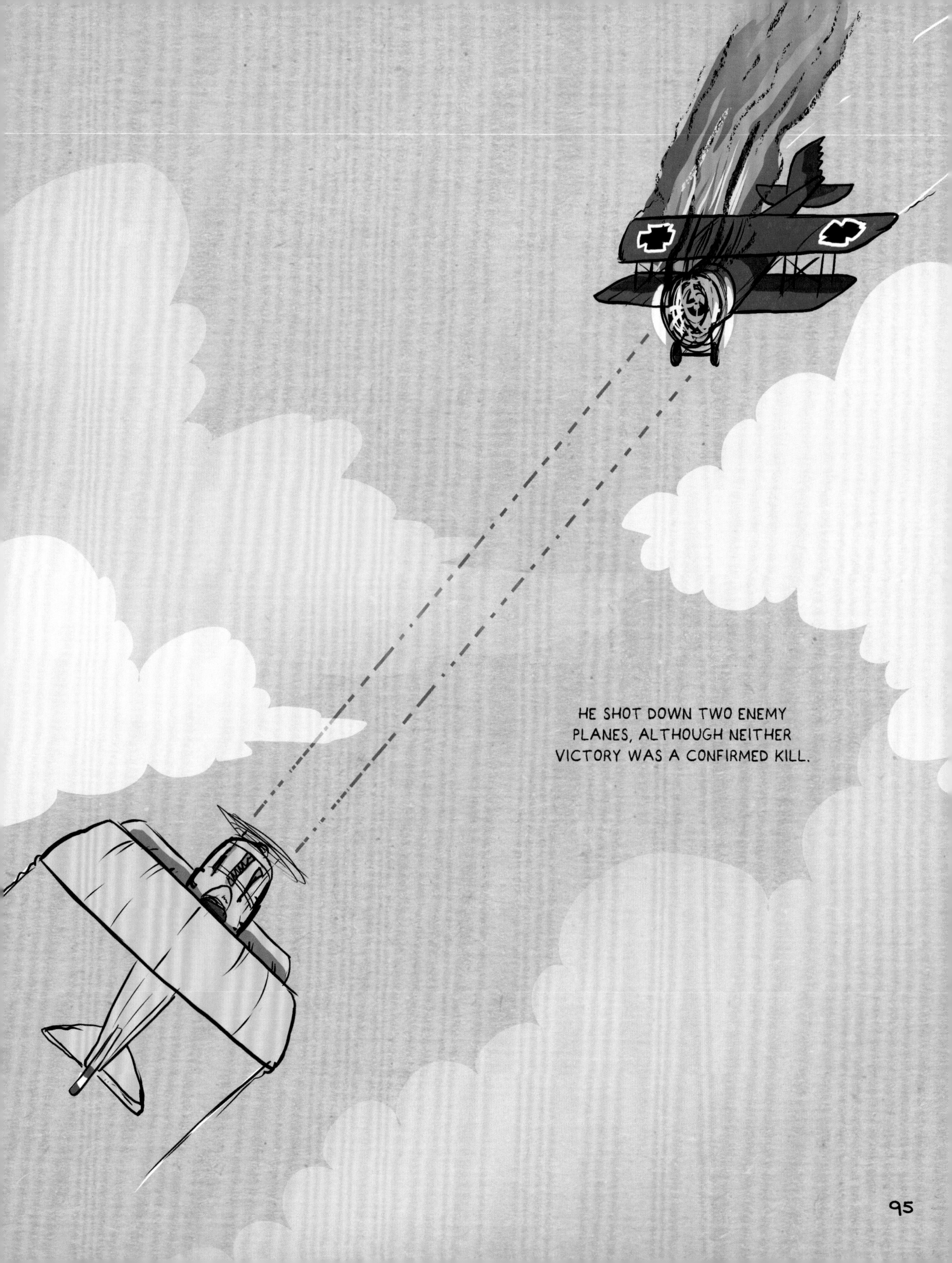
HE SHOT DOWN TWO ENEMY PLANES, ALTHOUGH NEITHER VICTORY WAS A CONFIRMED KILL.

EUGENE BULLARD HAD FOUND A HOME AND PURPOSE IN FRANCE, BUT HE LONGED TO SERVE HIS HOME COUNTRY.

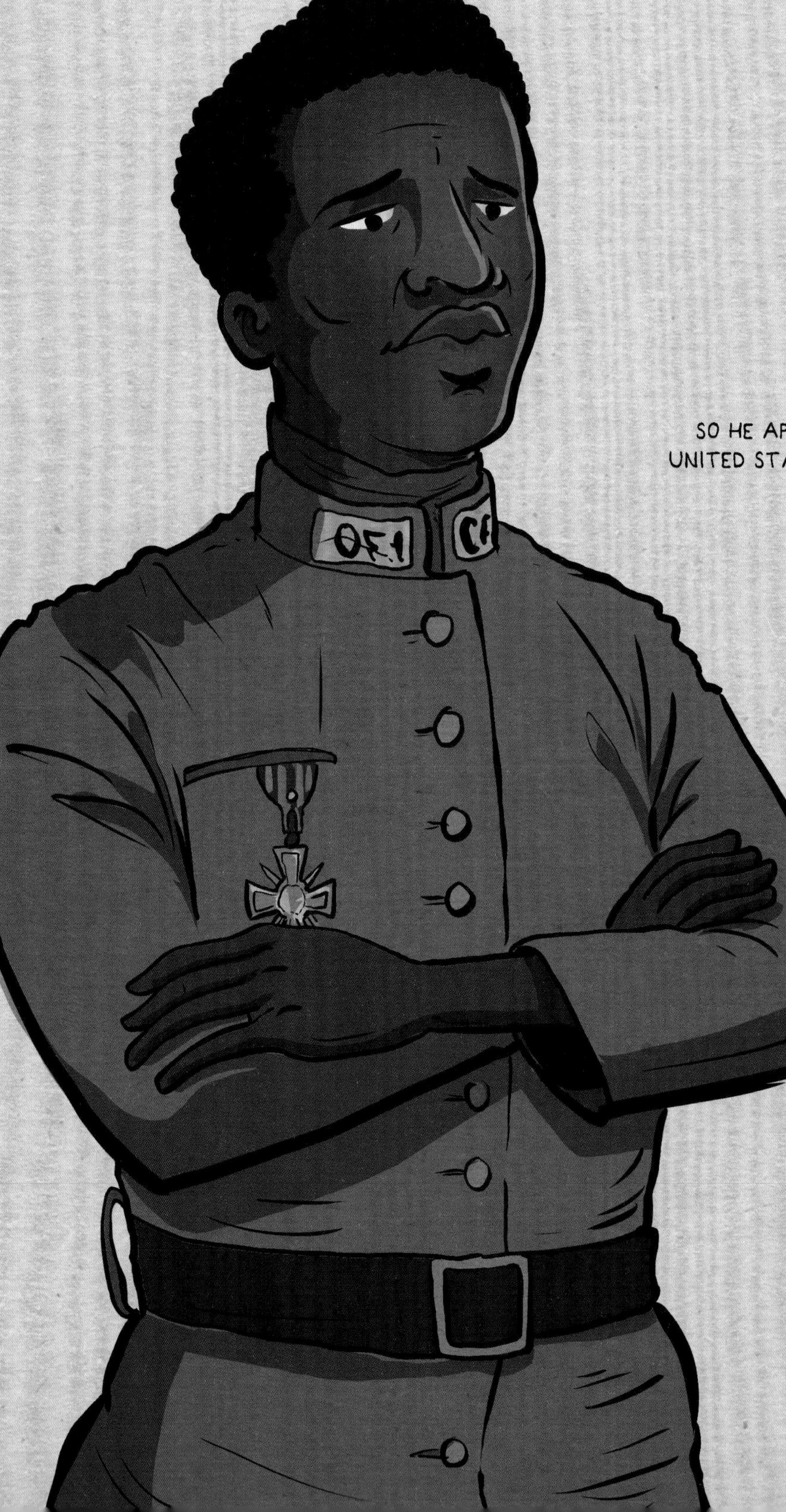
OF.1
CA

SO HE APPLIED TO THE UNITED STATES AIR FORCE.

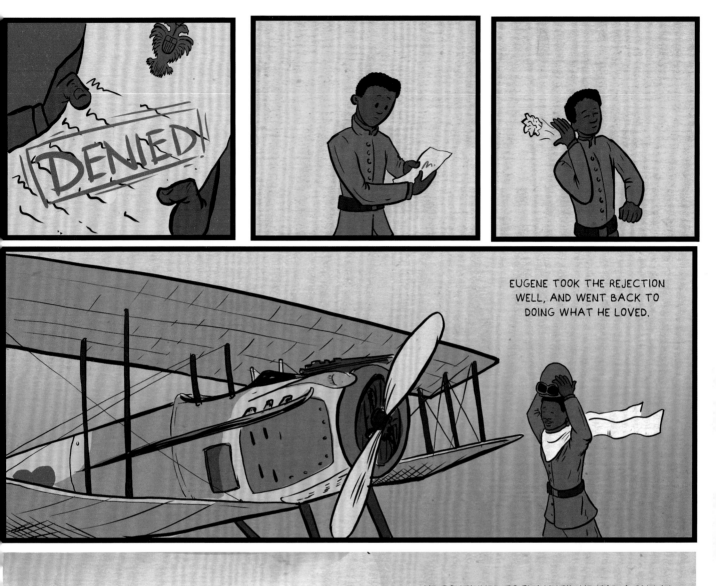

EUGENE TOOK THE REJECTION WELL, AND WENT BACK TO DOING WHAT HE LOVED.

HE CONTINUED TO FLY UNTIL HE HAD A RUN-IN WITH A RACIST COMMANDING OFFICER. AFTER THE INCIDENT, HE WAS DISMISSED.

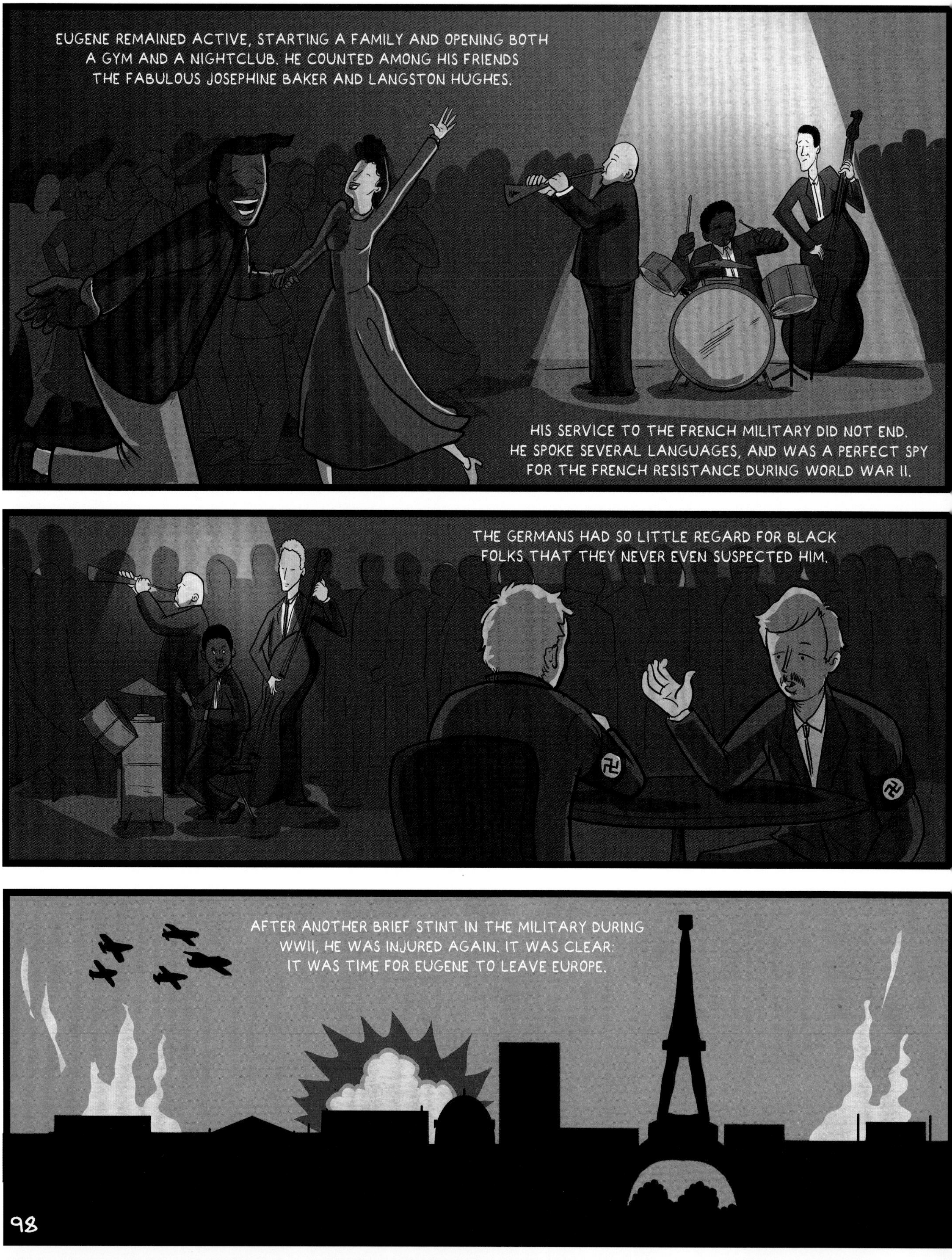
EUGENE REMAINED ACTIVE, STARTING A FAMILY AND OPENING BOTH A GYM AND A NIGHTCLUB. HE COUNTED AMONG HIS FRIENDS THE FABULOUS JOSEPHINE BAKER AND LANGSTON HUGHES.
HIS SERVICE TO THE FRENCH MILITARY DID NOT END. HE SPOKE SEVERAL LANGUAGES, AND WAS A PERFECT SPY FOR THE FRENCH RESISTANCE DURING WORLD WAR II.
THE GERMANS HAD SO LITTLE REGARD FOR BLACK FOLKS THAT THEY NEVER EVEN SUSPECTED HIM.
AFTER ANOTHER BRIEF STINT IN THE MILITARY DURING WWII, HE WAS INJURED AGAIN. IT WAS CLEAR: IT WAS TIME FOR EUGENE TO LEAVE EUROPE.

HE PACKED UP HIS FAMILY AND FLED.

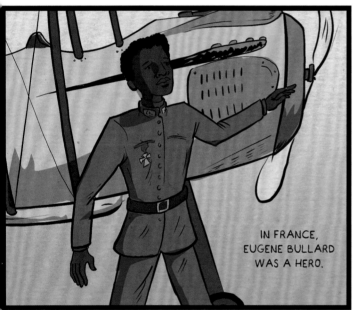

IN FRANCE, EUGENE BULLARD WAS A HERO.

IN AMERICA, HE WAS STILL BLACK.

IN EUROPE, HE WAS WIDELY LOVED AND RESPECTED. HEMINGWAY EVEN MODELED A CHARACTER AFTER HIM.

IN AMERICA, THIS WAR HERO BECAME AN ELEVATOR OPERATOR.

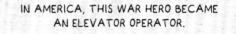

99

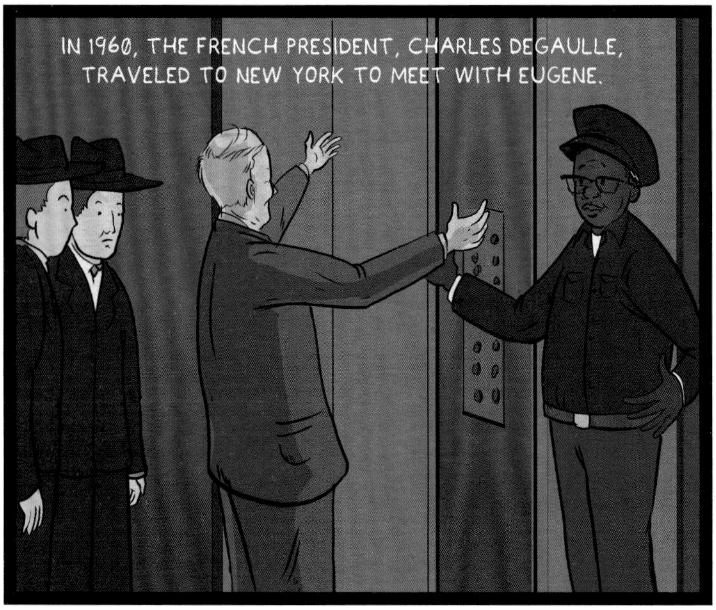
IN 1960, THE FRENCH PRESIDENT, CHARLES DEGAULLE, TRAVELED TO NEW YORK TO MEET WITH EUGENE.

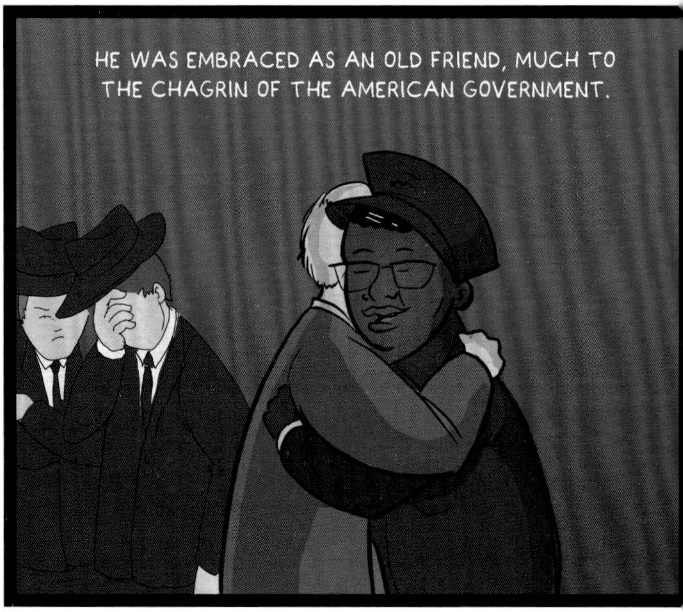
HE WAS EMBRACED AS AN OLD FRIEND, MUCH TO THE CHAGRIN OF THE AMERICAN GOVERNMENT.

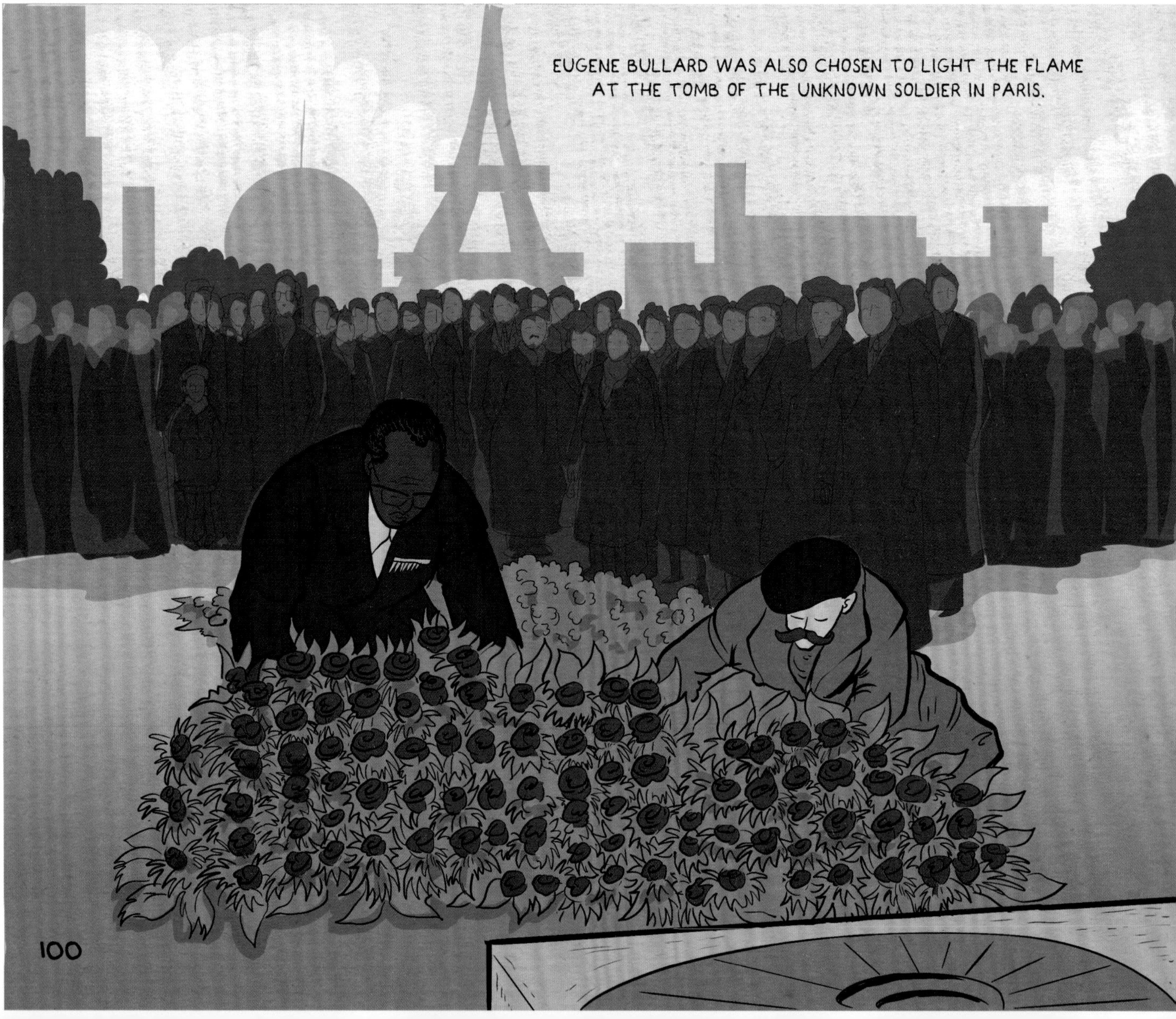
EUGENE BULLARD WAS ALSO CHOSEN TO LIGHT THE FLAME AT THE TOMB OF THE UNKNOWN SOLDIER IN PARIS.

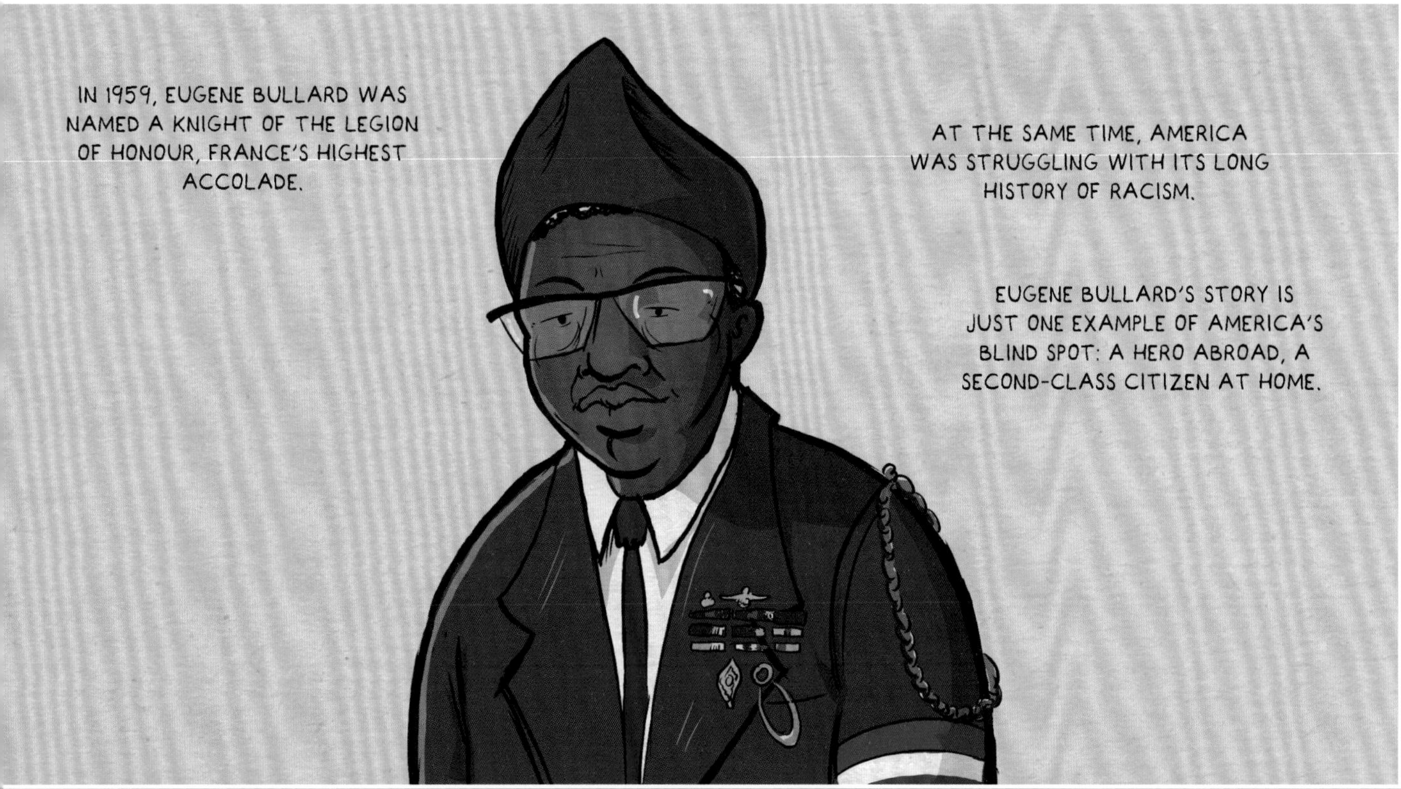
IN 1959, EUGENE BULLARD WAS NAMED A KNIGHT OF THE LEGION OF HONOUR, FRANCE'S HIGHEST ACCOLADE.
AT THE SAME TIME, AMERICA WAS STRUGGLING WITH ITS LONG HISTORY OF RACISM.
EUGENE BULLARD'S STORY IS JUST ONE EXAMPLE OF AMERICA'S BLIND SPOT: A HERO ABROAD, A SECOND-CLASS CITIZEN AT HOME.

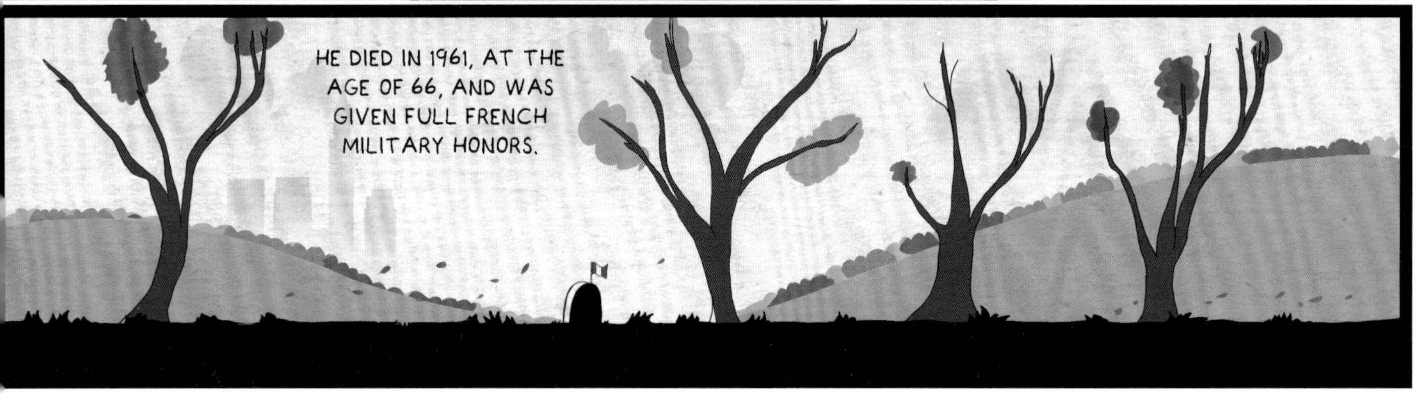
HE DIED IN 1961, AT THE AGE OF 66, AND WAS GIVEN FULL FRENCH MILITARY HONORS.

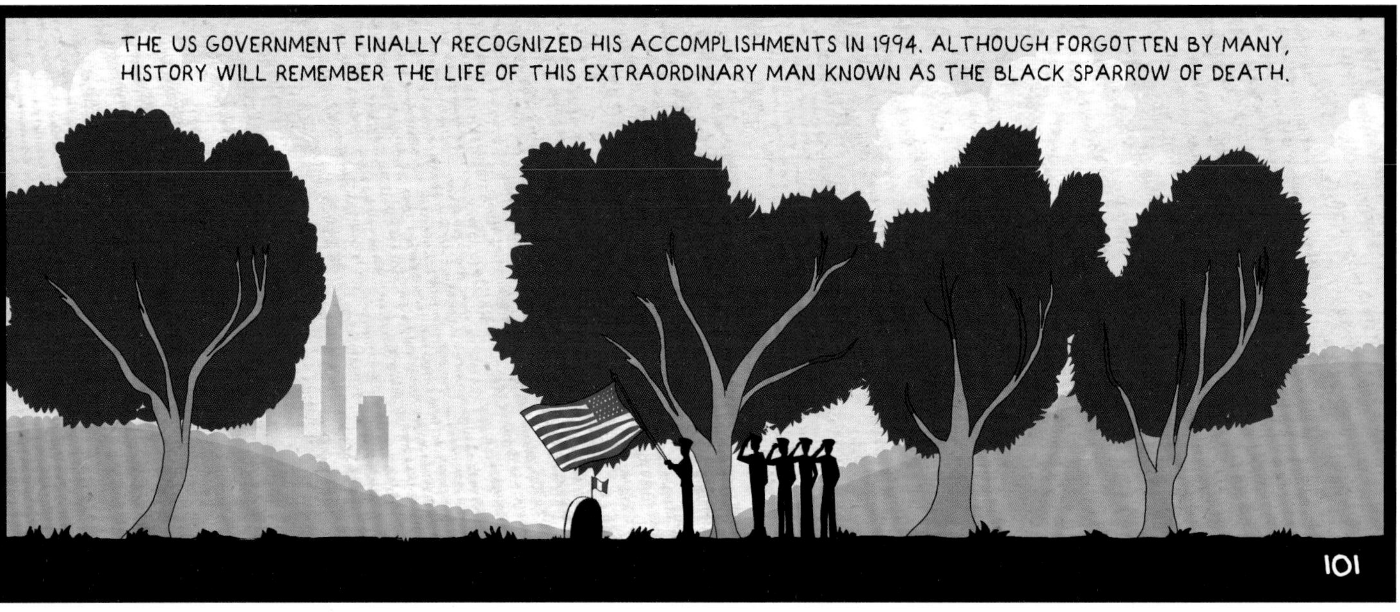
THE US GOVERNMENT FINALLY RECOGNIZED HIS ACCOMPLISHMENTS IN 1994. ALTHOUGH FORGOTTEN BY MANY, HISTORY WILL REMEMBER THE LIFE OF THIS EXTRAORDINARY MAN KNOWN AS THE BLACK SPARROW OF DEATH.

Did You Know?

Jourdon Anderson

After Jourdon wrote his letter, it was picked up by the press and reprinted in several newspapers, including the *New York Daily Tribune* and the *Cincinnati Commercial*. Readers loved his dry sense of humor, which some called "slave humor" because of its wry, indirect critique of the white upper class.

Mary Fields

When the postal service hired contract workers, it tended to award the route to the lowest bidder who could provide "celerity [swiftness], certainty, and security." When written down, the phrase was often shortened to three stars: ***. That's how the star route got its name.

Willie Kennard

During the latter years of the Civil War, the Union Army formed several all–African American regiments of soldiers, many of whom were escaped slaves. These regiments were all stationed west of the Mississippi. Native American people who encountered the regiments nicknamed the soldiers "Buffalo Soldiers"—a name many historians think referred to the soldiers' thick, curly hair, or the fact that they fought as fiercely as wild buffalo.

Cathay Williams

Cathay was not the only woman to apply for a military pension in early American history. A few other women fought in the Revolutionary War while disguised as men, such as Anna Maria Lane, who was severely wounded in the Battle of Germantown. Unlike Cathay, Lane was honored by the Virginia General Assembly after the war, and was permitted to draw a pension for her service.

Tom Wiggins

Although autism wasn't specifically identified until 1943, Tom Wiggins was probably an autistic savant. Before autism was understood, many people with this condition were misdiagnosed as suffering from schizophrenia or insanity. Some people even believed supernatural forces caused savant abilities. In Tom's case, spiritualists claimed he was a medium channeling the music of the great masters.

Millie and Christine McCoy

Several doctors offered to surgically separate Millie and Christine. They were especially concerned later in the twins' life, when Millie's health started to fail. The operation would have been risky, however, so the sisters elected to remain together.

Victor Green

In its heyday, the Idlewild Resort was not only hugely popular among African Americans, but also the largest resort in the Midwest. Many celebrities, including W. E. B. Du Bois and Louis Armstrong, spent time there. After the passage of the Civil Rights Act, however, vacationers had other options, and Idlewild faded to a shell of its former self. Now residents of the town of Idlewild are working to revive the resort and preserve its cultural legacy.

Eugene Bullard

Eugene's friend Josephine Baker also received French military honors for her work during the war. Baker was an actress and dancer who became one of the biggest celebrities of her era. During the war, she not only spied for the French Resistance, but also performed for Allied troops and joined the Red Cross. She even smuggled messages in her sheet music while on tour.

Bibliography

$11,680

Fessenden, Marissa. "A Free Man's Letter to A Former Slaveowner in 1865." November 16, 2015. Smithsonian, https://www.smithsonian-mag.com/smart-news/free-mans-1865-letter-his-former-slave-owner-180957278/.

Usher, Shaun. "To My Old Master." January 30, 2012. Letters of Note, http://www.lettersofnote.com/2012/01/to-my-old-master.html.

Nevertheless, She Persisted

Cooper, Gary, as told to Marc Crawford. "Stagecoach Mary: A Gun-Toting Black Woman Delivered the U.S. Mail in Montana." *Ebony* (October 1959), repr. *Ebony* (October 1977).

Kelly, Kate. "Mary Fields (ca. 1832–1914): First African-American Woman to Carry the Mail." America Comes Alive! https://americacomesalive.com/2014/01/05/mary-fields-ca-1832-1914-known-as-stagecoach-mary/.

"Stagecoach Mary: 'You Got A Problem With That?'" Growing Bolder, https://www.growingbolder.com/stagecoach-mary-got-problem-3007670/.

The Sheriff of Yankee Hill

Eberle, Jeff. "Yankee Hill, Colorado – And the Legend of 'The Black Marshal' Willie Kennard." July 25, 2014. Life... Death... Iron, https://lifedeathiron.com/2014/07/25/yankee-hill-colorado-and-the-legend-of-the-black-marshall-willie-kennard/.

Lindemann, Gerald. "Willie Kennard: Yankee Hill's Black Marshal." June 12, 2006. History-Net, www.historynet.com/willie-kennard-yankee-hills-black-marshal.htm.

Contraband

"Disapproved Pension Application File for Cathay Williams (AKA William Cathay), 38th U.S. Infantry Regiment, Company A (SO-1032593)." National Archives Catalog, https://catalog.archives.gov/id/20848612 (image courtesy of citizen contributor: Madeline Espesth, Carolyn Grier, Rose Buchanan).

"Living Contraband: Former Slaves in the Nation's Capital During the Civil War." August 15, 2017. National Park Service, https://www.nps.gov/articles/living-contraband-former-slaves-in-the-nation-s-capital-during-the-civil-war.htm.

Weiser, Kathy. "Cathay Williams – Female Buffalo Soldier." March 2017. Legends of America, https://www.legendsofamerica.com/cathay-williams/.

All Sound Was Music

"Blind Piano Prodigy Thomas Greene Bethune: The First African American Artist to Perform at the White House." The White House Historical Association, https://www.whitehousehistory.org/blind-piano-prodigy-thomas-greene-bethune.

O'Connell, Deirdre. "The Ballad of Blind Tom: Slave Pianist, American's Lost Musical Genius." The Ballad of Blind Tom, www.blindtom.org.

Zick, William J. "Thomas 'Blind Tom' Wiggins (1849 – 1908): African American Pianist and Composer." January 1, 2016. AfriClassical.com, http://chevalierdesaintgeorges.homestead.com/wiggins.html.

Stronger Together

Keene, Ann T. "Millie and Christine McKoy." September 2005. American National Biography Online, http://www.anb.org/articles/20/20-01879.html.

Macfie, John. "McCoy, Millie-Christine [McKoy]." 1991. NCPedia, https://www.ncpedia.org/biography/mccoy-millie-christine.

McCormick, Ginny. "Review of *The Two-Headed Nightingale*." May/June 2000. Stanford Alumni, https://alumni.stanford.edu/get/page/magazine/article/?article_id=39956.

Samuels, Ellen. "Examining Millie and Christine McKoy: Where Enslavement and Enfreakment Meet." *Signs: Journal of Women in Culture and Society* [serial online] (September 2011), 37(1): 53–81. Available from: Academic Search Premier, Ipswich, MA.

The Green Book

Andrews, Evan. "The Green Book: The Black Travelers' Guide to Jim Crow America." February 6, 2017. History, http://www.history.com/news/the-green-book-the-black-travelers-guide-to-jim-crow-america.

Brown, DeNeen L. "'Life or Death for Black Travelers': How Fear Led to 'The Negro Motorist Green-Book.'" June 1, 2017. *The Washington Post*, https://www.washingtonpost.com/news/retropolis/wp/2017/06/01/life-or-death-for-black-travelers-how-fear-led-to-the-negro-motorist-green-book/.

Carlisle, John. "Once a Paradise, Idlewild Hopes to Rise Again." November 30, 2014. Detroit Free Press, http://www.freep.com/story/news/columnists/john-carlisle/2014/11/30/idlewild-michigan-hard-times/19668773/.

Goodavage, Maria. "'Green Book' Helped Keep African Americans Safe on the Road." January, 10, 2013, http://www.pbs.org/independentlens/blog/green-book-helped-keep-african-americans-safe-on-the-road/.

All Blood Runs Red

Ayubu, Kani Saburi. "9 Facts about Eugene Jacques Bullard." February 8, 2012. Black Art Depot Today, http://blackartblog.blackartdepot.com/features/black-historical-facts/9-facts-about-eugene-jacques-bullard.html.

Brosnahan, Cori. "The Two Lives of Eugene Bullard." PBS, http://www.pbs.org/wgbh/americanexperience/features/the-great-war-two-lives-eugene-bullard/.

Garner, Carla W. "Bullard, Eugene James ['Jacques'] (1895–1961)." Black Past: The Online Reference Guide to African American History, http://www.blackpast.org/aah/bullard-eugene-jacques-18941961.

Lloyd, Craig. "Eugene Bullard (1895–1961)." November 19, 2002. New Georgia Encyclopedia, http://www.georgiaencyclopedia.org/articles/history-archaeology/eugene-bullard-1895-1961.

Pisano, Dominick. "Eugene J. Bullard." October 12, 2010. Smithsonian National Air and Space Museum, https://airandspace.si.edu/stories/editorial/eugene-j-bullard.

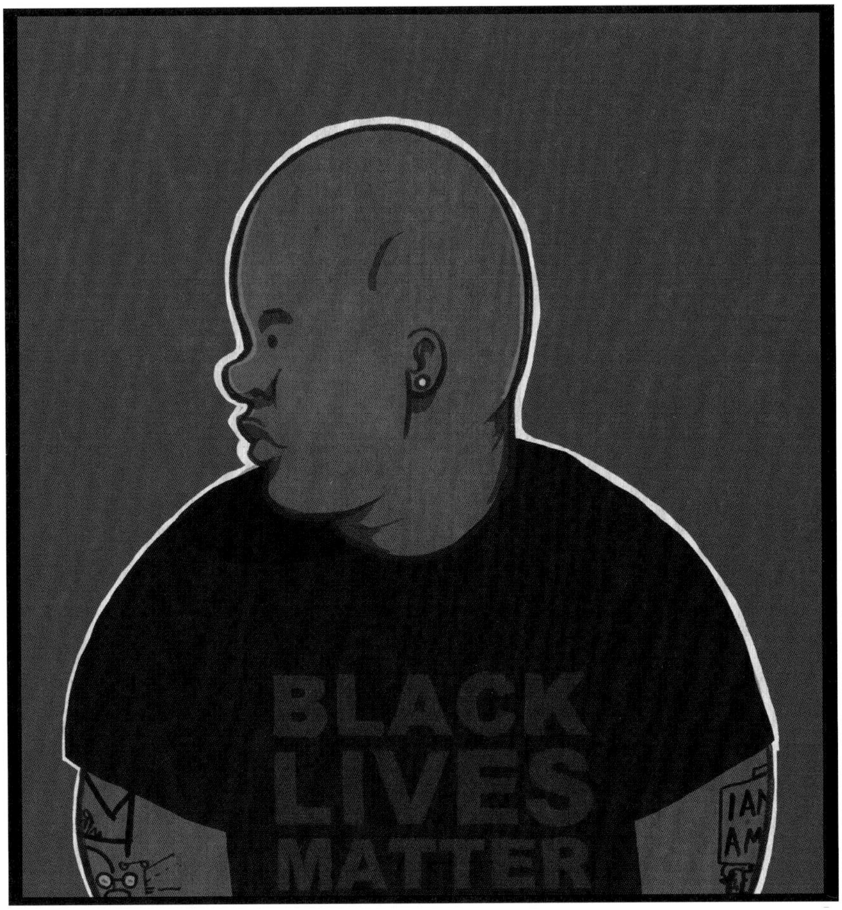
BLACK
LIVES
MATTER

JOEL CHRISTIAN GILL

Joel Christian Gill is the Chair of Foundations at the New Hampshire Institute of Art and recipient of the 2016 Boston University College of Fine Arts Alumni Award. He wrote the words and drew the pictures in *Strange Fruit, Volume I: Uncelebrated Narratives from Black History*, *Bass Reeves: Tales of the Talented Tenth, no. 1*, and *Bessie Stringfield: Tales of the Talented Tenth, no. 2*.

Joel received his MFA from Boston University and a BA from Roanoke College. His secret lair is behind a secret panel in the kitchen of his house (sold separately) in New Boston, New Hampshire. For more information about Joel Christian Gill, reread this paragraph and enjoy.

Joel Christian Gill believes that 28 days are not enough when it comes to Black History. Join the discussion on social media by following Joel's #28DaysAreNotEnough, his call-to-action about Black History. Visit his website at www.joelchristiangill.com or connect with him on Twitter (@jcg007).

Thank you to my wife, April.
You saved my life.

Thank you to my mom, Judy.
You gave me life.

Thank you to the countless people
who shared their stories with me.

Praise for *Strange Fruit*, Volume I

Strange Fruit is an evocative and richly illustrated tour through the shadowed corners of Black History. Gill shares these nine stories simply and with deep thoughtfulness and reverence to voices that—the reader will quickly be convinced—need to be heard.

> — Andrew Aydin, creator and co-author with Rep. John Lewis of the National Book Award recipient and bestselling *MARCH* series

By the time I finished reading *Strange Fruit*, I thought, let the comic-book sellers have their mythic superheroes; through Joel Christian Gill, we can have our own. But, instead of flying around in capes or spinning webs, the superheroes in *Strange Fruit* are extraordinary-ordinary black folks making "a way out of no way." The difference: they really lived.

> — Dr. Henry Louis Gates, Alphonse Fletcher University Professor, Harvard University

Still more thoughtful reflections come from Joel Christian Gill's graphic novel *Strange Fruit*, which unpacks its power through drawings and pointed text that chronicle the trials and triumphs of black Americans who struggled against prejudice more than a century ago. At a moment when racial inequities have ignited this nation, Mr. Gill offers direction for the road ahead from the road behind. — *The New York Times*

Strange Fruit is black history as you've never seen it before. Working with a striking palette of ruby reds, rich browns, bleached-out blues and deep piney greens, author/artist Joel Christian Gill conjures up forgotten firsts and impassioned everymen in a cartoon style that's at once cheeky and epic, naive and majestic. — *The Chicago Tribune*

The short narratives are conversational in tone and the accompanying detailed images convey tragic beauty. Gill doesn't shy away from portraying brutal scenes, but does so without sensationalism. —*School Library Journal*

Gill's book fills a definite void in America's painfully white history books, but on top of that, it's just a really good read. Gill doesn't sugarcoat—not everyone gets a happy ending—but the book is visually witty, engaging, and well researched. History truly comes to life under Gill's skillful hand. —*Foreword Reviews*

Gill's graphic novel series is a tool with which to discuss African Americans, social justice and a shared history. —*The Philadelphia Tribune*